Priorities in Health

D1306168

Advisory Committee to the Editors

J. R. Aluoch
Jacques Baudouy
Fred Binka
Mayra Buvinić
David Challoner
Guy de Thé
Timothy Evans
Richard Horton
Sharon Hrynkow
Gerald Keusch
Kiyoshi Kurokawa
Peter Lachmann
Mary Ann Lansang

Christopher Lovelace
Anthony Mbewu
Rajiv Misra
Perla Santos Ocampo
G. B. A. Okelo
Sevket Ruacan
Pramilla Senanayake
Jaime Sepúlveda
Chitr Sitthi-amorn
Sally Stansfield
Misael Uribe
Zhengguo Wang
Witold Zatonski

Contributing Writers

William D. Savedoff and Anne-Marie Smith, Social Insight

Priorities in Health

Editors

Dean T. Jamison
Joel G. Breman
Anthony R. Measham
George Alleyne
Mariam Claeson
David B. Evans
Prabhat Jha
Anne Mills
Philip Musgrove

THE WORLD BANK
Washington, D.C.

362.1
Priorities
2006

3 1712 01278 3661

This volume was funded in part by a grant from the Bill & Melinda Gates Foundation and is a product of the staff of the International Bank for Reconstruction and Development / The World Bank, the World Health Organization, and the Fogarty International Center of the National Institutes of Health. The findings, interpretations, and conclusions expressed in this volume do not necessarily reflect the views of the Executive Directors of The World Bank or the governments they represent, the World Health Organization, or the Fogarty International Center of the National Institutes of Health.

ISBN-10: 0-8213-6260-7
ISBN-13: 978-0-8213-6260-0
eISBN: 978-0-8213-6261-7
DOI: 10.1596/978-0-8213-6260-0

Library of Congress Cataloging-in-Publication data has been applied for.

Contents

Foreword

Priorities in Health is the companion volume to the second edition of *Disease Control Priorities in Developing Countries (DCP2)*, a successor to the first edition (*DCP1*) published in 1993, but with a vastly expanded mandate. *DCP1* proved to be a highly influential document in shaping health policies globally. The World Bank's (1993) path-breaking publication *World Development Report 1993: Investing in Health*, which incorporated *DCP1*'s main concepts and messages, became the standard reference for health policy makers worldwide and even today continues to enjoy that status.

In India, the impact was dramatic, and I was greatly privileged to be in a position to manage and oversee the transition to greatly improved implementation of public health interventions in terms of both coverage and effectiveness. A serendipitous set of circumstances facilitated this, namely: an unprecedented fiscal and balance of payments crisis that compelled India to seek structural adjustment lending from the International Monetary Fund and the World Bank and resulted in severe fiscal compression; a shift in World Bank lending policies whereby the International Development Association was to emphasize social sectors; a paucity of health and education projects in the pipeline to use the highly concessional International Development Association allocation at a time when India was experiencing a severe foreign exchange crunch; and finally, an extraordinarily sympathetic and supportive team at the World Bank's India desk.

We became aware of *DCP1*'s main concepts well before its publication by means of a seminar at Delhi's All India Institute of Medical Sciences in early 1992, at which Dean Jamison and his colleagues presented the main findings of *DCP1* and the *World Development Report 1993*, including the concepts of disability-adjusted life years, burden of disease, epidemiological transition, and cost-effectiveness analysis as a tool for priority setting. These concepts provided a completely new way of determining priorities objectively based on evidence and economic analysis. Despite some initial and understandable skepticism about the methodologies and the estimates, the overall response was highly favorable.

At the same time, the World Bank was looking for objective criteria for identifying projects in the health sector. A commonality of approach developed between the World Bank and the Ministry of Health to use *DCP1* techniques, which led to the revamping and scaling up of all major disease control projects in record time—particularly those against leprosy, blindness, tuberculosis, and malaria—in addition to new initiatives for dealing with the emerging threat of HIV/AIDS. Simultaneously, projects for system strengthening were also undertaken in several states to improve capacity. As a result, the developmental outlays for the Department of Health rose more than 5-fold and the external component rose more than 25-fold between 1990–1 and 2001–2 (*India Health Report 2003*), which not only increased available financial resources beyond anyone's expectations, but also completely changed how projects were formulated and implemented. This is a success story of which both the Indian government and the World Bank can legitimately be proud, that is, the contribution of *DCP1* to channeling additional resources to cost-effective interventions to deal with the conditions responsible for a major share of the burden of disease.

COVERING NEW GROUND

DCP2 is a much more comprehensive, and indeed ambitious, effort. It goes well beyond updating the technical content, burden of disease, and cost-effectiveness estimates of *DCP1*. It covers new ground by examining important, complex areas, such as the delivery, management, and financing of health care and health research. It clearly recognizes that objective priority setting is only the first step: identified interventions have to be delivered to the targeted population efficiently to derive the full benefits of cost-effectiveness exercises; individual health interventions are rarely effective in isolation; and not only must the entire health system perform well to achieve positive outcomes but so do such related sectors like nutrition, drinking water, sanitation, and education. Raising the capabilities of the whole system along with establishing close linkages with other players is the key to success.

PRESENTING LEADING EXPERTS

DCP2 assembled an impressive array of the world's leading experts on health-related disciplines as contributors and is thus a treasure house of the latest knowledge, technical information, and international experience along with expert analyses on a multitude of health-related subjects. It should therefore legitimately expect to be an influential publication and a standard reference for health professionals and policy makers.

PROMOTING EFFECTIVE DECISION MAKING

DCP2 has the potential to contribute significantly to global health by promoting evidence-based and better-informed decision making at all levels. It comes at a particularly opportune time for my country, India, where for the first time since independence, the government is committed to giving high priority to health and raising public health expenditure from the current level of less than 1 percent to 2 or 3 percent of gross domestic product. *DCP2* could therefore have a far greater impact than its predecessor, not only in the rational allocation of additional resources, but also in revitalizing and upgrading the public health delivery system, which has been performing poorly in much of the country.

EXPLAINING MORTALITY AND MORBIDITY MEASUREMENT

The Disease Control Priorities Project has also resulted in a separate book, the *Global Burden of Disease and Risk Factors,* which summarizes the concepts and estimates of the burden of disease and the attribution of this burden to several major risk factors. This volume is a definitive explanation of how mortality and morbidity are measured, including health damage such as stillbirths, which were not previously included in estimates of the global burden of disease, and of how these losses are combined into overall measures of health status. The book also provides estimates of how mortality has changed over time.

HIGHLIGHTING CRITICAL ISSUES

DCP2 highlights some critical issues that are widely recognized, but are often inadequately addressed in the international health literature. First and foremost, it recognizes equity as a key objective of health policy. The concern for equity arises not merely from a moral or human welfare standpoint, but also from the recognition of the critical role of health in alleviating poverty. Second, it clearly states that "unless equity considerations become part of policy making and of monitoring outcomes, interventions may widen instead of narrowing equity gaps." The book rightly attributes much of the progress in global health to technical progress in its broadest sense and the current glaring disparities in health status between and within countries to uneven application of this knowledge. The greatest challenge before the international community is thus "assuring that the benefits of technical progress are shared quickly and effectively on a global scale." A more forceful or clearer presentation of the case for equity would be hard to find.

COMBINING BALANCED VIEWS AND PRACTICAL APPROACHES

Another quality that stands out in *DCP2* is its total freedom from ideological bias along with a highly pragmatic approach. This results in the complete absence of prescriptive preaching and a refreshing open-mindedness. It clearly recognizes that socioeconomic, cultural, and governance diversities make a "one size fits all" solution to complex global health issues impossible. It therefore attempts to pool all relevant knowledge and lessons drawn from international experience to enable policy makers to make well-informed decisions suited to their particular situations. Another feature is that unlike many other publications, it takes a balanced view between the relative importance of mobilizing resources and of using them effectively and efficiently. Similarly, it exhibits a refreshing even-handedness in dealing with the responsibilities of the donor community and those of the developing countries themselves. The clear message is that while the rich countries should greatly step up their assistance, the poor countries must put their own houses in order to make good use of the money. While enlightened self-interest is necessarily the main motivation for donor support, a marked improvement in the quality of aid utilization would undoubtedly contribute significantly to improving the aid climate.

OFFERING A COMPREHENSIVE ARRAY OF INFORMATION

DCP2 is a voluminous, well-researched publication divided into 73 chapters, which might not be easy reading for lay readers. Even academics and health professionals may not be equally interested in all the subjects covered and may prefer to read selectively. The audience for *DCP2* is intended to be wide: from academics and health professionals to health policy makers and program managers. Indeed, to derive the maximum benefits, the net would need to be cast wider to include the media, political parties, legislators, and the informed lay public. How often have we lamented that the lack of political will has been responsible for the neglect and failure of many health initiatives in the developing countries? Similarly, the lack of response from donor countries to admittedly deserving causes is often attributed to apathy and indifference to the problems of the poor among the populations of the rich countries.

PRESENTING *DCP2*'s CONTENT SUCCINCTLY

In democratic societies in both the industrial and developing countries, public opinion plays a critical role and needs to be systemically mobilized. Key messages therefore have to reach the media and lay readers on a wide scale to generate general awareness of and informed debate on key global health issues. We needed a companion volume that distills the essence of *DCP2* into a succinct, lucid, and easy-to-read document. *Priorities in Health* addresses this need admirably. If the work of *DCP1* became better known through the *World Development Report 1993*, this companion volume is the instrument for wide dissemination of *DCP2*. In barely 200 pages, it brings out clearly, in readable prose unencumbered by technical jargon and an overload of statistics, the essence of the entire document. It also opens a window to the main document for those interested in particular aspects to encourage them to read the relevant chapters. It can be read by busy policy makers during the course of a long flight. It is my sincere hope that *Priorities in Health* will be widely read in both developed and developing countries and that its messages will be actively debated to derive the maximum advantage from this magnificent effort. I consider *Priorities in Health* as a must-read for all those interested in health and related sectors.

Rajiv Misra
Former Secretary of Health, India

Acknowledgments

In early 2001, convinced that advances in global health demanded a second edition of *Disease Control Priorities in Developing Countries (DCP2)*, Dean T. Jamison and Prabhat Jha enlisted Anthony R. Measham into the enterprise, and the Disease Control Priorities Project (DCPP) was born. Gerald Keusch, then director of the Fogarty International Center at the National Institutes of Health (NIH), generously offered to support and host the DCPP at NIH. Six more editors joined the DCPP soon after: George Alleyne, Joel G. Breman, Mariam Claeson, David B. Evans, Anne Mills, and Philip Musgrove.

The first edition of *Disease Control Priorities in Developing Countries* was based at the World Bank. Christopher Lovelace was director of the Health, Nutrition, and Population Unit at the World Bank in 2001, when it became another core partner of the DCPP. The World Health Organization (WHO) soon followed suit, led by Gro Harlem Bruntland, then director-general, and Christopher Murray, Executive Director of the Evidence and Information for Policy Division. The project was launched in early 2002 with major support from the Bill & Melinda Gates Foundation. J. W. Lee at WHO, Jacques Baudouy at the World Bank, and Sharon Hrynkow at the Fogarty International Center of NIH each continued the strong support of the DCPP initiated by their predecessors.

The DCPP is a joint enterprise of the Fogarty International Center of the NIH, WHO, the World Bank, and the Population Reference Bureau. The Fogarty International Center is the international component of the NIH. It addresses global health challenges through innovative and collaborative research and training programs and supports and advances the NIH mission through international partnerships.

WHO is the United Nations' specialized agency for health. Its objective, as set out in its constitution, is the attainment by all peoples of the highest possible level of health. WHO's constitution defines health as a state of complete physical, mental, and social well-being and not merely the absence of disease or infirmity.

The World Bank Group is one of the world's largest sources of development assistance. The Bank, which provides US$18 billion to US$22 billion each year in loans to its client countries, provided $1.27 billion for health, nutrition, and population in 2004. The World Bank is now working in more than 100 developing economies, bringing a mix of analytical work, policy dialogue, and lending to improve living standards—including health and education—and reduce poverty.

The Population Reference Bureau informs people around the world about health, population, and the environment and empowers them to use that information to advance the well-being of current and future generations. For 75 years, the bureau has analyzed complex data and research results to provide objective and timely information in a format easily understood by advocates, journalists, and decision makers; conducted workshops around the world to give key audiences the tools they need to understand and communicate effectively about relevant issues; and worked to ensure that developing country policy makers base policy decisions on sound evidence rather than on anecdotal or outdated information.

The idea for this companion volume for policy makers and other influential individuals arose at the first meeting of the DCPP Advisory Committee to the Editors, held in Cuernavaca, Mexico, in June 2003. The Executive Committee of the Advisory Committee to the Editors, composed of David Challoner, Guy de Thé, and Jaime Sepúlveda (chair), immediately endorsed it.

Priorities in Health was written by William Savedoff and Amy Smith based on *DCP2*. The editors, authors, and staff of the DCPP acknowledge a deep debt of gratitude to Bill and Amy for their singular success in capturing, in relatively few pages, the essence of the 1,400-page volume. Philip Musgrove, Sonbol A. Shahid-Salles, and Anthony Measham reviewed and edited this companion volume and are responsible for any failure to fully capture that essence.

Carlos Rossel, Mary Fisk, Randi Park, Nancy Lammers, Alice Faintich, Andres Meneses, and their colleagues at the World Bank's Office of the Publisher have done outstanding work on every aspect of the production of the DCPP books, including this one. Without their professionalism, meticulous attention to detail, hard work, and unstinting support and advice, publishing this book in tandem with *DCP2* would have been impossible.

Finally, the DCPP editors wish to pay tribute to the 350-plus chapter authors of *DCP2* for their outstanding contributions to *Priorities in Health.* We hope that this companion volume will help ensure that *DCP2* substantially reduces death, illness, and disability around the globe, especially among the poor in developing countries.

Abbreviations and Acronyms

ART   antiretroviral therapy
BCG   Bacille Calmette-Guérin
CVD   cardiovascular disease
DCP2   *Disease Control Priorities in Developing Countries,*
            second edition
DALY   disability-adjusted life year
DOTS   an internationally disseminated strategy that has effectively
            combated the spread of tuberculosis
GDP   gross domestic product
Hib   *Haemophilus influenzae* type B
IMCI   Integrated Management of Childhood Illness
ITN   insecticide-treated net
MDG   Millennium Development Goal
NGO   nongovernmental organization
ORT   oral rehydration therapy
SARS   severe acute respiratory syndrome
STI   sexually transmitted infection
TB   tuberculosis
WHO   World Health Organization

All dollar amounts are U.S. dollars unless otherwise indicated.

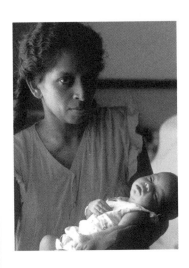

Chapter **1**

Accomplishments, Challenges, and Priorities

It is time for a checkup of human health around the globe. Many people are living longer, healthier lives than ever before, but many others still lack access to the most basic health care, and the gap between the health care haves and have-nots has actually widened for some fundamental services. As for infectious diseases, while the medical community is successfully controlling some of them—and has even eradicated one—new diseases are emerging, some of which are caused by mysterious viruses that cross species or mutate quickly. Other major components in the global disease burden arise from human behavior and the harmful choices that people make both individually and collectively.

Disease Control Priorities in Developing Countries, 2nd edition (*DCP2*) (Jamison and others 2006) is intended as a checkup both for health and for health care. What progress has the medical community made in identifying and reducing the global disease burden? How much have countries accomplished in developing and providing efficient, effective, and equitable health care? How should countries set and achieve priorities in health?

In 1993, the first edition of *Disease Control Priorities in Developing Countries* (Jamison and others 1993) presented knowledge about the distribution of the disease burden in developing countries, up-to-date information about many of these diseases, and data on the cost-effectiveness of interventions available to address them. The book helped to inform and galvanize health sector policies in countries around the world by demonstrating the benefits of redirecting efforts toward diseases with large burdens and doing so with cost-effective interventions. It provided a conceptual basis for discussing the allocation of resources in the health sector while illustrating the linkages between prevention and treatment, between public health care and personal health care services, and between the health sector and other sectors. The information and analysis provided in the 1993 publication helped many developing countries define basic packages of health care; guided their management decisions about training, supplies, and equipment; and aided the design of social insurance programs. The book also informed numerous other publications during the 1990s, including the *World Development Report 1993: Investing in Health* (World Bank 1993).

Now, 13 years later, *DCP2* assesses subsequent accomplishments, remaining and emerging challenges, and new opportunities for improving health in the developing world. This new publication goes beyond its predecessor in several ways, namely:

- It includes discussion of a larger number of diseases and conditions, covering the full range of infectious diseases, reproductive issues, children's health issues, noncommunicable diseases, and injuries, as well as risk factors and consequences of disease.
- It provides cost-effectiveness analysis that is more thorough and more comparable across conditions and regions than was possible in the earlier edition.
- It devotes considerable attention to implementation, examining the delivery, management, and financing of health care.
- It addresses cross-cutting issues, such as gender differences in health status and the ethics of resource allocation.

Thus this new publication is a comprehensive, updated assessment of the medical, economic, and management knowledge that can now be harnessed to ease the global burden of disease and improve human health.

HISTORICAL ACHIEVEMENTS IN WORLD HEALTH

"Until the 19th century, deaths of infants and children were commonplace worldwide."

Any checkup should include a case history.[1] A review of the unprecedented improvements in human health in the last century provides important perspectives on the current situation.

Until the 19th century, deaths of infants and children were commonplace worldwide. Poor nourishment left most people stunted by today's standards. Infectious diseases such as smallpox, measles, and

[1] For historical perspectives on health and health care, see *DCP2* chapter 1.

Figure 1.1 Limits and Convergence for National Average Female Life-Expectancy at Birth

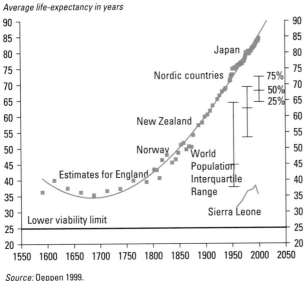

Average life-expectancy in years

Source: Oeppen 1999.

tuberculosis decimated entire communities and left many people scarred and crippled. Life expectancy was low throughout the world. Even for women in England, who had the world's highest average lifespan between 1600 and 1840, life expectancy fluctuated between 35 and 45 years, half what it is today (figure 1.1).

This overall picture has changed rapidly and dramatically since the mid-19th century. The medical community brought many infectious diseases under control, and even eradicated smallpox; better nutrition and overall health conditions lowered mortality rates for everyone, especially children; and life spans increased dramatically. After 1840, the upward trend in life spans proceeded at a surprisingly sustained and uniform rate of increase of 2.5 years per decade for the next 160 years. By 1900, the highest average life expectancy just surpassed 60 years; by 2000, it exceeded 80 years.

However, even though the gains in health and life expectancy have not been uniform around the globe and have not occurred at the same time or to the same extent, they have been widespread:

- Smallpox was eradicated worldwide by 1977.
- Polio remains in only a handful of countries.

Table 1.1 Levels and changes in Life Expectancy, 1960–2002, by World Bank Region

Region	Life expectancy (years)			Rate of change per decade (years)	
	1960	1990	2002	1960–90	1990–2002
Low- and middle-income	45.2	63	65	6.3	1.7
East Asia and the Pacific	39	67	70	9.3	2.5
(China)	(36)	(69)	(71)	(11)	(1.7)
Europe and Central Asia	n/a	69	69	n/a	0.0
Latin America and the Caribbean	56	68	71	4.0	2.5
Middle East and N. Africa	47	64	69	5.7	4.2
South Asia	44	58	63	4.7	4.2
(India)	(44)	(59)	(64)	(5)	(4.6)
Sub-Saharan Africa	40	50	46	3.3	−3.3
High-income	69	76	78	2.3	1.7
World	57	70	72	4.3	1.7

Source: World Bank 2004.
Note: Entries are the average of male and female life expectancies.

- Diphtheria, whooping cough, measles, and tetanus are rare or absent in many parts of the world.
- Child mortality, while still high in many places, has declined almost everywhere.
- Average life expectancy has increased—albeit with setbacks— around the world. Between 1960 and 2002, average life expectancy rose from 36 to 71 years in China, from 56 to 71 years in Latin America and the Caribbean, from 47 to 69 years in the Middle East and North Africa, and from 44 to 63 years in South Asia. Even in Sub-Saharan Africa, average life expectancy rose from 40 to 50 years in 1990 before falling back to 46 years in 2002, largely because of the spreading HIV/AIDS epidemic (table 1.1).

Even though life expectancy in high-income countries exceeds that in developing regions, convergence is notable. In 1910, for example, a male born in the United States could expect to live 49 years, but had he been born in Chile, his life expectancy would have been only 29 years. By the late 1990s, in contrast, U.S. life expectancy had reached 73 years and that of Chile had reached 72 years.

ACCOUNTING FOR HEALTH GAINS

A host of factors account for the remarkable and widespread gains in human health during the 20th century, including changing demographics, rising productivity, urbanization, increased food supplies, medical science, sanitation, and institutional change. Some historical analyses emphasize one critical factor in a search for the one that underpins the rest, while other approaches emphasize the interplay of several factors. Efforts to understand the unprecedented changes in human health in the 20th century have involved exploration of theories of history and the nature of causation and how they have contributed to the study of epidemiology. Many different accounts are possible, but for our purposes—deriving lessons from this unprecedented historical trajectory—the following two clear messages emerge:

- Income growth by itself cannot account for the dramatic improvements in health in the last century, nor can it be relied upon as the only strategy for making progress on health in the future.
- Technical progress, in the broadest sense, works. It has been, and can be, the basis for substantial health gains, even when income growth is slow or stagnant.

While economic development and income growth are certainly among the factors that help explain the remarkable health gains of the 20th century, declining mortality in Europe was only weakly correlated with periods of economic growth in the 19th and early 20th centuries, and more recent experiences in many places, including Cuba, Sri Lanka, and the state of Kerala in India, demonstrate that dramatic improvements in health can occur without high or rapidly growing incomes. The pace of health improvements in so many different countries at different levels of economic development and with disparate rates of income growth demonstrates that other factors can and do play a leading role.

An increasing number of studies attribute last century's remarkable health gains not so much to increased wealth as to technical progress. In this context, technical progress refers to any advance in knowledge that leads to practical improvements. It includes the development and application of sophisticated treatments, such as organ transplants and angioplasty, and also simple treatments, such as oral rehydration

"Technical progress, . . . has been, . . . the basis for substantial health gains, even when income growth is slow or stagnant."

therapy, whereby a child suffering from diarrhea is given liquids containing a few simple ingredients to drink to prevent death from dehydration. It includes progress in preventive care, such as new, more effective, or easier to administer vaccines along with simple behavioral changes, like keeping newborns warm and ensuring that their umbilical cords are clean and free of infection. It also includes innovative methods for delivering standard treatment, such as directly observed therapy short course (DOTS), an internationally disseminated strategy that has effectively combated the spread of tuberculosis (TB) in many countries.

Technical progress also comprises institutional and managerial innovations. These may include organizing and administering public health functions for the first time in a country or doing so in novel and more effective ways. They may involve identifying and training new cadres of health workers, developing new means of surveillance to track a disease and then target vaccination campaigns, or taking steps to improve the accessibility and quality of care.

In the sphere of economics and public policy, technical progress comprises improvements in allocating funds as a result of studying the efficacy of interventions and strategies and assessing their cost-effectiveness. It encompasses the development of new methods for financing health systems, such as mobilizing public resources or pooling existing financial resources, and new strategies for paying providers and purchasing health services. The creation of social security systems and national health services is another form of this kind of technical progress that helps to insure millions of families against the high costs of serious illnesses and injuries. *DCP2* illustrates the many ways that collective action through public financing has led to substantial health gains for society.

Technical progress outside the health sector has also contributed to improving health. Notably, rising agricultural productivity has improved nourishment for a large part of the world's growing population. In addition, improvements in such infrastructure as housing, sanitation, potable water, and safe roads have made significant contributions to health. Investments in education, which help increase literacy and thereby facilitate the diffusion of messages about healthy living, have had an important impact as well.

The boundary between institutional innovations and broader social change is not easily defined, and social changes have contributed substantially to progress in health. One of the most prominent of these social

"The creation of social security systems and national health services is another form of . . . technical progress . . ."

changes has involved women's status, including their political rights, education, and other forms of empowerment. These improvements in women's status have contributed to improving not only women's own health, but also the health of their families and societies.

When countries have adopted technical changes such as these, people's health has improved even in the absence of societal wealth or economic growth. Between 1950 and 1980, low- and middle-income countries such as Chile, Costa Rica, Cuba, and Sri Lanka adopted basic approaches to improving public health, including sanitation, routine immunization, and improved birth attendance, with remarkable reductions in infant, child, and maternal mortality. Countries with similar economic profiles that failed to adopt such measures lagged behind. A cross-country econometric analysis shows that countries that made rapid technical progress reduced infant mortality by as much as 5 percent annually compared with countries that made little or no technical progress.[2] Even poor countries with weak public institutions, as well as those mired in violent conflict, have made important health gains through vaccination campaigns that eradicated smallpox worldwide, eliminated polio in most of the world, or controlled other endemic infectious diseases. By embracing technical progress in its myriad forms, progress in health is possible.

Health gains in the last century were not only unprecedented but were dramatic relative to trends in economic growth and to local institutional capacity. Indeed, "income growth is neither necessary nor sufficient for sustained improvements in health. Today's tools for improving health are so powerful and inexpensive that health conditions can be reasonably good even in countries with low incomes" (*DCP2*, chapter 1, p. 8).

"... countries that made rapid technical progress reduced infant mortality by as much as 5 percent annually compared with countries that made little or no technical progress."

HEALTH AND ECONOMIC GROWTH

Researchers have frequently overlooked the importance of the dramatic health gains of the 20th century for human welfare because they have been difficult to quantify, and also because another measure of well-being, growth in national income, has been the standard indicator of a country's progress. Several studies have sought to redress this problem by estimating the value, in monetary terms, of increased longevity.

[2] Specifically accounting for the different pace of technical progress has also demonstrated that the effect of health on income is significantly stronger than the effect of income on health. For further discussion of the economic benefits of health, see *DCP2*, chapter 1.

When the value of these additional life years is added to national income, the resulting sum, known as full income, comes closer to measuring human welfare. Calculations of this kind for the United States have shown that the rate at which increasing longevity raised Americans' well-being matched or exceeded the sixfold increase in real income during the first half of the 20th century. Paying attention to the value of increased longevity also tempers assessments of global inequality because, since the 1950s, life expectancy in poorer countries has converged toward the life expectancy high-income countries enjoy.

Researchers have also underestimated the importance of health improvements to human welfare: better health itself contributes to economic growth. Indeed, while economic growth is not essential for health, health may be crucial for economic growth. Numerous studies have demonstrated that the healthier people are the more productive they are. These studies include focused experiments, such as demonstrations that agricultural workers are more productive after being treated for anemia. They also include broad historical research indicating, for example, that as much as half of British growth during the Industrial Revolution could be attributed to improved nourishment, and therefore to healthier and more productive workers. Cross-country studies have demonstrated that reductions in adult mortality accounted for 10 to 15 percent of economic growth between 1960 and 1990 and that one additional year of life expectancy is associated with a sustained increment of 4 percent in national income.

EQUITY

The broad historical perspective on human health is reassuring in many ways. The overarching trends are positive, with unprecedented gains, widespread advances, and converging health status. However, these positive trends mask the uneven progress that has left large numbers of people behind and at a disadvantage. No process of setting priorities and designing strategies for improving health can ignore the pervasive large inequities. As *DCP2* (chapter 1, p. 5) observes, "In far too many countries health conditions remain unacceptably—and unnecessarily—poor. This factor is a source of grief and misery, and it is a sharp brake on economic growth and poverty reduction."

Given today's tools and resources, health conditions could be reasonable everywhere, but for far too many people "reasonable" health conditions are not the norm. Children born in low-income countries have much smaller chances of leading a long life with good health than those born in higher-income countries. Women generally lead longer lives than men, but their lives tend to be marked by poorer health (*DCP2*, chapter 10). Where societies deny women rights of inheritance, political voice, legal standing, or education, those women suffer from more diseases and injuries and have less access to treatment and services. Other socially marginalized groups, whether large groups like indigenous populations, rural dwellers, and migrant workers or smaller groups like sex workers and street children, suffer from similar excessive disease burdens.

Equity is a major subtext throughout *DCP2*.[3] Each disease-specific chapter notes the distribution of the disease burden and identifies where this burden is concentrated, whether in particular regions or populations. Discussions of interventions assess their effectiveness relative to different age, gender, cultural, and social groupings, and analyses of delivery mechanisms address the barriers to accessing appropriate and timely health care as those barriers vary across population groups. As the authors of the chapter on integrated management of childhood illness (IMCI) observe, "The challenge of improving equity is not unique to IMCI or to child survival; it affects virtually every intervention and delivery strategy. *Unless equity considerations become a key part of policy making and of monitoring outcomes, interventions may widen instead of narrow inequity gaps*" (*DCP2*, chapter 63, p. 1189, emphasis added).

Health inequities, many of which are plainly visible, can be documented when researchers disaggregate analyses by the relevant divisions in society, for example, age, gender, income, ethnicity, or region. The resulting patterns of inequity can be seen at three different levels: large disparities in health status, differential access to and use of health care services, and disproportionate exposure to health risks.

Patterns of Inequity in Health Status

The reassuring picture painted by rising global averages obscures substantial disparities in health among different regions of the world and different income brackets, genders, and age groups. A child born in Ethiopia today, for example, has a 20 percent chance of dying before the age of five compared with a less than 1 percent chance for a child born in North America or Western Europe. During 1990–2002, the mortality rate

"Women generally lead longer lives than men, but their lives tend to be marked by poorer health . . ."

"During 1990–2002, the mortality rate for children under five remained stagnant or increased in 27 countries."

[3] The issue of equity is addressed in virtually every chapter of *DCP2*. The most explicit discussion is contained in chapter 3, but see also chapters 9, 10, 59, and 63.

for children under five remained stagnant or increased in 27 countries. A woman's risk of death in childbirth is less than 20 per 100,000 births in high-income countries, but the average exceeds 900 per 100,000 births in the lowest-income countries. Progress on reducing maternal mortality has slowed, and has even reversed, in some countries, and thus the gap is widening.

The excess disease burden for women is not exclusively a result of diseases related to maternal conditions, but includes a higher incidence of illnesses that derive from inequitable gender roles; for example, in Sub-Saharan Africa, teenage girls are 5 to 16 times more likely to be infected with HIV than teenage boys. In China, India, and other parts of South Asia, neglect of female children, gender-selective abortions, violence, and other causes of excess mortality mar the lives of women, leading to the haunting estimates of millions of women who are therefore missing from population counts.

In many of the former Soviet republics, life expectancy declined among men in the 1990s because of a rise in alcoholism and social dislocation and the deterioration of basic health infrastructure. By far the worst calamity of recent years has hit Sub-Saharan Africa, where HIV/AIDS is reducing average life expectancy and increasing mortality from opportunistic infections, TB, malaria, and malnutrition.

Large disparities in health can also be found within countries. Western China, for example, lags far behind China's wealthier coastal regions in its health profile, and indigenous populations in Latin American countries have shorter, less healthy lives than other segments of the population. Indeed, researchers regularly find that in most countries the poor live shorter, less healthy lives than the rich.

Patterns of Inequity in Health Care Provision

Inequity is also evident from disparities in health care services, for instance:

- Coverage levels for effective interventions to improve child survival are remarkably low in most developing countries. A review of the 42 countries that account for 90 percent of global child deaths showed that only two out of nine key interventions reached more than half of all children.
- In 1999, skilled birth attendants assisted less than half the women giving birth in Sub-Saharan Africa.

- One-third of the world's population has no effective access to essential modern medicines or vaccines. Some 65 percent of people in India and 47 percent of those in Sub-Saharan Africa simply cannot obtain essential drugs when they need them.

Many different barriers exclude people from getting appropriate health care. As noted in the *DCP2* chapter on gender differentials (chapter 10), these barriers can be divided into those related to services, to clients, or to institutions and tend to affect women disproportionately as follows:

- *Service factors* include high costs of care and transportation, distances to services and the time needed to reach them, poor quality care, inappropriate care, negative staff attitudes, and cultural and linguistic differences.
- *Client factors* include social and cultural constraints on women's mobility and women's lower incomes and wealth, women's greater time burdens because of their socially assigned family roles, and women's limited information about their health needs and rights and about the availability of services.
- *Institutional factors* include men's control over decision making, health budgets, and facilities; local perceptions of illness; local treatment norms; and stigma and discrimination in health settings.

Although the particulars vary, other *DCP2* chapters delineate a wide range of barriers that constrain access to care for infants, children, sex workers, and a number of other disadvantaged populations.

Patterns of Inequity in Exposure to Health Risks

Differences in health status are also the result of differential exposure to health risks. Many of these differences are associated with poverty and are discussed in a number of *DCP2* chapters, including those on water and sanitation (chapter 41), neonatal care (chapter 27), malnourishment (chapter 28), and indoor air pollution from stoves (chapter 42). Many risks are associated with risky and physically demanding occupations (chapter 60). Still others are associated with climatic and geographic conditions, which are particularly relevant to malaria (chapter 21), river blindness (chapter 50), helminthic infections (chapter 24), and a wide range of tropical diseases (chapters 22 and 23).

"... 65 percent of people in India and 47 percent ... in Sub-Saharan Africa simply cannot obtain essential drugs ..."

"Many risks are associated with climatic and geographic conditions ... relevant to malaria, river blindness, helminthic infections, and ... tropical diseases."

Equity and Technical Progress

How did these inequities in health status, health care services, and exposure to risk arise? Many factors play a role, ranging from accidents of climate or geography to political repression and neglect. Yet despite ample debate about some aspects of the nature and origins of inequities in health, most experts tend to agree that health inequities have arisen largely from the uneven adoption and implementation of health interventions associated with technical progress; that is, they have arisen largely because cost-effective interventions have been applied in some places and not others or for privileged groups and not other groups.

Where the fruits of technical progress have not been available, people have been left behind, with some gaps growing ever deeper. For example, among 12 million childhood deaths analyzed in 1998, close to 4 million resulted from diseases for which effective vaccines are available. Cost-effective and relatively inexpensive interventions for many vaccine-preventable illnesses, diarrhea, pneumonia, TB, and malaria have resulted in a reduction of the disease burden from these diseases to as little as 0.3 percent of the total where such interventions have been applied. Where such interventions are not deployed, these preventable diseases account for 11.7 percent of the disease burden (table 1.2, figure 1.2).

". . . health inequities have arisen largely from the uneven adoption and implementation of health interventions associated with technical progress . . ."

Table 1.2 Health Expenditures by Country Income Level, Public and Private, 2001

Country Group	Health expenditure per capita (2001 US$)	Health expenditure (% of GDP)	Public sector expenditures (% of total)
Low-income	23	4.4	26.3
Middle-income	118	6.0	51.1
High-income	2,841	10.8	62.1
(countries in European Monetary Union)	*1,856*	*9.3*	*73.5*
World	500	9.8	59.2

Source: World Bank 2004, Table 2.14.

Figure 1.2 Major Causes of Death in Persons of All Ages, by World Bank Region

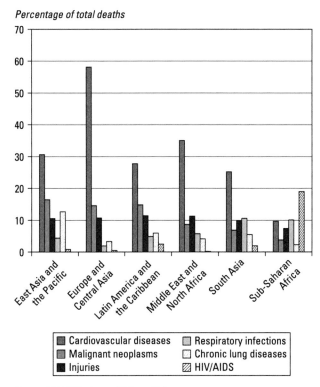

Percentage of total deaths

Legend:
- Cardiovascular diseases
- Malignant neoplasms
- Injuries
- Respiratory infections
- Chronic lung diseases
- HIV/AIDS

Source: DCP2 2006, chapter 33, figure 33.1.

AN AGENDA FOR ACTION

The general improvement in world health status is still marred by too many cases of neglect or failure in the application of life-saving public policy actions. What can be done to redress inequities while also sustaining and furthering historic gains in health? *DCP2* tackles this challenge with the latest evidence and cost-effectiveness analysis. It identifies the specific interventions and policy changes that hold the most potential for progress in health. These measures include applying knowledge about cost-effective health interventions in more settings, improving the policies and platforms that support quality health care delivery and reduce barriers to access, generating knowledge in priority areas, and mobilizing additional financial and human resources.

Applying Knowledge to Select Interventions Well

DCP2 presents what we know about which health interventions work for a comprehensive range of diseases, injuries, and disabilities in many different contexts. A large share of the disease burden in low- and middle-income countries is attributable to diseases for which cost-effective interventions are already known and feasible. Selecting the right intervention for a given disease and context matters. *DCP2* demonstrates how decision makers could use cost-effectiveness information along with information on disease prevalence and avertable illness to determine which interventions should be extended and which ones should be questioned. If countries scale up interventions and extend health care services that are cost-effective, the impact on the disease burden could be large.

"A large . . . disease burden in low- and middle-income countries is attributable to diseases for which cost-effective interventions are already known . . ."

Improving Health Systems

Improving health systems and reducing barriers to health care will improve the implementation of health interventions. *DCP2* gives substantial attention to strengthening health systems, because interventions—no matter how carefully selected—are almost impossible to deliver without such systems. As noted in *DCP2* (chapter 3, p. 85), "Cost-effectiveness data reflect largely what can be achieved given a reasonably well-functioning health system. In that sense they can be considered to represent *potential* cost-effectiveness and need to be supplemented with evidence and guidance on how health systems can be strengthened to provide interventions effectively, efficiently, and equitably" (emphasis added).

Systems can be strengthened, coverage can be extended, and equitable distribution can be achieved in a variety of ways, including increasing service infrastructure, reducing costs, improving quality, and establishing transparency in resource allocation. Increasing input from underserved populations is also imperative, because, as discussed in *DCP2* (chapter 3, p. 89), "Strengthening structures of accountability to communities, and introducing mechanisms to ensure that users have a voice in the local health system and can influence priorities, are likely to be important in encouraging good performance."

Determining Priorities for Research

The returns from research in health are extremely high, as illustrated by the potential health gains that could be reached by applying the knowledge available today. Putting resources into research now will permit greater health gains tomorrow, but such resources need to be well targeted. One priority area for research is finding cost-effective interventions for neglected diseases that account for a high burden, particularly among underserved populations. Another essential area of research is on all aspects of the delivery of health care, that is, devising the best and most effective means to get interventions to people who have so far been excluded from its benefits.

Current imbalances in attention to diseases and delivery include the following areas:

- *Drug development.* Of 1,233 new drugs marketed between 1975 and 1999, only 13 were approved specifically for tropical diseases.
- *Research funding.* Even though 85 percent of the global burden of disability and premature mortality occurs in the developing world, less than 4 percent of global research funding is devoted to the communicable, maternal, neonatal, and nutritional disorders that constitute the major burden of disease in developing countries.
- *Underutilization of health services by women.* This has been well documented overall and for specific diseases. For instance, even though women in India report more illness than men, hospital records show that men receive more treatment. Similarly, in Thailand, men are six times more likely to seek clinical treatment for malaria, a disease that affects women and men similarly (*DCP2*, chapter 10).

DCP2 identifies priority areas for research in epidemiology, interventions, and health care delivery.

Mobilizing More Resources

DCP2's attention to cost-effectiveness is motivated by the goal of achieving the most value for every dollar spent, but this does not imply that no more dollars are needed. A comprehensive effort to improve health around the world will involve substantial costs.

In most low-income countries, the total resources available for health interventions are grossly insufficient relative to the scale of the disease burden and the need for health interventions. Countries need to finance their own health interventions as much as possible, but for the world's low-income countries, external assistance is already, and will continue to be, an important source of funding. Even though

"One priority area for research is finding cost-effective interventions for neglected diseases that account for a high burden . . ."

"In most low-income countries, the total resources available for health interventions are grossly insufficient . . ."

development assistance has increased in the last decade, including participation by new private foundations and the formation of new global initiatives, more has been promised than delivered and further commitments are still needed.

In middle-income countries, financial resources may be a less binding constraint in absolute terms, but health interventions must still compete with other uses for resources. If existing resources are misspent or ineffective, lobbying for more resources for health when public allocation decisions are being made becomes more difficult. *DCP2* can assist in that process by helping the health sector become more effective and efficient.

PUTTING *DCP2* TO USE

The research, insight, and analysis undertaken in *DCP2* discerns trends in the leading causes of disease and injury over the last decade and has great significance for policy debates on how to respond to and diminish the burden of disease worldwide. Health policy actors and health system decision makers, whether at the level of national health ministries, large regional programs, or smaller programs, will find in *DCP2* up-to-date information on the burden of disease, on cost-effective interventions, and on the interplay of prevention and treatment. Together with their own knowledge about local burdens, resources, and institutional capacities, they will be better able to define priorities and select the best interventions to implement in their context. Others more involved in managing and administering health systems will find current best practice in the delivery of health care, recommendations for innovation, ways to improve quality, and strategies to overcome system constraints. Those primarily concerned with financing health care, whether national finance ministries or those involved in international assistance, will gain an appreciation for the role of health in economic growth and find evidence of the great health effect that is possible when resources are applied well. Researchers will learn of key priorities for their fields, while educators in public health will find a useful teaching tool.

The wealth of information and analysis covered in *DCP2* is structured into three parts (box 1.1). Part One provides perspective, context, and overview. It articulates the volume's main messages and policy implications. Chapter 1, "Investing in Health," provides historical perspectives; argues for investing in health; and highlights some of *DCP2*'s new

Box 1.1 DCP2 Table of Contents (see appendix for full list of authors)

(Continued on the following page.)

Box 1.1 (*Continued*)

36. Diseases of the Kidney and the Urinary System
37. Skin Diseases
38. Oral and Craniofacial Diseases and Disorders
39. Unintentional Injuries
40. Interpersonal Violence

C. Risk Factors

41. Water Supply, Sanitation, and Hygiene Promotion
42. Indoor Air Pollution
43. Air and Water Pollution: Burden and Strategies for Control
44. Prevention of Chronic Disease by Diet and Lifestyle Changes
45. The Growing Burden of Risk from High Blood Pressure, Cholesterol, and Bodyweight
46. Tobacco Addiction
47. Alcohol
48. Illicit Opiate Abuse

D. Consequences of Disease and Injury

49. Learning and Development Disabilities
50. Loss of Vision and Hearing
51. Cost-Effectiveness of Interventions for Musculoskeletal Conditions
52. Pain Control for People with Cancer and AIDS

Part Three: Strengthening Health Systems

A. Strengthening Public Health Services

53. Surveillance and Response
54. Information to Improve Decision-Making in Health
55. Drug Resistance
56. Community Health and Nutrition Programs
57. Contraception
58. School-Based Health and Nutrition Programs
59. Adolescent Health
60. Occupational Health
61. Natural Disaster Mitigation and Relief
62. Control and Eradication
63. Integrated Management of the Sick Child

B. Strengthening Personal Health Services

64. General Primary Care
65. The District Hospital
66. Referral Hospitals
67. Surgery
68. Emergency Medical Services
69. Complementary and Alternative Medicine

C. Capacity Strengthening and Management Reform

70. Improving the Quality of Care in Developing Countries
71. Workers: Building and Motivating the Workforce
72. Ensuring Supplies of Appropriate Drugs and Vaccines
73. Strategic Management of Clinical Services

findings, such as the unexpectedly high burden of cardiovascular illness in developing countries and the importance of care during a child's first 28 days of life for reducing infant mortality. Chapter 2, "Intervention Cost-Effectiveness," reviews the set of cost-effective interventions for all diseases discussed in *DCP2* and then identifies "best buys" among these. Coupled with information on local disease prevalence and health system capacity, readers will be able to use this analysis to decide which interventions are most suitable for their own contexts. While selecting interventions is crucial, no intervention will reach its target without good delivery mechanisms. Chapter 3, "Strengthening Health Systems," therefore reviews the evidence on health systems, identifying aspects of best practice and defining key areas for further research and improvement in the delivery and management of health care. Chapter 4, "Priorities for Global Research and Development of Interventions," examines some of the current gaps in knowledge and urgent priorities for further study and progress.

These 4 initial summary chapters are followed by 11 chapters addressing cross-cutting themes, including the Millennium Development Goals (MDGs), women's health, recent public health successes, ethics of resource allocation, and cost-effectiveness methodology, plus a range of financial and economic issues. These chapters provide further demographic and economic context and general discussion that inform all the subsequent chapters on specific diseases, interventions, and modes of delivery.

Part Two of *DCP2* turns to particular diseases, risk factors, and sequelae and the selection of interventions. It is subdivided into four categories, the first of which is "Infectious Disease, Reproductive Health, and Undernutrition." Its 13 chapters include discussions of HIV/AIDS, TB, malaria, diarrhea, tropical diseases, and maternal and neonatal conditions. The second category is "Noncommunicable Disease and Injury," with 12 chapters on cancers, diabetes, psychiatric disorders, cardiovascular disease (CVD), hemoglobinopathies, and intentional and unintentional injuries. The third category, "Risk Factors," provides eight chapters on such topics as air and water pollution, sanitation, obesity, and tobacco and alcohol consumption. The final category, "Consequences of Disease and Injury," offers four chapters that address developmental and sensory disorders, disability and rehabilitation, and pain control.

Finally, part Three of *DCP2* turns to health systems. "Strengthening Public Health Services" is its first category, with 11 chapters addressing

"While selecting interventions is crucial, no intervention will reach its target without good delivery mechanisms."

such topics as family planning, school health programs, adolescent health, and occupational health. The second category, "Strengthening Personal Health Services," provides six chapters on general primary care, district and referral hospitals, surgery, emergency care, and alternative medicine. The concluding category is "Capacity Strengthening and Management Reform," with four chapters tackling quality of care, human resources, essential medicines, and management of clinical services.

In addition to its principal volume, the Disease Control Priorities Project has generated a number of related publications. These include the *Global Burden of Disease and Risk Factors* volume (Lopez and others 2006), which updates the 1990 global burden of disease study. In the years that have elapsed since that earlier study, methods for measuring the disease burden have improved, new data sets have become available, and means to analyze existing data sets have been modified and strengthened. The *Global Burden of Disease and Risk Factors* presents these new methods, data sets, and analyses; compiles epidemiological data of deaths and disability for 2001 by age, gender, cause, and region; and includes information on exposure to risk factors.

The Disease Control Priorities Project also generated a review of public health successes that was published as *Millions Saved: Proven Successes in Global Health* (Levine and others 2004), a special issue of the *American Journal of Tropical Medicine and Hygiene* entitled "The Intolerable Burden of Malaria: What's New, What's Needed" (Breman, Alilio, and Mills 2004); the Disease Control Priorities Project Working Paper Series and Reprint Series (for a full list, visit the Disease Control Priorities Project Web site at http://www.fic.nih.gov/dcpp), and this volume.

THIS VOLUME

Priorities in Health is a companion volume to *DCP2*. It was written to facilitate access to the substantial content of *DCP2*, to synthesize some of *DCP2*'s major themes and findings, and to help readers identify which chapters will be of greatest significance and relevance to them. Via this companion volume, policy makers, practitioners, academics, and the interested public can learn about *DCP2*'s main messages, gain an understanding of its principal methods of analysis, appreciate the scope of diseases and issues covered, and be alerted to chapters of immediate interest. The companion volume will enable access to the massive amount of information and analysis contained in *DCP2* and facilitate discussion about disease control among colleagues, with constituents, and in the wider community.

The next chapter demonstrates that success is not only possible, but has been realized throughout the developing world. It relates a series of public health successes that have been documented as part of the Disease Control Priorities Project. Chapter 2 demonstrates that despite the high burden of disease in developing countries, success is possible and has been achieved even against great odds, and also that no single recipe for success exists.

Chapter 3 describes the cost-effectiveness methodology employed in *DCP2* and explains its uses, interpretation, and limitations.

Chapters 4 and 5 provide an update on selected diseases, highlighting some of the significant discoveries and sound strategies that emerged from *DCP2*'s comprehensive review of the global disease burden and the range of health interventions currently available. Chapter 4 reviews diseases such as diarrhea, maternal ill health, HIV/AIDS, and malaria, which account for much of the difference in health status between people living in the developing and the industrialized world. By contrast, chapter 5 addresses diseases for which the burden is shared and the challenges to improving health may be similar, as in the cases of CVD, diabetes, tobacco addiction, and neurological disorders.

Chapters 6 and 7 address issues related to implementing interventions and delivering care. Chapter 6 looks specifically at *DCP2*'s findings regarding different levels of health care services and how they relate to one another; particular health service functions, such as surgery and drug supplies, that are important throughout the health care system; and ways that health care services can be integrated around the needs of particular subgroups, such as schoolchildren and adolescents. Chapter 7 then takes a more in-depth look at four dimensions of the health care system that are key to making it effective: generating and using information, managing services to assure good quality, training and deploying qualified health care personnel, and mobilizing and allocating financial resources.

Chapter 8 urges the global community to adopt the strategies and priorities identified in *DCP2* so that progress in health for all can continue.

"... despite the high burden of disease in developing countries, success is possible and has been achieved even against great odds ..."

"... the challenges to improving health may be similar, as in the cases of CVD, diabetes, tobacco addiction, and neurological disorders."

Chapter **2**

Success in Addressing Priorities

At the most general level, priorities in health are clear: identify the cost-effective interventions for those diseases that impose the largest burdens—around the globe or in target regions or populations that exhibit grave need or inequity—and determine how to deliver those interventions effectively, efficiently, and equitably. Science and medicine have shown that many interventions can be effective. Combining this knowledge with economic analyses of cost-effectiveness identifies which interventions can achieve the greatest health gains with a given level of resources. Making such health gains a reality requires implementing the selected interventions, a challenge that countries with effective health systems are better able to handle, but one that countries without effective health systems can deal with by improving their existing health systems or constructing them where they are lacking.

Thus while health priorities are relatively easy to define, they are far more difficult to address, but doing so is possible. Indeed, investigators have carefully documented a number of recent public health successes in a search for lessons that will enable further successes.

The What Works Working Group, convened by the Center for Global Development's Global Health Policy Research Network, collected nominations from *DCP2* authors regarding successful public health interventions (Levine and others 2004). The working group examined the nominations and identified 17 cases that met 5 explicit criteria:

- They were implemented on a significant scale: national, regional, or global.
- They addressed a problem of major public health significance as measured by disability-adjusted life years (DALYs).

- They lasted at least five consecutive years.
- They were proven to be cost-effective, costing less than about $100 per DALY averted.
- They documented evidence of a clear and measurable effect on health outcomes, not just coverage rates or process indicators.

The stories behind these 17 cases were then researched and published in *Millions Saved: Proven Successes in Global Health* (Levine and others 2004). *DCP2,* chapter 8 summarizes these cases and provides additional insights into these public health successes, including some of the factors that helped make success possible (box 2.1).

The 17 cases that emerged from the selection process are not the only public health successes, nor are they necessarily representative of public health successes in recent decades,[1] but the collection is a treasure trove for those involved in public health. All the cases have been carefully analyzed for lessons regarding leadership, financing, collaboration, strategies, role of the public sector, constraints, and much more.

An important message for policy making that emerges from this collection is that success can come in many forms. Countries have achieved successes in the most trying institutional contexts and policy environments; against diseases of many different kinds, both infectious and noncommunicable; and with many different intervention methods, including those based on providing products (for example, vaccines), providing services (such as prenatal care or simple surgery), promoting behavior change (for instance, using condoms, filtering water, or practicing good hygiene), or reducing environmental risks (for example, spraying larvicides or building latrines). Some key elements recur, namely, political leadership, technological innovation, expert consensus regarding the approach, effective use of information, and sufficient public financial resources, and some types of challenges may be easier to meet than others, but no single ingredient is sufficient and no single combination ensures success. Rather, these stories convey the message that success is possible, demonstrated, and varied.

The wide range of approaches adopted to improve health presented in *DCP2* further demonstrate this point. *DCP2* does not offer a single prescription for improving health, but assesses the many interventions

---

[1] Indeed, the *DCP2* authors nominated another 26 interventions as clear examples of success in public health, but these had to be set aside because of a lack of formal evidence regarding their effect on health. Thus the absence of more cases in Levine and others (2004) may be attributed more to weaknesses inherent in current evaluation practices than to any paucity of accomplishments in public health.

Box 2.1 Successful Programs from Around the World

In addition to the six cases selected for discussion in the text, other public health successes presented in *DCP2* (chapter 8) include the following:

- *Improved health among children and adults.* In 1997, the Mexican government launched a new social welfare program design to help lift poor families out of poverty by providing cash payments in exchange for their participation in nutritional and supplementation programs, use of preventive and basic health care services, and children's school attendance. After five years, the children of participating families were 12 percent less likely to experience illness than those of nonparticipating families and their nutritional status had improved. Adult health indicators had also improved.
- *Chagas disease control.* In 1991, seven countries—Argentina, Bolivia, Brazil, Chile, Paraguay, Uruguay, and later Peru—joined forces as part of the Pan American Health Organization's Initiative for the Southern Cone Countries to combat Chagas disease through a combination of surveillance activities, house-to-house spraying, and other vector control methods. By 2000, disease incidence had fallen by 94 percent, and by 2001, disease transmission had been halted in Chile, Uruguay, and large parts of Brazil and Paraguay.
- *Diarrheal treatment.* In Egypt, the government launched a national program in the early 1980s to promote the use of locally manufactured oral rehydration salts by mothers by means of a four-part strategy that included: tailoring product design and branding to accommodate local preferences and customs; strengthening production and distribution channels, both public and private; training health workers; and engaging in social marketing and a mass media campaign. Between 1982 and 1987, infant and child mortality dropped by 36 and 43 percent, respectively. Mortality attributed to diarrhea fell 82 percent among infants and 62 percent among children.
- *Guinea worm control.* Twenty countries in Asia and Sub-Saharan Africa began a global campaign to eradicate guinea worm in the mid 1980s. Led by the Carter Center, the United Nations Children's Fund, the U.S. Centers for Disease Control and Prevention, and the World Health Organization, the campaign promoted improved water safety through deep well digging, environmental control, and the use of cloth filters for drinking water; health education programs; and case management, containment, and surveillance. By 1998, between 9 million and 13 million cases of guinea worm had been prevented, and global prevalence had dropped by 99 percent.
- *Family planning.* Since the 1970s, Bangladesh has promoted family planning through a door-to-door outreach program conducted by young, married women who provide information about limiting family size or spacing pregnancies and pertinent products. The outreach program is accompanied by an extensive media campaign. Contraceptive use among married women in Bangladesh is now approximately 50 percent, compared with only 8 percent in the mid 1970s, and the average number of children per family is 3.3, down from 7.0 during the same period.
- *HIV/AIDS prevention.* Thailand launched the 100 Percent Condom Use Program in 1991 to address the rising incidence of HIV/AIDS. The program provided boxes of

(Continued on the following page.)

"Between 1982 and 1987, infant and child mortality dropped by 36 and 43 percent, respectively. Mortality attributed to diarrhea fell 82 percent among infants and 62 percent among children."

"By 1998, between 9 million and 13 million cases of guinea worm had been prevented, and global prevalence had dropped by 99 percent."

Box 2.1 (*Continued*)

"... measles cases reported annually ... fell from 60,000 in 1996 to 117 in 2000."

condoms to brothels free of charge, mandated the use of condoms among sex workers, and threatened brothels with penalties and closure for noncompliance. Condom use in brothels rose from 14 percent in 1989 to more than 90 percent by 1992. The number of new sexually transmitted infections fell from 200,000 in 1989 to 15,000 in 2001, and the rate of new HIV infections fell five-fold between 1991 and 1993–95.

- *Measles elimination.* In 1996, the seven southern African countries agreed to a coordinated immunization strategy, supported by improved surveillance and laboratory capacity, to eliminate measles by including it as part of routine immunization for all nine-month old babies and organizing nationwide catch-up and follow-up campaigns for children age 9 months to 14 years. The number of measles cases reported annually in the region fell from 60,000 in 1996 to 117 in 2000. The number of deaths attributed to measles fell from 166 to none during the same period.

- *Salt fluoridation.* In Jamaica, a formal agreement between the Ministry of Health and the country's only salt producer introduced salt fluoridation in 1987 to prevent caries. By 1995, the prevalence of caries in children between the ages of 6 and 12 had fallen by more than 80 percent.

- *Salt iodination.* China launched the National Iodine Deficiency Disorders Elimination Program in 1993. The government requires producers to iodize salt and has stepped up its monitoring and enforcement capacity to ensure compliance. Total goiter rates among children between the ages of 8 and 10 fell from 20.4 percent in 1995 to 8.8 percent in 1999.

- *Tobacco control.* Poland passed groundbreaking legislation in 1995, imposing strong warning labels on cigarette packages, banning smoking from enclosed workplaces, and prohibiting tobacco sales to minors. South Africa passed similar legislation in 1999 to strengthen a previously imposed tax of 50 percent on the value of the retail price of cigarettes. Between 1990 and 1998, Poland experienced a 30 percent decline in lung cancer among men age 20 to 44, a nearly 7 percent decline in CVD, and a decline in the number of babies born with low birthweights. In the 1990s, South Africa witnessed a 30 percent decline in cigarette consumption, especially among youth and the poor.

- *Tuberculosis control.* In 1991, China launched a 10-year program in 13 of its 31 mainland provinces to apply the DOTS strategy to TB control. Peru, previously one of 23 high-burden countries that collectively account for 80 percent of the world's new TB cases each year, launched a similar effort the same year. Within two years of initiating its program, China had achieved a 95 percent cure rate for new cases and a cure rate of 90 percent for those patients whose treatment had previously been unsuccessful. Between 1999 and 2000, the number of people in these provinces with TB declined by more than 37 percent. In Peru, the DOTS program achieved a case detection rate of 70 percent and an 85 percent cure rate. As a result, disease incidence declined 6 percent a year.

Source: Adapted from *DCP2*, chapter 8.

"Between 1990 and 1998, Poland experienced a 30 percent decline in lung cancer among men age 20 to 44, a nearly 7 percent decline in CVD, and a decline in the number of babies born with low birthweights."

and implementation strategies that have worked in different places. This section presents just a few of these public health success stories, selected to illustrate some of the important messages in *DCP2* about the nexus between selecting cost-effective interventions and delivering them effectively. Specifically, these cases

- succeeded despite weak, or even absent, health systems (smallpox eradication)
- were conducted in ways that built or strengthened weak health systems (control of onchocerciasis [river blindness] and polio)
- were aimed directly at building a health system (improving maternal health)
- furthered existing health systems (*Haemophilus influenzae* type B [Hib] vaccination)
- moved beyond health systems (control of trachoma).

SUCCESSES DESPITE WEAK HEALTH SYSTEMS

Countries have implemented cost-effective interventions and accomplished major public health successes even under conditions of dire poverty, weak or nonexistent health care infrastructure, and civil unrest or war. Consider the worldwide eradication of smallpox. In 1980, the World Health Assembly declared that smallpox, which has been known since at least 1160 BC, was the first disease in history to have been eradicated. That eradication was accomplished through a global campaign that reached even the most distant rural parts of the world's poorest countries, war-torn countries, and countries whose health systems were barely functional.

Certain distinctive characteristics of smallpox shaped the strategy and influenced the success of the eradication. The disease was transmitted directly from person to person without any other hosts or vectors and was relatively easy to identify. Once an individual contracted smallpox, that person took 10 to 14 days to become infectious, but by then that individual was usually already bedridden, thereby reducing contact with others. People who survived the illness or were adequately vaccinated were immune for the rest of their lives. Thus features of the disease itself made its eradication feasible.

Essential technological breakthroughs for battling the disease included not only the actual smallpox vaccine but also the bifurcated

"Countries have . . . accomplished major public health successes even under conditions of dire poverty, weak or nonexistent health care infrastructure, and civil unrest or war."

". . . smallpox, which has been known since at least 1160 BC, was the first disease in history to have been eradicated."

needle, which reduced costs and made vaccinating people easier. Sustained leadership and funding were also crucial to the eradication campaign, but were not at first readily available. Initially proposed in 1958, the campaign to eradicate smallpox did not really begin until 1967 because of fortuitous changes in leadership and staffing at the World Health Organization (WHO) and decisions in the United States to commit substantial funding to the campaign.

Another important turning point involved shifting from a strategy of generalized vaccination of entire populations to a strategy of surveillance and containment. This so-called ring strategy involved highly refined epidemiological surveillance, selective containment, and vaccination of patients and communities in response to specific outbreaks. This strategy was crucial to eliminating the last remaining reservoirs of smallpox in five countries—Bangladesh, Ethiopia, India, Nepal, and Pakistan—even when one or more of these countries were in crisis, were suffering from war or civil unrest, or were facing massive refugee flows or extreme poverty.

The campaign against smallpox developed an intervention strategy independent of the existence or nonexistence of health systems and infrastructure in any of the countries, and it achieved its goal. A disease that at the start of the campaign had been responsible for millions of cases and 1.5 million to 2.0 million deaths a year, and that left many survivors deeply scarred or blind, had ceased to exist only three decades later.

SUCCESSES THAT STRENGTHENED WEAK HEALTH SYSTEMS

Countries have achieved other successful public health interventions in contexts of weak health systems and implemented them in ways that also strengthened these health systems. Controlling onchocerciasis in Sub-Saharan Africa and eliminating polio in Latin America and the Caribbean are two illustrations of this process.

Approximately 18 million people live in areas where onchocerciasis is endemic, 99 percent of them in Sub-Saharan Africa (*DCP2*, chapter 22). The disease is caused by a microscopic worm that infects humans through the bite of an infected blackfly that breeds in the fast-moving waterways of Sub-Saharan Africa. The victim's body is eventually infested with worms, resulting in a range of debilitating symptoms, including blindness. In endemic areas, more than a third of the adult population may be blind, and infection often approaches 90 percent of the population. Because of fear of the disease, people abandoned vast areas of fertile riverside land.

Control efforts, which were launched in 1974, have included weekly aerial spraying of breeding sites to kill the blackfly that spreads the disease and distribution of a new drug, ivermectin, that kills the worms in human beings. The impact has been immense. Key features of the effort included collaboration by many organizations and agencies, public-private partnership with the producer of ivermectin, and long-term funding. Initial successes led to subsequent and larger commitments such that from 1974 to 2002, the control efforts halted transmission in 11 West African countries, prevented 600,000 cases of blindness, permitted 18 million children to be born free from the risk of river blindness, and rendered about 25 million hectares of arable land safe for resettlement and cultivation. The control efforts achieved this despite the extreme poverty of these countries, the dispersal of populations in remote villages, the countries' inadequate health systems, a shortage of health workers, and the imperative of maintaining activities (including uninterrupted weekly aerial spraying of larvicide) despite civil and regional conflicts and coups.

Follow-up programs have emphasized long-term sustainability, because killing all the worms requires annual drug treatment for 15 to 20 years, and to this end have pioneered a system of community-directed treatment. This is a framework through which thousands of communities organize and manage ivermectin treatment locally. In some areas, the coordinators of the ivermectin distribution program are the only health workers to reach every village. Indeed, some people have suggested that even though the community-directed treatment framework was originally designed for onchocerciasis control, it could become the backbone of health systems and be used to distribute vitamin A, azithromycin (to treat trachoma), albendazole (to treat lymphatic filariasis), and even vaccines and HIV/AIDS drugs. Thus "the impact of the successful ComDT [community directed treatment] system extends beyond the treatment and prevention of river blindness. The system offers a valuable entry point for other community-directed health interventions in neglected communities with little or no access to traditional health services and a vehicle for strengthening the overall health system in developing countries" (Levine and others 2004, p. 62).

The elimination of polio in Latin America and the Caribbean offers some parallels. As recently as 1988, 125 countries were endemic

" . . . from 1974 to 2002, the control efforts . . . prevented 600,000 cases of blindness, permitted 18 million children to be born free from the risk of river blindness, and rendered about 25 million hectares . . . safe for resettlement and cultivation."

"As recently as 1988, 125 countries were endemic for polio. By the end of 2003, . . . just six countries reported polio . . ."

for polio (*DCP2*, chapters 20 and 62). By the end of 2003, because of a massive, well-targeted vaccination and surveillance campaign, just six countries reported polio cases and none of these were in Latin America and the Caribbean.

The elimination of polio faces particular challenges because of the nature of the disease. The causative virus is extremely contagious and, while usually transmitted by fecal-oral contact, can survive for as long as two months outside the body, residing in pools, drinking water, food, and clothing. Transmission can go undetected because 90 percent or more of carriers develop no symptoms. When symptoms do develop, they are not always recognizable as polio. Indeed, one distinctive and confirmed case of polio paralysis implies that the community has another 2,000 to 3,000 contagious carriers whose only sign of infection may be a fever (Levine and others 2004, p. 40). Eliminating such a disease is challenging even where health systems are strong.

With the inclusion of the oral polio vaccine in the Expanded Program on Immunization as of 1977, the success of initial efforts in Latin America was impressive. By 1981, the incidence of polio in the region had been halved and the number of countries reporting cases of polio had dropped from 19 to 11. By 1984, coverage with the vaccine reached 80 percent. This improvement encouraged the Pan American Health Organization to mount an all-out campaign to eliminate polio from the region.

Launched in 1985, the campaign had a striking feature—the coordination among international, regional, and national public and private organizations. This unprecedented coalition pursued a strategy to strengthen surveillance so that health workers could identify, rapidly respond to, and contain any outbreaks. It also bolstered polio immunization coverage, so that even countries with less robust health infrastructures and weaker routine immunization programs could achieve impressive results. This was done through such means as national vaccine days, which took place twice a year and during which children under five were inoculated regardless of whether or not they had been vaccinated previously.

The polio campaign left an enduring legacy for health systems in Latin America and the Caribbean by tackling polio in such a way that the campaign became "a stepping stone to strengthening the entire Expanded Program on Immunization . . . , to improving health infrastructure throughout the region, and to establishing a greatly needed

"The polio campaign left an enduring legacy for health systems in Latin America and the Caribbean . . ."

surveillance system to monitor the impact of interventions on the reduction of polio and other diseases" (Levine and others 2004, p. 41). In addition to enhancing infrastructure and improving the capacity for disease control, the polio campaign also built capacity for national health planning in that countries are now adapting the process of developing annual action plans for the polio campaign for other initiatives, including improving and extending maternal and child health services.

COST-EFFECTIVE INTERVENTIONS AIMED AT BUILDING HEALTH SYSTEMS

Vaccines will halt some diseases, and larvicides will wipe out some vectors, but such approaches have no bearing on prenatal care and childbirth. For these, a robust, functioning health system with equitable access is crucial for good results. The experience of Sri Lanka shows how this can be achieved.

Pregnancy and childbirth are natural events and typically require little or no medical intervention for either mother or baby (*DCP2*, chapter 26). However, if a woman is in poor health because of, say, malnutrition, malaria, immune deficiency, TB, or heart disease, she can face serious risks during pregnancy and childbirth. Reducing maternal and infant mortality requires preventive measures, such as proper nutrition and screening for possible risks. It also requires a sanitary environment for giving birth and swift, effective care in case of emergencies, such as obstructions at birth or hemorrhaging. Unsafe abortions are another major risk factor for women's health. Where health systems are poor and populations consequently lack appropriate care, a much higher proportion of pregnancies can result in complications, illness, permanent disability, or death of the mother or child. *Millions Saved* notes that "interventions to detect pregnancy-related health problems before they become life-threatening, and to manage major complications when they do occur, are well known and require relatively little in the way of advanced technology. What is required, however, is a health system that is organized and accessible—physically, financially, and culturally—so that women deliver in hygienic circumstances, those who are at particularly high risk for complications are identified early, and help is available to respond to emergencies when they occur" (Levine and others 2004, p. 48).

" . . . if a woman is in poor health because of . . . , malnutrition, malaria, immune deficiency, TB, or heart disease, she can face serious risks during pregnancy and childbirth."

Despite its poverty, this is what Sri Lanka has provided. In the 1950s, estimates indicated that Sri Lanka's maternal mortality ratio was 500 to 600 per 100,000 live births. By 2003 it had plummeted to 60, and skilled practitioners were attending 97 percent of births. This was an outcome of continued, dedicated efforts by the government to extend health services, including essential maternal health care, equitably. Sri Lanka has pursued its goal of building a system accessible to all in many different ways: it has purposely located facilities in rural areas, made care universally free, provided transportation networks, and strengthened referral systems. In developing human resources, it has paid particular attention to midwifery. Other basic attributes of the Sri Lankan system have been making good use of information for monitoring and planning, improving the quality of care, and targeting underserved populations.

The country's step-by-step strategy to provide broad access to specific clinical services, to encourage the use of those services, and to systematically improve quality has been facilitated by its excellent civil registration system and reinforced by a good education system notable for its gender equity (89 percent of Sri Lankan women are literate, compared with the South Asian average of 43 percent). Moreover, its dedication to providing social services for all has been sustained and predates independence in 1948.

Sri Lanka has been and remains a poor country. It has achieved its exemplary performance in maternal health not only without major technological innovations but also without high levels of spending. Indeed, it accomplished all this on a spartan budget. Absolute national spending on maternal health was almost the same in the 1990s as it had been in the 1950s; but income growth over that interval meant that the share of gross domestic product (GDP) fell from 0.28 to 0.16 percent. Furthermore, financing was mostly domestic, coming from government revenues. *Millions Saved* suggests that "others can take inspiration from the country's record: In the late 1950s, when the first efforts were made to address the problem of maternal deaths, the GNP [gross national product] of Sri Lanka was equivalent, in constant dollars, to the national income of Bangladesh, Uganda, or Mali today and far lower than that of Pakistan, Egypt, or the Philippines. In relative terms, Sri Lanka has spent far less on health—and achieved far more—than any of these countries" (Levine and others 2004, p. 54).

The success of Sri Lanka is related to maternal health specifically, but it could not have been achieved without building a robust, equitable health system overall.

COST-EFFECTIVE INTERVENTIONS THAT FURTHERED EXISTING HEALTH SYSTEMS

Even where countries have strong, functioning health systems, specific needs for new initiatives arise, perhaps because of a new disease, a serious inequity, an obstinate problem, or a generalized need for improvement. Solutions can come from within the health system, especially if that system is open to ideas, conducts research, and looks for ways to improve its performance and the health of its population. Vaccination against *Haemophilus influenzae* type B (Hib) in Chile offers such a story (*DCP2*, chapter 20).

Hib disease includes Hib meningitis, which is particularly lethal, killing 20 to 40 percent of the children who contract it and fewer of the adults who contract it and leaving half the survivors with lasting impairments such as deafness or mental retardation. Worldwide, Hib disease is the leading cause of bacterial meningitis in children under five and the second most common cause of bacterial pneumonia deaths in this age group. An estimated 450,000 children die from Hib disease each year. A highly effective, and relatively expensive, conjugate vaccine against Hib has been available since the late 1980s.

Chile is a middle-income country with a modern health infrastructure and efficient immunization services where 95 percent of infants receive routine vaccines. In the late 1980s, Ministry of Health researchers undertook the first estimates of the incidence of Hib in the Santiago area. Until that time, no information about the extent of the disease in Chile had been available. The researchers analyzed clinical and laboratory records; matched the data with census records; and assessed the quality of the data, including the probability that it understated the true extent of the disease. They concluded that Hib was a widespread problem and had a high death rate in Chile.

Even though Hib vaccines were available, they were costly, and despite substantial proof of their efficacy (their biological protective effect), less evidence of their effectiveness (impact on a large population of infants receiving the vaccine under the normal conditions of a routine immunization service) was available. Thus the Ministry of Health devised and conducted an intent-to-vaccinate study, testing a combination of Hib vaccine with the usual diphtheria-pertussis-tetanus vaccine administered at 36 health centers in the Santiago area, and compared the outcome with that at 35 centers that did not offer the Hib vaccine.

The results of this pilot program were dramatic. The study demonstrated not only that the Hib vaccine was effective but also that combining diphtheria-pertussis-tetanus and Hib vaccines and delivering them within Chile's established system was feasible for health centers. As a result, in July 1996 the Ministry of Health introduced the vaccine into the routine immunization program for babies nationwide. The incidence of Hib meningitis in Chile has fallen by 91 percent and that of pneumonia and other forms of Hib disease by 80 percent.

While the cost of the vaccine was initially substantial, the Chilean government funded it in full with public funds from general taxes. The price has since fallen from around US$15 per dose in 1996 to around US$3 in 2003. In 1998, researchers concluded that the nation saves US$78 for every case of Hib prevented, providing further evidence to support the public expenditure, which has continued.

The reasons behind Chile's success included its existing research strengths and ability to act on the results. Having a delivery system already in place, with a routine vaccine program reaching 95 percent of infants, was also key. In other words, Chile's successful Hib vaccine program was an intervention that succeeded by taking full advantage of the strengths of an already good health system.

COST-EFFECTIVE INTERVENTIONS BEYOND HEALTH SYSTEMS

The preceding examples show that health interventions can succeed in situations of dire poverty and even during violent conflict. In addition, a look at the history of the unprecedented gains in human health in the 20th century reveals that improvements in health are not dependent upon economic development. As noted in chapter 1, technical progress—embodied in scientific knowledge, cost-effectiveness analyses, and managerial expertise—can define and deliver cost-effective interventions in almost any setting. Nonetheless, as the battle against trachoma in Morocco illustrates, the potential synergies between health interventions and improvements in general social conditions are significant (*DCP2*, chapters 50 and 67).

Trachoma is a disease of poverty. It is a highly contagious bacterial infection, and repeated infections lead to corneal scarring and eventually blindness, usually at the age of 40 to 50. The disease is spread by direct contact with eye and nose secretions from affected individuals, by contact with contaminated towels and clothing, and by flies. Disease transmission is rapid and intense in conditions of overcrowding, poor hygiene, and poverty.

With economic development and improved hygiene, trachoma has disappeared from Europe and North America, but it continues to afflict the developing world, particularly the millions of people living in hot, dry regions where access to clean water, sanitation, and health care is limited. Children are its first victims. In endemic areas, prevalence rates in children age two to five years reach 90 percent. The disease also disproportionately affects women, who because of their close contact with children are infected two or three time more frequently than men. The heaviest burden of blindness from trachoma affects the populations of Sub-Saharan Africa. Trachoma is linked to poverty as both a symptom and a cause, because trachoma-related blindness strikes people in their economically most productive years.

Initially, Morocco handled trachoma as though it were primarily a medical problem. In the 1970s and 1980s, schoolchildren in the most affected provinces were treated with tetracycline eye ointment twice a year, but this did nothing to improve the standard of living among the rural poor. Thus, while trachoma virtually disappeared from developing urban areas, it pervaded poorer, rural areas. In the early 1990s, a national survey found that more than 5 percent of Morocco's population exhibited signs of trachoma and that virtually all the cases were concentrated in five poor, rural provinces.

In 1991, Morocco set up the National Blindness Control Program. This expansive partnership included the five government divisions responsible for health, education, employment, equipment, and water; international organizations; bilateral and multilateral agencies; and local nongovernmental organizations (NGOs). Between 1997 and 1999, the government incorporated the so-called SAFE (surgery, antibiotics, face washing, environmental change) community strategy into the National Blindness Control Program. This strategy worked as follows:

- *Surgery:* a simple, quick, inexpensive procedure to save patients' vision with a success rate of 80 percent. In Morocco, mobile surgical units staffed by doctors and specialized nurses performed the surgery.
- *Antibiotics:* one-dose azithromycin to treat active infections and reduce the community pool of infections. The government

"... trachoma has disappeared from Europe and North America, but it continues to afflict the developing world ..."

"In the early 1990s, ... more than 5 percent of Morocco's population exhibited signs of trachoma ..."

developed multiple strategies for distributing the donated drug based on the recognition that trachoma is a community disease and that reinfection is likely to occur if only isolated cases are treated.

- *Face washing:* regular face washing can break the cycle of reinfection and prevent bacteria from spreading. Information, education, and communication campaigns have proven effective in changing people's behavior.
- *Environmental change:* improved living conditions and community hygiene are essential for reducing the spread of trachoma. The government oversaw the construction of latrines in 32 villages and the provision of potable water in 74 villages. Some 350 local village associations also undertook to build latrines, drill wells, and store animal dung safely so that it could be used for fertilizer without spreading flies. Access to potable water increased from 13 percent of all rural communities in 1992 to 60 percent in 2000. With the acknowledgment that reducing poverty and improving literacy among women is central to the fight against trachoma, the government undertook interventions to improve literacy among women and implemented economic programs to increase women's incomes.

The adoption of SAFE was driven by Morocco's recognition that, as the head of the National Blindness Control Program observed, "Trachoma at the level of these regions is not strictly a medical problem; it is essentially the reflection of a socioeconomic problem . . . The real enemies are the disfavored rural communities, illiteracy, family overcrowding, lack of water, the accumulation of animal wastes, and the proliferation of domestic flies. In sum, the enemy to combat is not *chlamydia* but poverty" (quoted in Levine and others 2004, p. 86).

With a health program that intentionally moves beyond the health system to include and encourage broader aspects of economic development, Morocco has achieved a 75 percent drop in the prevalence of trachoma since 1999 and its complete elimination from some provinces—the most rapid progress against trachoma in a single country ever recorded.

CONCLUSION

The brief discussion in this chapter has only touched on selected aspects of a few of the successful public health interventions discussed in *DCP2*. Much more can be learned from these stories, but perhaps

"... improved living conditions and community hygiene are essential for reducing the spread of trachoma."

"... Morocco has achieved a 75 percent drop in the prevalence of trachoma since 1999 and its complete elimination from some provinces ..."

the greatest value is to dispel cynicism in the face of what sometimes appear to be overwhelming challenges.

Ironically, when public health interventions forestall epidemics and prevent diseases, they are invisible successes: it is only the failures that make the news. By documenting how millions of people have been saved through concerted action, *DCP2* and *Millions Saved* provide an opportunity to acknowledge, celebrate, and learn from successes; to appreciate their variety; and to assume a degree of informed optimism, which may be another ingredient essential to success.

"... when public health interventions forestall epidemics and prevent diseases, they are invisible successes ..."

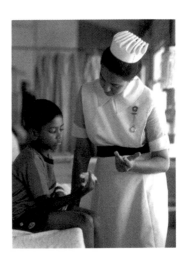

Chapter **3**

Cost-Effectiveness Analysis

Human health improved dramatically during the last century, yet grave inequities in health persist. To make further progress in health, meet new challenges, and redress inequities, resources must be deployed effectively. This requires knowledge about which interventions actually work, information about how much they cost, and experience with their implementation and delivery (*DCP2*, chapters 14 and 15).

WHY USE COST-EFFECTIVENESS ANALYSIS?

The 1993 edition of *Disease Control Priorities in Developing Countries* (Jamison and others 1993) was among the first efforts to guide choices about public health policies in developing countries by systematically combining information about effective interventions with information about their costs. It was motivated, in part, by a sense that developing countries were neglecting numerous opportunities for improving health and that better allocation of scarce resources could achieve better health outcomes. The publication presented cost-effectiveness analysis as an important tool for identifying these neglected opportunities and redirecting resources to better use.

Cost-effectiveness analysis helps identify neglected opportunities by highlighting interventions that are relatively inexpensive, yet have the potential to reduce the disease burden substantially. For example, each year more than a million young children die from dehydration when they become ill with diarrhea. Oral rehydration therapy (ORT) does not diminish the incidence of diarrhea, but dramatically reduces its severity and the associated mortality rate. The scientific evidence that ORT can save lives was an important step in identifying this as a neglected opportunity for improving health. Demonstrating that it could cost only US$2 to US$4 per life year saved helped make the case that this was something public policy should promote, and many countries responded by promoting ORT, saving millions of lives (*DCP2*, chapters 8 and 19).

Cost-effectiveness analysis helps identify ways to redirect resources to achieve more. It demonstrates not only the utility of allocating resources from ineffective to effective interventions, but also the utility of allocating resources from less to more cost-effective interventions. For example, a study by the National Center for Policy Analysis at Harvard University focused on 185 life-saving interventions that take place in the United States each year, costing US$21.4 billion and saving 592,000 life years. The study investigated different ways of allocating these funds and found that the number of life years saved could be doubled if resources were reallocated to more cost-effective interventions (*DCP2*, chapter 2, box 3).

DCP2 tells a similar story. It identifies dozens of interventions for a wide range of diseases and risk factors that are costly relative to the health gain they provide. These include hospital-based interventions, such as surgery for recurrent stroke, and community-based interventions for schizophrenia and bipolar disorder. Other interventions that are not particularly cost-effective include treating latent TB infections with isoniazid and regulations aimed at reducing alcohol abuse. If a country were to reallocate funds and efforts from these kinds of interventions and instead apply them to relatively more cost-effective interventions, substantially more people would be able to live longer and healthier lives. If reallocating funds from less cost-effective interventions is not feasible or appropriate, perhaps future increases in spending can be directed toward activities that will yield more health gains.

Studies of cost-effectiveness have multiplied since 1993, and the techniques have become more widely disseminated. *DCP2* has benefited from this expanding literature and has aimed for consistent comparisons across diseases and interventions. For example, wherever possible, the cost-effectiveness analyses in *DCP2* have used the same price units, health indicators, and definitions of included costs (box 3.1). This chapter introduces the basic concepts and methods of cost-effectiveness analysis, considers some of its limitations, and explains how it has been and can be put to use. The chapter also considers some of the other contextual factors that must complement cost-effectiveness analysis in the decision-making process if policy makers are to make the best use of the findings provided in *DCP2*.

Box 3.1 A Consistent Basis for Calculating Cost-Effectiveness in DCP2

Units for Cost-Effectiveness Ratios

The editors of *DCP2* asked the authors of the individual chapters to adopt a common method of cost-effectiveness analysis and to use consistent parameters. Authors were instructed to calculate cost-effectiveness in terms of U.S. dollars per DALY, where DALYs were calculated using disability weights provided by WHO and a 3 percent discount rate.

No Differentiation by Age

Unlike some studies, the editors of *DCP2* chose not to apply different weights by age. So, for example, the effect of saving an infant life counts for more than saving the life of an older person because of the difference in expected years of life, but not as the result of valuing a year of life saved at one age as higher or lower than a year of life saved at another age.

Basis for Calculating Years of Life

The calculations of expected years of life were based on regional average life expectancies at each age. This has the effect of reducing the cost-effectiveness of interventions in regions with lower life expectancy; however, within any region, this allows for a more realistic comparison of interventions that affect children and those that affect adults.

Currency Units

The main alternatives for measuring costs are to convert all currencies into a widely accepted currency such as U.S. dollars using market exchange rates or to convert them into international dollars by using a conversion factor based on purchasing power parity. The principal advantage of using international dollars is that they adjust for the real difference in purchasing power between one currency and another. However, *DCP2* elected to use U.S. dollars because they are more consistent with other cost estimates that are familiar to policy makers, and because available purchasing power indexes are based on aggregating a full spectrum of prices, and may therefore be misleading if used to analyze a specific sector with its own composition of tradable and nontradable goods. International dollars are harder to understand and do not correspond to financial feasibility as reflected in budgets.

Costs

DCP2 counts the costs of producing an intervention but not the costs of consuming it on the part of patients and their families. Indirect costs are often not monetary, especially the costs of people's time, and are hard to estimate consistently. When such costs are high, they make interventions appear not to be cost-effective, but the problem may lie with where facilities are sited and how they are staffed and operated rather than with the interventions they offer.

Source: Adapted from *DCP2,* chapter 15.

WHAT IS COST-EFFECTIVENESS ANALYSIS?

Cost-effectiveness analysis is a method for assessing the gains in health relative to the costs of different health interventions. It is not the only criterion for deciding how to allocate resources, but it is an important one, because it directly relates the financial and scientific implications of different interventions. The basic calculation involves dividing the cost of an intervention in monetary units by the expected health gain measured in natural units such as number of lives saved. For example, using volunteer paramedics and trained lay people as first responders to accidents costs about US$128 per life saved in South Asia and US$283 in the Middle East and North Africa, whereas using a community-based ambulance costs about US$1,100 and US$3,500 per life saved in the same two regions, respectively. By measuring cost-effectiveness in terms of lives saved, all lives are treated equally regardless of whether the person is an infant who might live another 80 years or a middle-aged person who can expect only another 40 years of life.

Some studies calculate cost-effectiveness using years of life lost as the natural unit for measuring the effect of interventions (box 3.2). This measure treats each additional year of life gained from an intervention as equal. It sums the number of years of life that would be saved by an intervention. Hence an intervention that saved an infant's life (for example, preventing dehydration from diarrhea) would count more than one aimed at saving an older person's life (for instance, preventing recurrence of a stroke).

Because the future is uncertain, common (but not universal) practice is to discount both health gains and costs in distant years. *DCP2* uses a discount rate of 3 percent per year, which has the effect of making 80 years of life expectancy at birth worth about 30 discounted years. With discounting, saving an infant's life still gains more years than saving that of a middle-aged person, but the difference shrinks considerably. Interventions that incur costs now but provide gains only years later look less cost-effective under discounting than when gains accrue immediately, but interventions whose costs and health benefits follow the same time pattern are all affected equally and their relative cost-effectiveness is unchanged.

Nevertheless, averting death or prolonging life is not the only goal of health interventions. Investigators have proposed other measures to differentiate between a year of life in perfect health and a year of life with some health impairment. One of the more commonly used measures

Cost-effectiveness ratio: The cost of an intervention divided by the resulting change in health status. The choice of currency units for measuring costs and the health units for measuring impact may vary. Wherever possible, *DCP2* reports U.S. dollars per DALY.

Average cost-effectiveness: The total cost of addressing a particular health problem using a particular intervention divided by the total health gain.

Incremental cost-effectiveness: The additional cost of extending a particular intervention divided by the additional health gain that would result.

DALY: A unit for measuring the amount of health lost because of a particular disease or injury. It is calculated as the present value of the future years of disability-free life that are lost as the result of the premature deaths or cases of disability occurring in a particular year.

Discount rate: A rate that is used to convert future costs and benefits into equivalent present values. For example, at a 3 percent discount rate, a cost of US$1 next year would be equivalent to US$0.97 today and a cost of US$1 in 10 years time would be equivalent to US$0.74 today.

Intervention: An activity using human, physical, and financial resources in a deliberate attempt to improve health by reducing the risk, duration, or severity of a health problem (Jamison 2002, table 2).

Quality-adjusted life year: A unit for measuring the health gain of an intervention calculated as the number of years of life saved and adjusted for quality.

Years of life lost: A measure of the impact of an adverse health event, generally calculated by subtracting the age at which death occurs from life expectancy at that age.

---

that addresses this issue is the disability-adjusted life year. A DALY measures not only the additional years of life gained by an intervention but also the improved health that people enjoy as a consequence. It assigns a value of 1 to a single year lived in perfect health. Any health impairment or disability is assigned a disability weight that describes the magnitude of the impairment, with a larger weight if the impairment is severe and a smaller one if the disability is modest. The value of a year lived with a disability then gets a value of 1 minus the disability weight, which measures the remaining degree of health. Researchers have assigned disability weights to various chronic conditions, pain, disability, and loss of bodily functions using a variety of methods, including international surveys that ask individuals to compare the quality of life under different health conditions. *DCP2* relied on disability weights calculated by

WHO's disease burden studies, sometimes using these to estimate disability from conditions that WHO had not explicitly considered.

DALYs are useful for policy makers because they are a more comprehensive measure of population health than merely counting deaths and because they allow comparisons among a wide range of health interventions. Some health interventions are aimed directly at reducing mortality, but many are aimed at reducing the severity of illness and improving the quality of life. With DALYs, these different interventions can be compared against a common standard. For example, a cost-effectiveness analysis that measured health gain by the number of averted deaths would find little value in preventing onchocerciasis, but measuring health gain in DALYs assigns a high value to preserving people's vision because the disability weight of blindness is large.

One of the advantages of using cost-effectiveness ratios is that they avoid some ethical dilemmas and analytical difficulties that arise when attempting cost-benefit analyses. Applying the alternative analytical technique of cost-benefit analysis requires assigning a monetary value to each year of life. By foregoing this step, cost-effectiveness analysis draws attention exclusively to health benefits, which are not monetized. When an intervention leads to health savings, the costs should be subtracted from intervention costs when compared to health outcomes. Many health interventions yield benefits beyond the immediate improvement of health status. For example, healthier parents will be able to provide better care for their children, healthier workers will be more productive in the workplace, and healthier families may avoid falling into poverty. Some health interventions can induce virtuous cycles. For instance, preventing the death of a parent may mean that a family has more income to provide nourishment for growing children. Other health interventions provide important ancillary benefits that are valued independently. For example, the cost-effectiveness of water and sanitation services in reducing gastrointestinal diseases is low, but piped water and sanitation services are valued in and of themselves as a convenience and an environmental improvement.

The values people place on nonhealth benefits are quite high as demonstrated by their willingness to pay for such services, but cost-effectiveness will not measure additional nonhealth-related benefits. Therefore comparing interventions according to cost-effectiveness criteria must be done with a clear understanding that it compares interventions only in terms of their efficiency at improving health, and if nonhealth benefits are going to be introduced into a debate, then they should be considered for all the interventions under discussion and not for a select few.

Cost-effectiveness analysis also requires comparable units for measuring costs. For domestic studies, the cost units in domestic currency will have a clear meaning. In the absence of unit prices of the inputs into interventions, for comparison across countries, *DCP2* authors were provided costs for each World Bank region in a widely used currency, usually U.S. dollars. The main question involves whether to use market foreign exchange rates to convert domestic currency costs and compare them to the value of imported and importable inputs expressed in dollars, or whether to use a different conversion factor based on studies of the relative purchasing power of the domestic currency. Because market exchange rates are easier to understand and correspond better to actual financial constraints, *DCP2* has used such rates for such conversions.

Cost estimates are affected by prices and prices can vary considerably between, and even within, countries. The authors of *DCP2* were unable to collect unit prices of the inputs into interventions in every country, so instead they were provided with average unit prices in each of six developing regions: East Asia and the Pacific, Europe and Central Asia, Latin America and the Caribbean, the Middle East and North Africa, South Asia, and Sub-Saharan Africa (previously published analyses, however, sometimes used WHO regional groupings). In the most complete analyses, the authors multiplied these regional unit prices by the estimated quantities of inputs required for each intervention and then divided by the estimated health effect to derive the cost-effectiveness ratios. In cases where the authors could not find disaggregated information on inputs but some cost-effectiveness measures were reported, they made extrapolations. In some cases, input ratios were available for one region and the authors extrapolated these to other regions (see, for example, *DCP2*, chapter 30).

To conduct a cost-effectiveness analysis, researchers also need to specify the health intervention in some detail. A health intervention is a deliberate activity that aims to improve someone's health by reducing the risk, the duration, or the severity of a health problem. Such interventions can be defined relative to adverse health events, such as being involved in an accident, contracting an infection, or suffering from a malignant tumor. Primary prevention seeks to avert an adverse health event, while secondary prevention aims to keep an adverse health event from recurring or causing a related problem once it has occurred. Following an adverse health event, interventions can also fall into several categories of case management, including cures, acute care, chronic care, rehabilitation, and palliation (box 3.3).

Box 3.3 Intervention Categories with Examples

The figure illustrates how interventions are related to a health event. The definitions of these categories are given below.

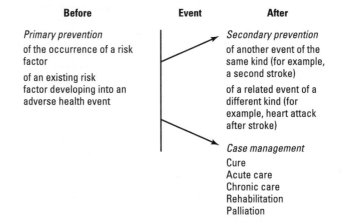

Population-based interventions all aim at primary prevention (as defined below), are directed to entire populations or large subgroups, and fall into three categories:

- Promoting personal behavior change (diet, exercise, smoking, sexual activity)
- Control of environment hazards (air and water pollution, disease vectors)
- Medical interventions (immunization, mass chemoprophylaxis, large-scale screening, and referral)

Personal interventions are directed to individuals, and can be intended for the following:

- Primary prevention—to reduce the level of one or more risk factors, to reduce the probability of initial occurrence of disease (medication for hypertension to prevent stroke, or heart attack), or to reduce the likelihood of disease when the risk factor is already present (prophylaxis for sickle-cell anemia).
- Secondary prevention following the occurrence of disease—to prevent another event of the same kind (medication to reduce the likelihood of a second coronary event) or to reduce the risk of a different but related event (medication to reduce the likelihood of a first heart attack after stroke).
- Cure—to remove the cause of a condition and restore function to the status quo ante (surgery for appendicitis).

- Acute management—to provide short-term activity to decrease the severity of acute events or the level of established risk factors, to minimize their long-term impacts (thrombolytic medication following heart attack, angioplasty to reduce stenosis in coronary arteries).
- Chronic management—to provide continued activity to decrease the severity of chronic conditions or prevent deterioration (medication for unipolar depression, insulin for diabetes). Chronic management can include some secondary prevention.
- Rehabilitation—to provide full or partial restoration of physical, psychological, or social function that has been damaged by a previous disease or condition (therapy following musculoskeletal injury, counseling for psychological problems).
- Palliation—to reduce pain and suffering from a condition for which no cure or rehabilitation is currently available (analgesics for headache, opiates for terminal cancer).

Source: DCP2, chapter 15, box 15.1.

Characterizing an intervention fully also requires defining the level of care at which it is delivered; the particular supplies and processes involved; and the types of health care workers and any associated services required, such as laboratory tests. The more detailed and accurate the analysis, the more readily investigators can assess whether it is similar to or diverges from how that intervention is characterized in other contexts. For example, health interventions might be provided by a less specialized facility or involve more visits in one country than another.

The scope of the costs included will also affect the cost-effectiveness analysis. Researchers may choose a narrow definition of costs and focus exclusively on the direct variable costs of providing a service; that is, they may only include the costs of additional materials and staff that are required and exclude costs associated with the use of existing infrastructure or installed capacity. In other cases researchers may use wider definitions of costs by apportioning some share of the fixed costs of facilities and administration to the costs of the service. The *DCP2* authors were asked to follow the latter approach.

In some studies, researchers include other costs, such as the value of the time patients and family members spend in obtaining a service or the cost of transportation to reach facilities. When more costs are included, the cost per unit of health gain will be higher and the intervention will appear to be less cost-effective. If the interventions that are being compared have similar characteristics, such as all being offered at a similar facility, then including these other costs will not alter the ranking of interventions, but comparisons across interventions that are dissimilar could yield different results if the ratios are otherwise close.

To be consistent, *DCP2* chapters use only direct costs, because estimates of these other costs are both difficult to obtain and rarely consistent across studies. An ethical problem is also involved if poor people's time is valued only on the basis of their low wages or incomes.

HOW RELIABLE IS COST-EFFECTIVENESS ANALYSIS?

Though the basic cost-effectiveness calculation appears to be simple, choices about units of measurement, definitions of interventions, scope of costs, and prices to be included not only will alter the numerical results but also will affect the interpretation of the cost-effectiveness ratio. In many cases the differences are so large that refining the underlying analyses is unnecessary. For instance, no amount of refinement will make coronary artery bypass grafting (>US$25,000 per DALY averted) more cost-effective than using new antimalarial drugs where resistance to older ones has developed (US$8 to US$20 per DALY averted) or taxing tobacco products (US$3 to US$50 per DALY averted) (table 3.1). For this reason, readers of *DCP2* are encouraged to pay attention to different orders of magnitude, distinguishing extremely or moderately cost-effective interventions from those interventions that are not cost-effective.

When cost-effectiveness ratios are within a similar range, policy decisions become more difficult. In such situations, closer scrutiny of the cost-effectiveness ratios may be warranted to improve confidence that the measures are close. This would entail verifying whether the units of measurement, the definition of interventions, and the scope of costs that are included were similar.

Note also that the quality of the evidence available to assess cost-effectiveness varies, especially given the wide range of interventions being looked at. *DCP2* notes that the best evidence comes from studies with randomized controls or systematic overviews and that the next best available evidence comes from nonrandomized studies that were nevertheless able to use rigorous statistical methods. The weakest evidence comes from limited case studies or surveys of expert opinion. However, a lack of evidence does not mean that an intervention is not cost-effective. It simply means that researchers do not know how cost-effective the intervention is. Nor does it mean that readers should ignore the cost-effectiveness numbers. Rather, readers should be cautious, should not rely heavily on point estimates, and should pay attention to orders of magnitude and quality of evidence.

Table 3.1 The Amount of Health US$1 Million Will Buy

Service or Intervention	Cost per DALY (US$)	DALYs averted per US$1 million spent
Reducing Under-Five Mortality		
1. Improved care of children under 28 days old (including resuscitation of newborns)	10–400	2,500–100,000
2.1 Expansion of immunization coverage with standard child vaccines	2–20	50,000–500,000
2.2 Adding vaccines against additional diseases to the standard child immunization program (particularly against haemophilus influenza and hepatitis B)	40–250	4,000–24,000
3. Switching to the use of combination drugs (ACTs) against malaria where there is resistance to current inexpensive and highly effective drugs (Sub-Saharan Africa)	8–20	50,000–125,000
Preventing and Treating HIV/AIDS		
4. Prevention of mother-to-child transmission (ARV–nevirapine–prophylaxis of the mother; breast-feeding substitutes)	50–200	5,000–20,000
5. STI treatment to interrupt HIV transmission	10–100	10,000–100,000
6.1 ARV treatment achieving high adherence for a large percentage of patients	350–500	2,000–3,000
6.2 ARV treatment that achieves high adherence for a small percentage of patients		because of very limited gains by individual patients and the potential for adverse changes in population behavior, there is the possibility that more life years would be lost than saved
Preventing and Treating Noncommunicable Disease		
7. Taxation of tobacco products	3–50	20,000–330,000
8.1 Treatment of acute myocardial infarction (AMI) or heart attacks with an inexpensive set of drugs	10–25	40,000–100,000
8.2 Treatment of AMI with inexpensive drugs plus streptoki-nase (costs and DALYs for this are in addition to what would have occurred with inexpensive drugs only)	600–750	1,300–1,600
9. Lifelong treatment of heart attack and stroke survivors with a daily "polypill" combining 4 or 5 off-patent preventive medications.	700–1,000	1,000–1,400
10.1 CABG or bypass surgery in specific identifiable high risk cases, such as disease of the left main coronary artery (incremental to 9)	>25,000	<40
10.2 Bypass surgery for less severe coronary artery disease (incremental to 9)	very high	very small

(Continued on the following page.)

Table 3.1 (*Continued*)

Service or Intervention	Cost per DALY (US$)	DALYs averted per US$1 million spent
Other		
11. Detection and treatment of cervical cancer	15–50	20,000–60,000
12. Operation of a basic surgical ward at the district hospital level focusing on trauma, high risk pregnancy, and other common surgically-treatable conditions	70–250	4,000–15,000

Sources: DCP2, Chapter 1, table 1.3.
Note: DALYs averted per US$1 million spent on an intervention will vary enormously from country to country and in light of many other factors. This table aims only to provide a very *rough* sense of how much health can be bought with different interventions and to show that there is huge variation in the amount of different health interventions (or that the same intervention applied in different ways) can provide for the same amount of money.
ACT = artemisinin combination therapy
AMI = acute myocardial infarction
ARV = antiretroviral
CABG = coronary artery bypass graft
STI = sexually transmitted infection

WHAT ARE APPROPRIATE TASKS FOR COST-EFFECTIVENESS ANALYSIS?

"Cost-effectiveness analysis . . . provides information about the costs of improving health by means of a particular intervention."

Cost-effectiveness analysis can offer no help for many important policy-making tasks. It essentially provides information about the costs of improving health by means of a particular intervention. As with any investment decision, the price of something is an important, but not the only, consideration. For example, the cost of building a school—like the cost of building a clinic—will vary depending on its size and location and the materials used. Those choices will affect the cost of schooling per student, which may affect the number of children who can attend and perhaps the quality of their learning. However, without information about price, decision makers cannot see the trade-offs involved in addressing other concerns.

Thus the question becomes how policy makers, health program administrators, researchers, and others can make the best use of cost-effectiveness analysis. Three types of comparisons become immensely easier with cost-effectiveness analysis:

- comparisons of different interventions for the same disease
- comparisons of different interventions for reaching specific segments of a population
- comparisons of different interventions for different diseases.

Using the cost-effectiveness ratio is most straightforward when comparing interventions that address the same disease or risk factor and differ only in the mode of delivery. In this case, cheaper interventions generally result in greater health gains. For example, addressing vitamin A deficiency by means of capsule distribution has a similar impact on health as fortifying sugar; however, capsule distribution costs about US$6 to US$12 per DALY averted, whereas sugar fortification costs about US$33 to US$35 per DALY averted. Another way of looking at this is to note that for the same cost, capsule distribution could reach three to five times more people than fortified sugar (*DCP2*, Chapter 28). This is a clear indication that more health gain is possible by spending resources on capsule distribution.

However, even in this simple example, decision makers might need to take other factors into account, in particular, that different interventions may reach different people. The cost-effectiveness analysis treats all health gains equally, whereas in public policy, distribution issues are also important. For example, capsule distribution might only reach people who attend health centers, while sugar fortification would only reach people who buy sugar. Depending on the characteristics and behaviors of the population with vitamin A deficiency, fortification might, in practice, be both more effective and more equitable. Fortification would still be costlier per DALY, so decision makers would have to decide whether the additional cost of achieving the more equitable outcome is affordable relative to other uses of the same funds.

Cost-effectiveness analysis is also useful when comparing interventions that address different diseases or risk factors. Scarce resources will generate more health improvements when they are applied to interventions that are more cost-effective. If the cost-effectiveness analysis uses number of deaths averted as its measure of health gain, then allocating resources to more cost-effective interventions will avert the most deaths. For example, spending US$1 million on expanding the traditional vaccination schedule for children to include a second opportunity for measles immunization would avert between 800 and 66,000 deaths, depending largely on the prevalence of measles. In contrast, spending the same amount of money to expand the schedule to include Hib vaccine would avert between 10 and 800 deaths and including yellow fever vaccine would avert between 300 and 900 deaths.

If instead the analysis uses DALYs as the measure of health gain, then allocating resources to the most cost-effective interventions will maximize years of healthy life. For instance, US$1 million spent on

" . . . addressing vitamin A deficiency by . . . capsule distribution has a similar impact on health as fortifying sugar; however, capsule distribution costs about US$6 to US$12 per DALY averted, averted whereas sugar fortification costs about US$33 to US$35 . . ."

" . . . spending US$1 million . . . to include a second opportunity for measles immunization would avert between 800 and 66,000 deaths, . . ."

nevirapine and breastfeeding substitutes to prevent HIV-infected mothers from transmitting HIV to their children would yield a gain of 5,000 to 20,000 DALYs, whereas the same amount of money spent to expand immunization coverage with standard children's vaccines would yield a gain of between 50,000 and 500,000 DALYs.

Thus cost-effectiveness should not be the exclusive basis for making health-related public policy decisions and should be complemented with information about distributional consequences. For public policy makers, these two kinds of information establish the trade-offs inherent in allocating funds to different interventions.

HOW CAN POLICY MAKERS USE COST-EFFECTIVENESS ANALYSIS?

To provide good policy guidance, cost-effectiveness must be complemented with essential information about the larger context, in particular, the prevailing burden of diseases, the existing coverage of health interventions, and the overall capacity of the health system.

An essential contextual factor in using information on the cost-effectiveness of any intervention is the burden caused by a disease. Some interventions may be highly cost-effective but affect only a small number of people or provide a small improvement in health (figure 3.1). For example, leishmaniasis treatment is relatively cost-effective, but is only applicable to a relatively small number of cases. By contrast, antimalarials and insecticide-treated bednets are cost-effective measures that, in certain countries, would avert a large burden of disease. If possible,

Figure 3.1 Efficiency of Interventions

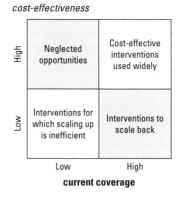

Source: DCP2, chapter 2, p. 34.

countries would finance all measures that would improve health, but as every country faces a tight budget or constrained capacity to deliver services, the avertable burden of disease is an essential piece of information that policy makers require when choosing between otherwise similarly cost-effective interventions.

Health interventions that are preventive will generally be more cost-effective in places where the burden of the targeted disease or risk factor is high and, consequently, where the intervention will avert more cases. Yet current prevalence is not always a good indicator of whether an intervention will be cost-effective, particularly in places where effective public health programs are responsible for the low rate of prevalence. For example, the prevalence of diphtheria, tetanus, pertussis, and measles is generally low in countries with effective vaccination programs, yet the cost-effectiveness of the vaccination program, which is needed to avoid a resurgence of these illnesses, is still quite high.

Prevalence also has a large effect on the cost-effectiveness of screening for illnesses and, indirectly, on the cost-effectiveness of a package to address a certain ailment. For example, screening and treatment for helicobacter, a bacterial risk factor for stomach cancer, is not cost-effective in the United States, but is cost-effective in Colombia, because the prevalence of stomach cancer is higher in Colombia and many of the costs of treatment are lower (*DCP2*, chapter 29).

The cost-effectiveness of screening for cancers and many other illnesses depends on the costs of identifying cases, on how many people do not follow up with treatment, and on the direct costs of treatment. Of course, if no treatment is available, screening is pointless. Testing for anemia among people with AIDS is cost-effective among those treated with zidovudine not only because screening is relatively cheap (less than US$0.02 per anemia test) but also because anemia occurs in 10 percent of these patients. When costs are higher or the likelihood of encountering conditions is small, screening may not be cost-effective.

Cost-effectiveness is also sensitive to the probabilities of transmission. For example, universal blood screening for HIV is costly, yet it is also cost-effective, even in countries with a low prevalence of HIV/AIDS, because receiving contaminated blood has such a high probability of leading to infection—almost 100 percent.

An appropriate time horizon is also imperative in assessing the weight of a disease burden and the value of an intervention for several reasons. One is that the gains from the intervention may accrue only in

"... the avertable burden of disease is an essential piece of information that policy makers require when choosing between otherwise similarly cost-effective interventions."

"... universal blood screening for HIV is costly, yet it is also cost-effective, even in countries with a low prevalence of HIV/AIDS ..."

the long term, so the intervention appears to be effective with a long horizon but not a short one. The discount rate matters greatly to this comparison because it makes the distant future less valuable. Another reason is that the intervention may have to be repeated for several years to assure the potential health gains. This is the case for ORT, which may need to be given many times over several years to prevent diarrheal disease deaths among young children, and for penicillin prophylaxis, to prevent deaths from infection in children with sickle cell disease (*DCP2,* chapters 19 and 34). Finally, an intervention may have substantial start-up costs that must be amortized over some period. *DCP2* uses 10 years as the standard in such cases.

The coverage of existing interventions is another crucial contextual factor in making use of cost-effectiveness analysis. When policy makers decide how to allocate resources, they can compare interventions that are relatively more or less cost-effective in light of the current supply of services. For example, some interventions may be extremely cost-effective but have low coverage. These are neglected opportunities that policy makers should look at more closely. Barring other contravening factors, these are likely to be interventions that would have a large effect on health for relatively little cost.

DCP2 mostly reports cost-effectiveness ratios as if they were independent of the level and scale of interventions, yet the incremental cost-effectiveness of most interventions will also vary with the level of service coverage. The cost of reaching the first 1 percent of a population may be quite high when the fixed costs of purchasing equipment, training staff, and setting up management systems are taken into consideration and may yield relatively few health gains. As coverage increases, however, the average cost may fall and health improvements may increase, resulting in a substantial improvement in the cost-effectiveness of reaching an additional group, for example, extending from 50 percent coverage to 51 percent coverage. Once coverage is high, reaching the remaining, and often marginalized, segments of the population may again be quite costly without a correspondingly large health gain, and consequently cost-effectiveness will worsen. Consider the experience of eradicating smallpox. At a certain point in the campaign, large parts of the world were free of smallpox and eradication became contingent on identifying the last few redoubts of the virus and responding massively and quickly to quarantine those infected and vaccinate everyone else in those areas. Today the polio campaign faces a similar challenge: reaching and vaccinating a few children in rural parts of India and Sudan is much costlier than treating many more in urban areas, but elimination of the disease can justify those high costs. A similar process is at play with the provision of basic health care in that it is generally less costly per person in areas with dense rather than sparse populations.

In addition to disease prevalence and existing coverage, policy makers need to take other local factors into consideration. *DCP2* provides estimates based on regional averages of unit prices,[1] but local prices and the availability of inputs may vary substantially from regional averages. Therefore a first consideration is whether a particular country's prices are near to or diverge sharply from the regional average. A second consideration is whether prices of key inputs have changed since the original analysis. One of the most dramatic changes since the earlier edition of *Disease Control Priorities in Developing Countries* (Jamison and others 1993) has been the fall in prices of antiretroviral drugs. Consequently, antiretroviral therapy is substantially more cost-effective today than it was a decade ago. Further reductions in the costs of diagnostic testing and alternative forms of delivery may increase the cost-effectiveness of antiretroviral therapy even further in the near future.

Finally, the cost-effectiveness of most health interventions also depends on how well the health system functions (*DCP2*, chapter 3). Most *DCP2* chapter authors calculate cost-effectiveness ratios based on the assumption that a functioning health system is available to deliver the intervention; however, this is an assumption whose validity varies greatly across countries. If a country has a particularly weak health system, then interventions that rely heavily on medical professionals, complex treatments, or sophisticated information systems will not be as cost-effective in practice as they would be in countries with stronger health systems.

The experience of introducing IMCI (*DCP2*, chapter 63) demonstrates the extent to which health system functioning can influence the cost-effectiveness of health interventions. Experiences in several districts in Brazil and Tanzania show that the IMCI package of interventions not only improves children's health outcomes but can actually be cost saving by reducing improper care and excessive use of medications. However, in most low- and middle-income countries the IMCI

---

[1] When price data were only available from a few countries in a region, *DCP2* authors tried to select a price that was most likely to be representative of that region, even if it was not a calculated average.

package has encountered difficulties in implementation and failed to realize its promise of cost-effectiveness because of high rotation and attrition of trained staff, inadequate supplies, and insufficient funds.

SUMMARY FOR USING COST-EFFECTIVENESS ANALYSIS PROPERLY

Applying resources effectively means spending money on things that influence health, and this requires scientific knowledge about risk factors, diseases, biochemistry, social behavior, and so on, but this scientific knowledge alone does not determine which interventions will have the most impact. To determine the best allocation of public funds, policy makers need information about relative costs to determine what combination of interventions can yield the greatest improvements in health. Cost-effectiveness analysis is the tool for weighing different costs and health outcomes when policy makers have to make resource allocation decisions. It does this by giving policy makers the "price" of achieving health improvements through different kinds of interventions, and thereby helps them make decisions that get the most out of their financial resources.

Ultimately, knowing which interventions work and at what cost has to be tempered by knowledge of institutions and implementation. Only when scientific and practical knowledge are combined can policy makers identify the interventions that will have the most impact in practice. Thus the cost-effectiveness analyses presented in *DCP2* and in this book provide an important contribution to broader debates about public policy decisions pertaining to health.

DCP2 compiles the best available evidence about the cost-effectiveness of different interventions. To use these numbers properly, readers should

- consider the cost-effectiveness ratios reported for their regions as a first approximation and rank the interventions in broad categories
- assess whether the calculated ratios would differ substantially in their countries because prices, demographics, epidemiology, or service coverage differ significantly from the regional average
- consider whether the cost-effective interventions would address major sources of the disease burden in their countries

- determine whether the cost-effective interventions would be feasible given existing institutions and experiences with implementation in their countries
- evaluate the cost-effective interventions in terms of how they would distribute health improvements and whether this would be equitable in their countries.

At the conclusion of such a review of the international evidence, countries will be able to achieve better health for their people because they can explicitly assess the costs and consequences of different courses of action.

Chapter **4**

Cost-Effective Strategies for the Excess Burden of Disease in Developing Countries

Many of the diseases and health conditions that account for a large part of the disease burden in low- and middle-income countries are far less common in high-income countries. These burdens are primarily associated with infectious diseases, reproductive health, and childhood illnesses. Just eight diseases and conditions account for 29 percent of all deaths in low- and middle-income countries: TB, HIV/AIDS, diarrheal diseases, vaccine-preventable diseases of childhood, malaria, respiratory infections, maternal conditions, and neonatal deaths.

Approximately 17.6 million people in low- and middle-income countries die each year from communicable diseases and maternal and neonatal conditions. Both the occurrence of and the death rates from such diseases and conditions are far lower in all high-income countries. This is due in part to greater wealth, better general living conditions, and different climatic and environmental factors, but also to the use of cost-effective health interventions. Many of the diseases that account for the largest differences in health status between low- and middle-income countries and high-income countries are also diseases for which cost-effective strategies are known, available, and feasible.

If low- and middle-income countries achieved the same rates of death from these diseases as high-income countries, the number of deaths would fall from 17.6 million to 3.0 million per year. The difference, some 14 million deaths, represents a measure of the excess burden of ill-health in low- and middle-income countries. Applying known and cost-effective measures to these diseases could substantially reduce many needless deaths.

A number of cost-effective measures for addressing communicable diseases and maternal and neonatal conditions were already known when the first edition of *Disease Control Priorities in Developing*

Countries (Jamison and others 1993) was published. ORT had been proven cost-effective for reducing case fatalities associated with childhood diarrhea. Prenatal care and skilled birth attendance, immunization against tetanus and hygienic care of a newborn's umbilical cord, immunization against childhood illnesses, and the DOTS strategy for controlling TB were also known, cost-effective measures for addressing this excess burden of disease. *DCP2* presents information confirming many of these earlier findings, but also surveys new evidence concerning, for example, the emergence of drug-resistant strains of malaria, TB, and HIV and the large concentration of childhood deaths that occur in the first 28 days of life.

This chapter can discuss only a selection of the diseases covered in *DCP2* that constitute the excess disease burden in low- and middle-income countries. (For a complete list of communicable diseases and maternal and neonatal conditions that are covered in *DCP2* see chapter 1, box 1.1, and the appendix.) Moreover, the following accounts can highlight only a few of the findings for each of the diseases included. For a fuller and more complete account, refer to the associated *DCP2* chapters as referenced in this chapter.

INFECTIOUS AND COMMUNICABLE DISEASES

"Infectious diseases account for less than 2 percent of deaths in high-income countries, but . . . 21 percent of deaths in low- and middle-income countries."

Infectious diseases account for less than 2 percent of deaths in high-income countries, but are responsible for 21 percent of deaths in low- and middle-income countries. Infectious diseases reveal a glaring difference in health status between rich and poor countries precisely because cost-effective interventions are available to prevent and treat so many of them.

Infectious diseases pose a range of challenges. Some are transmitted directly from one person to another, others through contact with insects or other animals. The human body's immune system readily resists some, whereas others, including auto-immune diseases, attack and weaken the immune system itself. Some present visible and obvious symptoms in a short time, while others are harbored for years before becoming active. Infectious diseases also vary in their virulence, infectiousness, and duration, and the infectious agents of some develop resistance to medications more rapidly than others.

Three communicable diseases, HIV/AIDS, TB, and malaria, account for about 10 percent of the deaths in low- and middle-income countries. Looking at just these three diseases suggests the immense variety of infectious diseases and demonstrates why strategies for dealing with them must be so different. HIV/AIDS is transmitted primarily through sexual contact, TB through inhaling infectious droplets in the air, and malaria exclusively from mosquito bites. HIV/AIDS attacks the body's immune system, while TB primarily attacks the lungs and malaria impairs the bloodstream and can attack the brain, liver, and other organs. Untreated HIV/AIDS is almost invariably lethal, and TB and malaria can also be fatal.

Another 10 percent of deaths in low- and middle-income countries are attributed to other diseases caused by infectious or communicable agents. For many of these diseases, such as pertussis, tetanus, and diphtheria, vaccines are available and universal coverage is practicable. Nevertheless, millions of children remain unvaccinated and consequently risk illness or death. Infections also cause diarrheal diseases that lead to needless deaths when children are not given proper treatment and die from dehydration.

HIV/AIDS

HIV has spread worldwide in a short time, but is disproportionately concentrated in low-income countries.[1] In 2004, some 2.9 million deaths attributed to AIDS occurred in the low- and middle-income countries, compared with an estimated 22,000 in the high-income countries. Sub-Saharan Africa is the region most affected by the epidemic. With only 10 percent of the world's population, it nonetheless accounts for 66 percent of all HIV cases and more than 75 percent of AIDS-related deaths. Countries in East Asia and the Pacific do not have prevalence rates as high as those in Sub-Saharan Africa, but their populations are large and prevalence is rising. In 2004, approximately 505,000 AIDS-related deaths occurred in this region, representing about 17 percent of all AIDS-related deaths.

When the disease was first identified in the early 1980s, most of those living with HIV/AIDS were men. The proportion of women affected by the epidemic has steadily grown: by 2004, women and girls accounted for nearly 50 percent of all people living with HIV/AIDS, and in Sub-Saharan Africa, women and girls represent 57 percent of those infected.

"... HIV/AIDS, TB, and malaria, account for about 10 percent of the deaths in low- and middle-income countries."

"In 2004, some 2.9 million deaths attributed to AIDS occurred in the low- and middle-income countries, compared with an estimated 22,000 in the high-income countries."

[1] This section is based on *DCP2*, chapters 17 and 18.

HIV is transmitted primarily through sexual intercourse, which accounts for approximately 80 percent of all infections. HIV is also transmitted via exposure to infected blood and from mother to child during childbirth or breastfeeding. Efforts to reverse the epidemic are founded on preventive strategies. For sexual transmission and exposure to infected blood, such measures include educating people about infection and how it is transmitted, encouraging condom use and decreased sexual contact with concurrent partners, screening blood that will be used for transfusions, establishing needle exchanges for injecting drug users, and promoting universal access to clean needles in health care settings. Antiretroviral drugs can be used to halt mother-to-child transmission (MTCT) during birth; perinatal transmission can also be reduced by limiting the duration of breastfeeding and preventing mixed feeding. Epidemic control strategies must also include treatment regimens using antiretroviral therapy (ART), which can extend lives and improve the quality of life for people living with AIDS.

In spite of these efforts, global attempts have not proved sufficient to control the spread of the pandemic or to extend the lives of the majority of those infected. The desired level of success has not yet been achieved for several reasons. Most people who could benefit from available control strategies (including treatment) do not have access to them. Modeling of the epidemic has determined that existing interventions could prevent 63 percent of all infections projected to occur between 2002 and 2010. However, as of now, fewer than one in five people at high risk of infection had access to the most basic prevention services, including condoms, AIDS education, MTCT prevention, voluntary counseling and testing (VCT), and harm reduction programs. Furthermore, care for those infected with HIV has historically been limited in developing country settings, and coverage of ART has been unavailable to most people living in resource-scare countries (notable exceptions include Argentina, Brazil, and Mexico). In short, national programs have lacked the means to undertake a comprehensive approach to HIV/AIDS.

Another enormous barrier to developing appropriate control strategies is lack of data about how to best implement packages of existing interventions at appropriate scale to maximize the effect of care interventions and to protect the human rights of people affected by the epidemic. During the past decade, governments and NGOs have accumulated limited but valuable experience with preventive and treatment strategies in a wide range of settings, making it possible to identify and

". . . existing interventions could prevent 63 percent of all infections projected to occur between 2002 and 2010."

emulate general principles of success. Nevertheless, the epidemic has continued to spread, but much less quickly in countries—including Brazil, Mexico, Senegal, Thailand, and Uganda—where national policies have taken the AIDS epidemic seriously and implemented national programs to control the disease (see box 4.1 and box 4.2). These successful programs had several features in common, including high-level political leadership, active engagement of civil society and religious leaders, population-based programs designed to change social norms, condom promotion, surveillance and control of sexually transmitted infections (STIs), programs to combat stigma and discrimination, and interventions targeting key "bridge" populations.

Perhaps the greatest challenge to effective global control of HIV/AIDS, however, is the lack of reliable evidence to guide the selection of prevention and care interventions for specific areas or populations. In the same way that global policy makers increasingly recognize the need for rigorous evaluation of development programs to ensure their success and eliminate waste, the need for reliable scientific evaluations of AIDS control programs is equally paramount for the same reasons. Lack of data on both the effectiveness and the cost of interventions to guide informed policy-making means that the current allocation of resources for HIV/AIDS prevention is seldom evidence-based.

Nevertheless, in spite of the paucity of rigorous data on effectiveness and costs of various control strategies, action is required. Guidelines

> "... the epidemic has continued to spread, but much less quickly in countries ... where national policies have taken the AIDS epidemic seriously ..."

Box 4.1 Uganda HIV/AIDS Epidemic

Like many countries in Sub-Saharan Africa, Uganda experienced a rapid increase in HIV incidence and a generalization of the epidemic in the late 1980s and early 1990s. By 1991, overall HIV prevalence was 21 percent (Low-Beer and Stoneburner 2003); however, the trajectory of Uganda's epidemic has differed markedly from that of its neighbors. By 2001, overall HIV prevalence had fallen to 5 percent, with dramatic decreases in incidence among key populations, such as soldiers, pregnant women, and young women (USAID 2002). Critical components of Uganda's HIV prevention program include the following:

- strong political support, especially from President Yoweri Museveni
- interventions to empower women and girls
- a strong focus on youths
- active efforts to fight stigma and discrimination
- emphasis on open communication about HIV/AIDS
- engagement of the religious leadership and faith-based organizations
- creation of Africa's first confidential VCT interventions
- emphasis on STI control and prevention.

Source: DCP2, chapter 18, box 18.5.

have been developed for selecting appropriate prevention and treatment strategies based on the epidemiological profile of a country (the characterization of individual epidemics, based on the prevalence of infection in particular key populations, such as sex workers, men who have sex with men, or intravenous drug users, and in the general population) and the unique political, cultural, and economic context.

These categories are listed in table 4.1, "Epidemic Profiles" (with the generalized epidemic category further subdivided into low and high categories). These categories can be used to develop prevention guidelines.

In countries where the prevalence of HIV infection is low, prompt, effective action is still imperative. Data collection is critical to evaluate the progress of the epidemic and guide public policy. Mapping key populations to learn about behaviors associated with infection and tracking the infection rate can provide valuable information for taking appropriate and timely actions. Basic knowledge about how HIV is transmitted and how to obtain and use condoms should be conveyed through limited mass media campaigns and school programs. Such information, education, and communication (IEC) activities should respond to prevailing attitudes toward sexual activity, as these will shape how people perceive educational materials. Public policies

". . . where the prevalence of HIV infection is low, prompt, effective action is still imperative.

Table 4.1 Epidemic Profiles

	Highest Prevalence in a key population (sex workers, drug injectors, MSMs)	Prevalence in the general population	WHO Regions
Low level	< 5%	< 1%	Middle East and North Africa
Concentrated	> 5%	< 1%	East Asia and the Pacific, Europe and Central Asia, Latin America and the Caribbean, South Asia
Generalized low	≥ 5%	1–10%	Sub-Saharan Africa
Generalized high	≥ 5%	≥ 10%	Sub-Saharan Africa

Source: UNAIDS 1997.

should also ensure that condoms are readily available through existing channels, such as pharmacies, clinics, and food stores. In addition, health facilities should screen all blood products to be used for transfusions and use sterile needles for all injections, because the rate of virus transmission through such means is high. Furthermore, because the infection spreads so rapidly among intravenous drug users, prevention programs are needed for this key population even where the infection is relatively unknown.

In countries with a concentrated epidemic, additional measures are needed. Programs aimed at preventing transmission among key populations at especially high risk of contracting or transmitting infection are of particular importance, including VCT for individuals and peer-based programs that educate individuals at risk, promote safe behaviors, and distribute condoms. Screening and treatment for STIs should be promoted, and pregnant women who fit a high-risk profile should be offered HIV screening and treatment, both to benefit them and to reduce the likelihood of mother-to-child transmission.

In a generalized low-level epidemic, such as in Tanzania, the emphasis on targeted interventions must be maintained or even strengthened, but interventions for broader populations must also be aggressively implemented. These prevention priorities should include surveillance of STIs, risk behaviors, and HIV infections in the entire population, with a particular focus on young people; extension of mass media IEC beyond basic education; routine voluntary and confidential HIV testing and STI screening and treatment promoted beyond key populations; subsidized and social marketing of condoms and strengthened distribution to ensure universal access; offering of HIV screening to all pregnant women; and broadening of peer approaches and targeted IEC to include all populations with higher rates of STIs and risk behavior.

In a generalized high-level epidemic, such as in Botswana and Zimbabwe, the epidemic is a national emergency that calls for the most vigorous possible public action. Routine HIV testing and STI screening and treatment should be promoted universally. Innovative mass strategies for reaching large numbers of people with information, screening, and condoms should be developed—for example, at workplaces, transit venues, political rallies, schools and universities, and military camps, and via youth brigades, workers' unions, and farmers' movements. Free distribution of condoms in all possible venues is imperative. VCT should be promoted for all couples initiating sexual relations. The poverty, education and social status of women, important factors in all epidemics, should be overriding concerns. Priority action should be taken to alter gender norms and reduce the economic, social, and legal restrictions on girls and women.

In addition to these preventive strategies, appropriate strategies for care and treatment are needed. Researchers have developed new therapies for treating HIV/AIDS, some of them easier to administer and less toxic than their predecessors. Treatment is also becoming a reality for many living in resource-constrained countries as the prices of antiretroviral drugs have dropped significantly because of international negotiations with and political pressure on drug companies, the manufacture of generics, and changes to international trade policy to allow compulsory licensing of pharmaceutical products in cases of emergency and to ease importation of generics. As ART becomes more widely available, HIV resistance to a number of antiretroviral drug regimes has emerged, frequently requiring patients to switch from first-line to second-line drugs that are more costly and have more problematic side effects.

The lives of people infected with HIV/AIDS can also be greatly improved and prolonged through psychosocial support, treatment of opportunistic infections, ART, and palliative care, which includes not only end of life and pain control, but also the psychological, social and spiritual problems of patients and their families. End-of-life care can be provided in numerous settings, ranging from hospitals and hospices to individuals' homes. Many inexpensive measures to treat pain,[2] diarrhea, nausea, and skin conditions[3] in infected individuals are available

[2] See *DCP2*, chapter 52.
[3] See *DCP2*, chapter 37.

and can improve patients' quality of life. Micronutrient supplements, which only cost US$15 a year, can increase body weight, reduce HIV viral load, improve CD4 counts, and reduce opportunistic infections in infected individuals. Despite the wide range of interventions to treat symptoms in people living with HIV/AIDS and their low cost, the need for palliative care for such people is far from being met.

Mass education campaigns can reduce the stigma of HIV infection and enable individuals to remain involved in their communities. Direct psychosocial support can also make a substantial difference. Studies in South Africa and Thailand have demonstrated that access to mental health services and counseling contribute significantly to patients' quality of life and, in some cases, was even associated with reduced mortality.

Diagnosing, treating, and managing life-threatening opportunistic infections (OIs) remains one of the most important aspects of caring for patients with HIV. When HIV begins to weaken patients' immune systems, which tends to occur five to seven years after infection, bacteria, fungi, viruses, and even cancers that would otherwise be held in check become active and damaging. Some infections such as pneumonia, tuberculosis[4] and oral and esophageal candidiasis are relatively easy to diagnose and cost-effective to treat, while others, such as cytomegalovirus, and *Mycobacterium avium* complex, are difficult to diagnose and costly to treat. In the latter case, ART, which reduces the viral load of HIV, thereby improving the immune system, may be more cost-effective than treating the actual infection. Certain OIs are cost-effective to prevent, and simple prophylaxis, such as co-trimoxazole to prevent *Pneumocystis jiroveci* pneumonia, positively influences survival. However, prophylaxis of OIs is underused in low- and middle-income countries, and unfortunately the benefit is short-lived, as it does not halt the relentless erosion of the immune system in infected individuals. The only way to halt the progression of disease in these individuals is to interrupt viral replication through ART.

The prospects for treating people infected with HIV with antiretroviral drugs in low- and middle-income countries have improved, but ART continues to be a costly and complex challenge. The cost of ART in some developing countries has fallen from US$15,000 per year per patient to less than US$150 per year. This lower price brings it within

[4] See *DCP2*, chapter 16.

reach of many middle-income countries, but is still a substantial burden for low-income countries, where annual public health expenditures are often less than US$20 per person per year. WHO and the Joint United Nations Programme on HIV/AIDS estimate that only about 7 percent of the nearly 6 million people in need of treatment receive it and that the number of people requiring ART increases by 8,000 each day.

DCP2 (chapter 18) describes the various regimens available for first-line treatment of HIV/AIDS when drug resistance is not encountered and for second- or third-line therapies when resistance is encountered. The preferred first-line medications in developing countries are dictated by differential efficacy of a number of combinations, as well as pricing and patent concerns. Nearly all highly active ART has some side effects, ranging from the fairly simple to treat (for example, anemia, with iron supplementation) to the more complex (lipodystropy and cardiovascular disease).

To achieve the full benefit of ART, adherence must be nearly perfect (in excess of 90 percent); in cases of suboptimal adherence, resistance can develop in as little as two weeks. Experiences with ART in Haiti and Uganda have shown that programs to implement directly-observed treatment can achieve high drug adherence rates in low-income countries, sometimes higher than in wealthy countries. Nevertheless, high adherence cannot be taken for granted, as studies in India, Mexico, and Senegal have shown poor adherence rates, demonstrating the need for more research on effective intervention to increase adherence.

Confronting the HIV epidemic requires appreciation of the myriad interconnections between technology, economics, politics, and behavior. When political leaders and celebrities endorse public campaigns to raise awareness and normalize public discussion of HIV, then technical and behavioral approaches gain wider acceptance. When technical developments make screening more accurate, cheaper, and easier, then voluntary counseling and testing can be better targeted and more effective. When generic competition reduces the cost of drugs, when international assistance is available for their purchase, and when social programs encourage adherence to drug regimes, then ART becomes more cost-effective and financially feasible.

Much more research is needed on the cost-effectiveness of interventions to combat HIV/AIDS, and figures in *DCP2* chapter 18 should be interpreted with the recognition that interventions and their costs are changing rapidly. *DCP2* chapter 2 reports that diagnosing and

"Much more research is needed on the cost-effectiveness of interventions to combat HIV/AIDS . . ."

treating STIs cost about US$57 per DALY averted, while blood and needle safety programs cost about US$84 per DALY averted. Treatment of OIs costs about US$150 per DALY averted and preventing and treating coinfection with TB costs about US$120 per DALY averted. The cost-effectiveness of ART is difficult to estimate, because it depends on the price of drugs, the prevalence of drug-resistant strains, the costs of diagnostics, and the effectiveness of the health system in delivering the drugs appropriately. While ART is not likely to be as cost-effective as these other interventions, treatment is an important component of an overall national strategy to combat and control HIV and cannot be ignored. Whether it can be effectively extended in hard-hit low-income countries is a major test for the affected countries themselves and for the international community.

The greatest research challenges in care and treatment for developing countries do not revolve around new drug development but rather around how to adapt care and treatment strategies to low-income, low-technology, low-human resource capacity settings in ways that maximize adherence; minimize toxicity, monitoring, and cost; and maximize the prolongation of high-quality life from ART—all without damaging the existing and often fragile health care infrastructures.

The synergy between prevention and treatment must be considered when struggling to allocate limited resources. Although preventing HIV/AIDS is often more cost-effective than treating it, decisions for allocating public funds are complicated by interactions between prevention and treatment. Making treatment available can remove some of the stigma and fear associated with AIDS and make those who are currently infected easier to contact and counsel so as to prevent future transmission. Treatment may also decrease infectiousness. However, there are concerns that the availability of treatment may reduce inhibitions and lead to increased risky behavior (as has been documented in the United States, Canada, and Europe). Poor adherence to treatment may also encourage drug resistance, while increased longevity as a result of treatment could expose more partners. The net effect of the interaction of prevention and treatment is likely to differ from one country to the next, and further study and monitoring of the interrelationships are imperative.

Controlling HIV/AIDS requires strategies and policies that address both prevention and treatment with limited resources. Much has been learned about the disease itself, the specific interventions and strategies,

"Although preventing HIV/AIDS is often more cost-effective than treating it, decisions for allocating public funds are complicated by interactions between prevention and treatment."

the interaction of prevention and treatment, and the larger contextual interconnections. *DCP2* presents the accumulated experience and evaluations conducted to date that permit policy makers to select appropriate strategies.

Tuberculosis

TB remains the second largest cause of death from an infectious agent in the world, even though drugs to cure the disease have been available for 50 years.[5] TB is high on the international public health agenda because of this enormous burden, because of the increase in TB cases associated with HIV infection and drug resistance, and because the internationally recommended TB control strategy known as DOTS has come to be recognized as one of the most cost-effective of all health interventions.

The resurgence of TB in high-income countries in the 1980s surprised public health officials, but effective public responses halted its spread and reduced the incidence in Western and Central Europe, Latin America and the Caribbean, and the Middle East and North Africa. TB has continued to spread and kill, however, wherever social conditions have deteriorated, public health measures are weak, and HIV/AIDS is prevalent. Thus the incidence of TB has been increasing in Eastern Europe, primarily in the former Soviet republics, since the political upheavals at the end of the 1980s and in Sub-Saharan Africa since the mid 1980s. By 2003, an estimated 8.8 million new cases of TB worldwide occurred annually. The highest incidence rate, 345 per 100,000 population per year, is in Sub-Saharan Africa, but the most populous countries of Asia—Bangladesh, China, India, Indonesia, and Pakistan—account for half of the world's cases of TB. Epidemiologists estimate that these upward trends can be reversed if 70 percent of cases are detected and 85 percent of those detected are cured. Reaching this target is necessary if the internationally sanctioned MDG of halving prevalence and death rates by 2015 is to be achieved.[6]

Interventions for controlling TB include preventing infection by means of vaccination, treating latent infections, and treating active disease. About 80 percent of infants worldwide currently receive a live attenuated vaccine, Bacille Calmette-Guérin (BCG). While the vaccine

[5] This section is based on *DCP2*, chapter 16.

[6] In 2000, the Group of Eight nations met in Okinawa, Japan, and informally set targets for reducing TB cases and deaths by 2010. The United Nations MDGs set targets for halving the number of cases and deaths by 2015 relative to their levels in 1990, and WHO is monitoring progress toward these targets.

is protective against meningitis and miliary TB in children, it has low efficacy against pulmonary TB in adults. Vaccination is still cost-effective in places with a high incidence, but is often discontinued in low-incidence countries, because the risk of infection is low and the immune response to the vaccine makes tuberculin skin tests less effective for disease surveillance purposes.

Identifying and treating active cases is currently the primary and most effective measure to control TB. The cornerstone of this approach is the DOTS strategy. DOTS entails diagnosis with a positive sputum sample, short-course treatment with effective case management, regular drug supplies, and systematic monitoring to evaluate outcomes for every patient. Effective case management includes regular supervision by a health worker or community volunteer to assure that the patient is actually taking the medication. The additional cost of monitoring patients and ensuring their adherence to the drug regimen even after symptoms have stopped has proven cost-effective because of its impact on cure rates, consequently both slowing the epidemic and limiting the development of drug resistance.

In all regions except Europe and Central Asia, DOTS costs between US$5 and US$50 per DALY averted. Under certain circumstances, DOTS can save money as well as prevent new cases and deaths. Treating people who have multidrug-resistant strains or are also infected with HIV/AIDS is less cost-effective, because treatment costs are higher and both efficacy and expected benefits are lower. Nevertheless, treating patients with multidrug-resistant TB costs relatively little for the likely gains in healthy life, typically less than US$400 per DALY averted. Treating people with latent infections, that is, people who are infected with TB but are not symptomatic, is the least cost-effective, at US$5,500 to US$26,000 per DALY averted, when TB is endemic (relatively stable) and HIV prevalence is low. However, during a TB epidemic among HIV-infected individuals, providing treatment for latent infection among those who have not yet developed active disease could cost less than US$100 per DALY averted in low-income countries. BCG vaccination is also cost-effective at US$40 to US$170 per DALY averted.

Research could provide a better range of interventions in the future, whether by improving the DOTS approach; tightening the link between private providers, who in many settings are the first to see TB patients, and the public sector; improving the understanding of risk factors; refining diagnostics; or actively seeking cases. Developing a low-cost vaccine that would be more effective than BCG in protecting adults against pulmonary TB would revolutionize the control of TB by shifting the emphasis from treatment to prevention. Until that time, DOTS or other treatment regimens will play the central role.

Success in controlling TB is closely related to the capacity of local health systems to maintain an effective system for identifying cases, beginning treatment, and assuring adherence. The cost is not unmanageable at the global level. In 2005, the high-burden countries that account for about 80 percent of global cases spent only US$1.2 billion, of which about US$200 million came from international donors. Continued international financial assistance is critical to ensuring that TB control can be maintained in the world's poorest countries, where the challenge of TB control is aligned with the challenge of building and implementing effective public health programs.

Malaria

Malaria is directly responsible for about 2 percent of all deaths in the world each year (an estimated 1.2 million deaths) and almost 3 percent of global DALYs.[7] In Sub-Saharan Africa, malaria accounts for a large share of the disease burden, causing about 9 percent of all deaths and 10 percent of all DALYs. The share in other regions is much lower, approximately 1 percent, but still accounts for a significant number of deaths and disabilities.

More than 3 billion people live in areas where malaria is present. Many countries outside Africa have successfully controlled the disease through a combination of preventive measures and treatment strategies. For those countries most afflicted by malaria, the implementation of such programs has been obstructed by the emergence and spread of drug-resistant strains of the parasite and of the vectors and hindered by the weakness of public health infrastructure.

Four species of malaria parasites infect human beings. *Plasmodium vivax* and *P. falciparum* are the most common, and the latter is the most dangerous. Virtually all deaths are caused by *P. falciparum*, which predominates in Haiti, Papua New Guinea, and Sub-Saharan Africa. *P. vivax* is more common in Central America and South Asia. The parasite is carried by mosquitoes, whose ability to reproduce and spread the parasite is strongly influenced by climate. Infestations occur when people are bitten by mosquitoes carrying the parasite. The incidence rate therefore depends on the number of bites per person that transmit the

[7] This section is based on *DCP2,* chapter 21.

Figure 4.1 Malaria Ecology and Burden: Clinical Manifestations

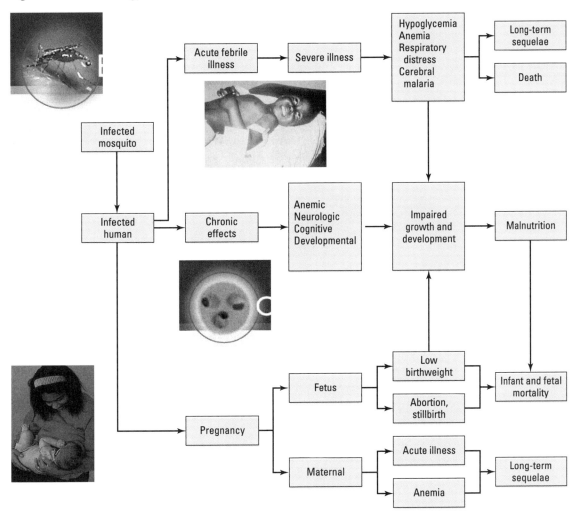

Source: Breman, Alilio, and Mills 2004.

parasite, or the entomological inoculation rate. This ranges from less than 1 bite per person per year in Latin America and Southeast Asia to more than 300 in parts of tropical Africa (figure 4.1).

Correctly treated, uncomplicated malaria has a mortality rate of only 0.1 percent. When the disease is left untreated and affects vital organs, mortality rises steeply. Coma may occur, in which case the likelihood of death is about 20 percent in adults and 15 percent in children. Cerebral malaria can lead to convulsions, neurological damage, and death. Malaria infections also lead to anemia that can be mild, moderate, or severe.

In addition, malaria has a significant impact on other health conditions. Women contracting malaria during pregnancy are more likely to develop anemia and bear children with low birthweight who are then at greater risk of disease, disability, or even death. About 3.7 percent of maternal deaths, or 5,300 deaths per year, are the result of malaria-related conditions. Estimates show that between 190,000 and 934,000 children die each year when malaria contributes to the development of anemia. Being ill with malaria has a variety of other consequences. One study in Africa estimated that 13 to 15 percent of school absenteeism was due to malaria in children (Holding and Kitsao-Wekulo 2004). Studies in The Gambia and Kenya showed that children who were protected by insecticide-treated bednets grew faster than those left unprotected.

Drug use and vector controls are the main antimalaria strategies and interventions for controlling malaria. Others aim at killing mosquitoes, preventing bites, blocking the development of the disease, or treating the disease itself. Environmental methods to kill the mosquitoes that spread malaria include eliminating breeding sites and spraying insecticides. Other efforts to kill mosquitoes or prevent bites include indoor residual spraying and the use of insecticide-treated bednets. A range of drugs work prophylactically and are taken by travelers to malaria-ridden areas and pregnant women. Finding drugs to treat the disease has become more of a challenge because of the emergence of drug-resistant strains of malaria globally.

The effectiveness and feasibility of some interventions depend heavily on whether malarial transmission is unstable (low, erratic, or focal) or stable (frequent, intense, and year round). Where malarial transmission is unstable, protective immunity is not acquired. Where malarial transmission is stable, survivors develop some immunity, and by adulthood, malarial infections are commonly asymptomatic.

In areas with unstable transmission, focused programs that eliminate breeding sites through judicious use of insecticides or through changes in construction practices may be feasible and effective, while in areas with stable transmission, identifying and controlling all potential breeding sites is generally infeasible. In unstable transmission areas, prophylaxis for pregnant women or intermittent preventive therapy will be most effective only during localized temporary epidemics. In stable transmission areas, however, more general use of intermittent preventive therapy can be extremely effective.

Many places have successfully used insecticide-treated nets (ITNs) to reduce transmission. ITNs have been associated with reductions in child mortality by 18 percent and reductions in malarial episodes by as much as 50 percent in different parts of Africa. The impact of ITNs is related not only to the technical effectiveness of the nets and the duration and efficacy of the insecticide used, but to the social and cultural acceptance of their use and to their affordability. China, Tanzania, and Vietnam have successfully promoted the use of ITNs and achieved substantial control of malaria in many places. Strategies to encourage ITN use have included social marketing in Kenya and Malawi; assisted commercial sector development in Mali, Senegal, and Tanzania; free generalized distribution in Togo; and vouchers for highly subsidized ITNs distributed to pregnant women in Tanzania.

Treatment programs have traditionally relied on relatively inexpensive drugs, principally chloroquine. The key to success is timely detection and treatment. In South Africa, where 83 percent of the population live within 10 kilometers of a health clinic, health professionals play a central role. In countries like Burkina Faso, Ethiopia, and Uganda, where health clinics are much less accessible, reducing mortality and morbidity through treatment has required training mothers and community health workers to dispense treatment based on presumptive diagnoses.

In many areas, strains of the parasite resistant to chloroquine and sulfadoxine-pyrimethamine are now common. Fortunately, researchers have developed a new array of drugs, including artemisinin combination therapy (ACT), which costs more than traditional first-line drugs but is cost-effective in areas where drug-resistant strains are highly prevalent.

Health education and counseling are also significant for controlling malaria. They improve the timeliness of treatment by helping people identify the disease and seek appropriate care. They also promote better and more regular use of ITNs and encourage re-treatment of nets with insecticide as required. In addition, they further improve adherence to treatments, thereby reducing transmission of the parasite and the development of drug resistance.

Most of the malarial interventions available are quite cost-effective. Almost all of them cost less than US$150 per DALY averted and many of them can be implemented at a cost of less than US$10 per DALY. *DCP2* estimates that ITNs cost between US$11 and US$17 per DALY averted, depending on the type of insecticide and the frequency of re-treatments required; indoor residual spraying costs between US$5 and US$18 per DALY averted; and intermittent preventive treatment for pregnant women costs US$13 to US$35 per DALY averted.

Among drug treatments, chloroquine remains the most cost-effective treatment as long as chloroquine resistance is less than about 35 percent. When the prevalence of resistance increases beyond this level, ACT becomes more cost-effective. Sulfadoxine-pyrimethamine can be more cost-effective than chloroquine and ACT, but sulfadoxine-pyrimethamine resistance appears to emerge fairly quickly, and ACT is more cost-effective than sulfadoxine-pyrimethamine when sulfadoxine-pyrimethamine–resistance surpasses approximately 12 percent.

While malaria interventions are cost-effective, their feasibility depends on the availability of financial resources and health infrastructure and local epidemiological conditions. The total cost of a program to promote ITN use for children is about US$2.80 per capita per year, and a program for indoor residual spraying would cost about US$4 per capita per year. While these costs may seem low by many standards, they are prohibitive for countries where malaria is endemic, because the entire public budgets for all health expenditures in such countries range between US$2 and US$10 per capita per year. Breaking the financial constraints for these cost-effective programs requires substantial external assistance.

Research for a vaccine against malaria has long been under way, and should be further encouraged, but developing such a vaccine will require many more years. In the meantime, research is also needed to improve patient care, including easier, cheaper home management and evaluation of alternative delivery systems; prevention, such as intermittent treatment and increased ITN use; technologies, such as insecticides and antiparasitic effector molecules using genomics; and field evaluations of transgenic methods for interrupting malaria transmission.

Such research into new forms of intervention, together with the implementation of known and cost-effective prevention and treatment strategies, will permit successful control of this disease. Since the greatest burden of malaria is concentrated in countries where high transmission rates are combined with limited resources and weak health systems, control of malaria also undoubtedly requires expanded international assistance.

Vaccine-Preventable Diseases

Illnesses for which relatively inexpensive and highly effective vaccines are available account for a significant portion of the disease burden in developing countries.[8] *DCP2* (chapter 20) discusses TB, diphtheria, tetanus, pertussis, polio, measles, rubella, Hib, hepatitis B, yellow fever, meningococcal disease, and Japanese encephalitis. Vaccines are also available or are being developed for two causes of diarrheal disease: rotavirus and cholera (*DCP2,* chapter 19).

Vaccine-preventable diseases are quite varied. Some vaccine-preventable diseases are bacterial and others are viral; some are found primarily in human beings, while others readily thrive in other species as well; some have high fatality rates, while others are debilitating; some are concentrated in particular regions, while others are widespread; and some are spread through respiratory contact, while others are transmitted through insect bites or contact with infected fecal matter or blood. Despite this variability, vaccine-preventable diseases generally share two important characteristics: people can be infected without signs or symptoms (with the exception of tetanus) and vaccine-induced immunity is generally lifelong (with the exception of pertussis).

Countries that immunize a large share of their populations against these illnesses have eliminated most of the mortality and morbidity associated with them. Regions with lower vaccination coverage continue to have thousands of deaths that would be relatively easy to avert. In 2001, seven vaccine-preventable diseases—measles, hepatitis B, Hib, pertussis, tetanus, yellow fever, and diphtheria—caused more than 2.3 million deaths, primarily in Africa and Asia. Some 80 percent of all deaths from yellow fever occur in Africa, as do 59 percent of deaths from measles, 58 percent of deaths from pertussis, and 41 percent of deaths from tetanus. East Asia and the Pacific faces the largest burden of deaths from hepatitis B and its associated conditions and accounts for 62 percent of all such deaths. South Asia also has high mortality from these diseases, especially tetanus and measles.

In recent decades, a number of global initiatives have sought to expand the coverage of vaccines. Since 1974, WHO's Expanded Program on Immunization (EPI) has provided guidance and support for expanding coverage by standardizing immunization schedules, promoting safe injection technologies, improving the stocking and availability of vaccines, and protecting vaccines' potency through cold chain management. Its Reaching Every District strategy aims at having 80 percent of children in each country receive three doses of diphtheria-pertussis-tetanus vaccine. In 2000, international agencies, bilateral donors, private foundations,

---

[8] This section is based on *DCP2,* chapters 16, 19, 20, 25, and 27.

NGOs, and pharmaceutical companies collaborated in launching the Global Alliance for Vaccines and Immunization (GAVI). Since that time, GAVI has raised more than US$1.3 billion to strengthen immunization systems; introduce new or underutilized vaccines, such as those for Hib, hepatitis B, and yellow fever; and support safe injection practices. In addition, major research efforts are aimed at developing new vaccines and delivery methods.

Once a vaccine is available, the most important aspect of designing immunization programs is organizing the logistics of vaccinating people. In most developing countries, children are brought to fixed health facilities to receive injections or to take oral vaccines. A substantial number of vaccines are also delivered through outreach, that is, mobile strategies in which health care workers travel to homes and villages. Immunization campaigns that focus on specific antigens are another approach. The most famous immunization campaigns have focused on smallpox, which was declared completely eradicated in 1980, and polio, which is now found in only a handful of countries (*DCP2,* chapter 8).

Vaccination is generally very cost-effective. In the best of cases, vaccines are relatively inexpensive and a single dose leads to lifetime immunity. Whenever such an intervention is available for a widespread and potentially fatal infection, it is likely to be cost-effective.

The mix of delivery strategies, the price of key inputs (the vaccine itself plus labor, transportation, and cold storage), and the overall scale of the program all affect costs. Recurrent costs represent some 80 percent of the costs associated with delivering vaccines through fixed health facilities and 92 percent of the costs of immunization campaigns. The cost per fully immunized child for the six original EPI vaccines—TB, diphtheria, pertussis, tetanus, polio, and measles—is approximately US$20. Investigators estimate that the incremental cost of replacing oral polio vaccine with injectable polio vaccine and adding new antigens for hepatitis B, yellow fever, Hib, measles, rubella, Japanese encephalitis, and meningoccocal disease to existing programs is between US$1 and US$16 per person.

Cost-effectiveness is influenced not only by differences in prices and strategies but also by existing levels of immunization coverage. The cost per death averted from successfully vaccinating children against the six original EPI diseases is US$205 per death averted in South Asia and Sub-Saharan Africa, and US$3,540 per death averted in Europe and Central Asia, with the relatively high coverage rates in the latter region being largely responsible for the difference. Nevertheless, even at

US$3,450 per death averted, vaccination is still highly cost-effective in Europe and Central Asia and compares favorably with many other uses of public money.

Future progress in controlling vaccine-preventable diseases depends on addressing financial and logistical constraints in low-income countries. Even though immunization programs are relatively inexpensive, the financial resources of many low-income countries are so constrained that even inexpensive programs account for substantial shares of available funding. On average, immunization programs account for 6 percent of government health expenditures in developing countries. However, among the world's lowest-income countries, expanding the coverage of traditional antigens, introducing new vaccines, and improving vaccine quality and safety could consume as much as 20 percent of a government's health budget in the absence of substantial foreign assistance.

The financial burden may be reduced through research and development into vaccines that require fewer doses and are cheaper to produce, easier to transport and store, and safer to administer. The development of new delivery strategies could also make a substantial difference to universalizing immunization coverage in low-income countries.

Diarrheal Diseases

Diarrheal disease is one of the top five preventable killers of children under five years old in developing countries.[9] It is most dangerous for the young, with about 90 percent of deaths from diarrhea occurring in small children. However, even though children in developing countries still experience an average of 3.2 episodes of diarrhea each year, the number of deaths appears to have fallen significantly from an estimated 4 million to 6 million deaths in 1979 to an average of 2.6 million per year in the 1990s, with the bulk of the improvement attributable to effective public health interventions (see, for example, the discussion on using ORT in the Arab Republic of Egypt in *DCP2*, chapter 8).

Dozens of viruses, bacteria, protozoa, and helminths cause diarrheal disease. Some of these agents rely almost exclusively on human hosts, whereas others also infect animals. They are generally acquired through fecal-oral transmission, often through the ingestion of contaminated water or unwashed foods. Infection by such agents causes severe bouts of diarrhea, compromises the body's immune system, weakens its ability to draw nourishment from food, and can lead to serious and

"... even though children in developing countries still experience an average of 3.2 episodes of diarrhea each year, the number of deaths appears to have fallen significantly from an estimated 4 million to 6 million deaths in 1979 to an average of 2.6 million per year in the 1990s ..."

[9] This section is based on *DCP2*, chapters 19 and 41.

rapid dehydration. Severe watery acute diarrhea, caused mostly by rotavirus, enterotoxigenic *Escherichia coli,* and *vibrio cholerae,* causes rapid dehydration and can lead to death. Persistent diarrhea is associated with malnutrition, and even though it accounts for a relatively small share of diarrheal cases, it is three times more likely to be fatal than watery diarrhea. Bloody diarrhea is often associated with intestinal damage and nutritional deterioration, some dehydration, and fevers.

The strategies for reducing the burden of diarrheal disease have not changed substantially since the first edition of *Disease Control Priorities in Developing Countries* (Jamison and others 1993) with the exception of some advances in vaccine technologies. Better and more hygienic feeding practices, immunization, improved water and sanitation, and better case management are the major interventions available for preventing and treating diarrheal disease.

Better and more hygienic feeding starts with programs that promote exclusive breastfeeding during a child's first six months of life. This reduces the likelihood that a child will ingest contaminated food or water during infancy and strengthens the child's immune system through the ingestion of beneficial elements in the mother's milk. Such programs include hospital policies that encourage breastfeeding, counseling and education from peers and health workers, mass media and community education campaigns, and mothers' support groups.[10]

Better feeding practices once a child is six months old can also be encouraged and effective. Some 800,000 lives per year could be saved by more hygienic food storage and preparation and by promoting education, providing good nutrition, and ensuring adequate weight gain. Researchers have also shown that vitamin A and zinc supplementation have beneficial effects on diarrhea: both are associated with reducing the frequency of severe diarrhea, and zinc supplementation also reduces the incidence of diarrhea.

Rotavirus immunization could prevent some 440,000 deaths per year from this common infection. Developing a safe and effective vaccine for cholera has also proven difficult, and it can usually be controlled through effective public health programs. Only Vietnam routinely deploys cholera vaccine. Other countries have decided that ORT is so

"Some 800,000 lives per year could be saved by more hygienic food storage and preparation and by promoting education, providing good nutrition, and ensuring adequate weight gain."

[10] The one important qualification to this approach is concern about mother to child transmission of HIV. The best practice in such cases would be safe replacement feeding for the child of an HIV-positive mother. However, when a mother's HIV status is unknown in countries with high HIV prevalence, a decision has to be made that balances the risks of HIV transmission against the likely benefits of exclusive breastfeeding (*DCP2*, chapter 19).

inexpensive and so effective in preventing deaths from cholera that the costs and risks of immunization are not worthwhile. Measles compromises the immune system and can thereby lead to acute diarrhea. By reducing the occurrence of measles, vaccines could reduce 6 to 26 percent of diarrheal deaths among children under five.

Another way to reduce diarrheal disease is by providing clean water and sanitation, because estimates indicate that contaminated water causes 90 percent of diarrheal cases among children. Nevertheless, *DCP2* (chapter 41, p. 778), notes that "domestic hygiene—particularly food and hand hygiene—is the principal determinant of endemic diarrheal disease rates and not drinking water quality." Rather than quality, the quantity, continuity, and convenience of water services is what reduces the incidence of diarrhea by encouraging more hygienic behavior with regard to personal care and food preparation.

Investment infrastructure for water and sanitation can be expensive relative to other preventive measures and case treatment. Nevertheless, water service has many health benefits beyond reducing diarrheal disease. When water service is associated with better personal hygiene, it interrupts the transmission of skin and eye infections such as trachoma from one person to the next; reduces the incidence of water-based illnesses such as schistosomiasis and guinea worm; and reduces exposure to water-related insect vectors responsible for dengue, malaria, and trypanosomiasis.

The most important benefit people popularly associate with water and sanitation services is greater convenience other than the effects on health. The savings in time and labor can be substantial, given that women and children in particular spend an average of more than an hour each day in rural East Africa and more than two hours each day in several Asian countries obtaining and hauling water. Surveys also show that people in developing countries value improved sanitation less for health reasons than for reasons of comfort, prestige, and safety.

In public policy debates, the health benefits of water and sanitation can best be viewed as an additional benefit conferred by water and sanitation investments that are justified for other reasons. Public health policy still has a role to play in regulating water quality, but public health authorities may be justified in expanding their regulatory authority to consider the quantity and continuity of water service given services' important influence on hygienic behaviors that reduce the incidence of disease.

When diarrhea prevention fails, simple and low-cost techniques are available for managing most cases. ORT, which consists of the oral

". . . women and children . . . spend an average of more than an hour each day in rural East Africa and more than two hours each day in several Asian countries obtaining and hauling water."

administration of fluids containing simple salts and sugars, is inexpensive, can be administered by family members with limited training, and is highly effective at reducing the severity of many diarrheal diseases and averting death. After its introduction in the 1980s, many countries rapidly expanded the use of ORT to reach 33 percent of children with diarrhea in the Philippines, 35 percent in Brazil, 50 percent in Egypt, and 81 percent in Mexico. Zinc supplementation for children with diarrheal disease also helps reduce the severity of the illness. For bloody diarrhea, treatment with antimicrobial drugs is indicated, but as with so many other diseases, resistance to first-line antimicrobials is spreading and making these drugs less effective.

In places where basic water and sanitation are not available, hygiene is poor, and ORT is not widely used, public health interventions aimed at preventing diarrheal diseases are extremely cost-effective. Promoting exclusive breastfeeding, measles immunization, ORT, and hygiene costs less than US$5 per DALY averted; promoting better sanitation through public policy costs about US$11 per DALY averted; investing in and maintaining hand pumps for water costs about US$94 per DALY averted; house connections for potable water cost about US$223 per DALY averted; and construction and promotion of basic sanitation facilities costs more than US$270 per DALY averted (*DCP2*, chapter 41).

Factors that encourage the transmission and development of diarrheal diseases are prevalent among people living in poverty. Impoverished people are more likely to be undernourished, to lack clean water and sanitary means of disposing of human waste, to cohabit with animals that harbor and transmit human pathogens, and to lack access to proper means of food storage such as refrigeration. Nevertheless, progress against diarrheal diseases can be made despite poverty. Effective programs can encourage such healthful behaviors as exclusive breastfeeding and personal hygiene; improve environmental conditions through the provision of safe water and sanitation; and train caregivers to recognize symptoms, especially of the more dangerous forms of diarrhea, and apply relatively simple treatments.

MATERNAL AND NEONATAL HEALTH

Along with infectious diseases, maternal and neonatal conditions account for a substantial part of the health gap between rich and poor countries; for example, more than 99 percent of maternal deaths occur in the developing world. This differential represents the largest single disparity in public health statistics between low-income and high-income countries. Overall, the average lifetime risk of maternal death is 1 in 4,000 in high-income countries, 1 in 61 in middle-income countries, and 1 in 17 in the lowest-income countries.

Death rates during the neonatal period (from birth to 28 days old) also reveal vast differences between rich and poor countries. Only 1 percent of all neonatal deaths occur in high-income countries, where the neonatal mortality rate averages 4 per 1,000 live births. In low-income countries, the average is about 33 per 1,000 live births. The majority of neonatal deaths occur in South Asia because of its sizable population; however, 20 of the countries with the highest neonatal mortality rates are in Sub-Saharan Africa. The highest rates are found in countries where civil wars and political instability have exacerbated poverty, such as Ethiopia, Liberia, and Sierra Leone. In these countries, neonatal mortality rates exceed 50 per 1,000 live births.

International agreements have recognized the importance of reducing maternal and child mortality in low- and middle-income countries. Indeed, two of the eight MDGs address these issues: the fourth goal calls for reducing mortality among children under five by two-thirds and the fifth calls for reducing the maternal mortality ratio by three-fourths, both by 2015. *DCP2* stresses that neonatal deaths account for 40 percent of all deaths of children under five, that the first week of life is when 75 percent of these neonatal deaths occur, and that 50 percent of maternal deaths occur in the first week after childbirth.

The maternal and infant mortality rates in a particular country may reveal more about the state of its health system than any other figures. Achieving low maternal and infant mortality rates requires an integrated and well-functioning health care delivery system that reaches communities with education and counseling, helps people avoid unwanted pregnancies, promotes good nutrition, screens for risks, assists healthy births, and responds to obstetric emergencies effectively.

The health sector alone, however, is unlikely to achieve or sustain maternal health improvements in many countries without concomitant social changes to increase girls' education; reduce gender biases in employment and pay; and confront imbalances in bargaining power within the household that affect women's access to nutrition, domestic workload, and physical safety. Nonetheless, the primary focus of *DCP2* is health sector interventions, and it shows that many cost-effective

"... more than 99 percent of maternal deaths occur in the developing world. This differential represents the largest single disparity in public health statistics between low-income and high-income countries."

"... neonatal deaths account for 40 percent of all deaths of children under five, ..."

interventions to prevent unwanted pregnancies, to make pregnancy and childbirth safer, and to improve neonatal health are available.

Family Planning

Globally, an estimated 210 million pregnancies occur each year, of which 60 million end in an abortion or with the death of the mother or baby.[11] Twenty-five percent of all pregnancies, about 52.5 million, end in abortions. More than 500,000 maternal deaths and 4 million neonatal deaths occur annually, but mortality is only one possible negative outcome. Every year, more than 54 million women also suffer from diseases or complications during pregnancy and childbirth. Indeed, conditions associated with maternity represent between 12 and 30 percent of the disease burden among women age 15 to 44 in developing countries. Reproductive health conditions are a major source of the difference in the disease burden between men and women, with women generally leading longer but less healthy lives.

Although pregnancy and childbirth are natural parts of a healthy life, they do entail risks. Women with high blood pressure, heart disease, malaria, anemia, TB, hepatitis, STIs, or HIV/AIDS face substantial risks during pregnancy. Providing appropriate screening, counseling, and contraception services is particularly important for these women. Unwanted pregnancies also have negative consequences. Data are patchy and regional variations are large, but estimates indicate that family planning programs could prevent between 20 and 40 percent of all infant deaths by preventing births among adolescents and older women and permitting intervals of three to five years between pregnancies.

Family planning can reduce unwanted pregnancies and help couples achieve their desired family size. Access to effective contraception is key. The unmet need for contraception is defined as the number of women who wish to avoid pregnancy but are not using contraception. The unmet need for contraception is highest in Sub-Saharan Africa, where an estimated 19.4 percent of women would like to avoid becoming pregnant but are not using any contraceptive. Major obstacles to meeting the need for contraception include lack of knowledge, health concerns, and social disapproval. With some variation across countries and contexts, these factors are more significant than contraceptive supply, availability, or cost. In countries where demand for contraception is mostly satisfied, such as Brazil, Colombia, and Vietnam, there are

[11] This section is based on *DCP2*, chapter 57.

lower fertility rates and lower maternal mortality. By contrast, in Sub-Saharan Africa, the share of women with unmet needs sometimes exceeds the share of women who are using contraception.

When women have unwanted pregnancies, many will seek an abortion whether or not it is legal or socially acceptable. In 1995, an estimated 35.5 million abortions were performed in developing countries. Most legal abortions take place in China and elsewhere in Asia, but because of population size and high fertility rates, the bulk of illegal abortions also occur in Asia. In countries where abortion is illegal, it is far riskier. Each year, unsafe abortions cause some 80,000 deaths, accounting for about 13 percent of the disease burden among women of reproductive age. The mortality rate for unsafe abortions ranges from 100 to 600 per 100,000 procedures, compared with a mortality rate for safe abortions of only 0.6 deaths per 100,000 procedures. Many of those who survive an unsafe abortion suffer from disabilities.

Contraception for those who wish to avoid a pregnancy can be permanent, long-term, or temporary. Permanent methods involve sterilization for women or men. This is the most popular and effective method of contraception: the 187 million sterilized women worldwide account for 34 percent of all contraceptive practices. Male sterilization by means of vasectomy is a simpler and safer procedure than female sterilization, but is less common. Nevertheless, the estimated 40 to 50 million sterilized men worldwide account for 8 percent of contraceptive practices. Intrauterine devices are the second most common method of contraception, used by 150 million women worldwide. These devices are long-term methods of contraception, as they are inserted in the uterus and prevent pregnancy until they are removed.

Temporary methods include pills, skin implants, and injectable products that alter a woman's hormone cycle to prevent conception. Although these methods are safe and effective, they can also cause irregular bleeding, a problem for women in societies that bar or restrict women from certain activities during menstruation. WHO estimates that 10 to 30 percent of women abandon these contraceptive methods for this reason. Other temporary methods include barriers, the most common of which are condoms. Unlike other forms of contraception, condoms are unique in providing protection against STIs. Male condoms account for about 4 percent of contraceptive use among couples of reproductive age. Strategies for meeting the demand for contraceptive services include education and outreach, subsidies, free distribution, and measures to facilitate or encourage sterilization

"Each year, unsafe abortions cause some 80,000 deaths, accounting for about 13 percent of the disease burden among women of reproductive age."

(box 4.3). Social marketing refers to a variety of strategies that adopt traditional commercial marketing techniques to promote socially beneficial behaviors, products, and services. Typically such programs will promote products, such as condoms, through the mass media. They will also repackage the products and promote them in ways that are effective within a particular culture and context. Sometimes governments will partner with commercial manufacturers to market existing brands. Social marketing programs have expanded contraceptive sales and use in many countries.

The cost of family planning programs is between US$5,000 and US$35,000 per maternal death averted, between US$1,300 and US$5,000 per infant death averted, and after including other health impacts along with averted deaths, between US$30 and US$60 per DALY averted. Interventions appear to be more cost-effective in South Asia and Sub-Saharan Africa than in East Asia and the Pacific. Cost-effectiveness within regions also varies by as much as two orders of magnitude because of differences in fertility rates, risks of mortality, and existing contraceptive prevalence rates.

Overall, the evidence is strong enough to show that family planning is cost-effective, but not strong enough to show which programs are the most cost-effective. The cost of contraception is not usually a major barrier to acceptance. Rather, social mores and health concerns are larger obstacles. Proximity to services and availability of supplies are also relevant. To be effective, programs need to ascertain local obstructions to family planning and then design an appropriate response.

Maternal Conditions

Family planning reduces the disease burden associated with pregnancy by averting unwanted pregnancies.[12] For women who are pregnant, a variety of maternal conditions (understood to occur in the period from conception to 42 days postpartum) can lead to death or disability even though pregnancy and childbirth are not inherently pathological. Providing care during normal, healthy pregnancy and childbirth while ensuring a state of readiness to deal with potential health problems is the goal of safe motherhood programs.

Of the 210 million pregnancies worldwide each year, some 500,000 end in maternal death, and each year more than 54 million women suffer from diseases or complications related to pregnancy and childbirth.

[12] This section is based on *DCP2*, chapter 26.

Box 4.3 The Bangladesh Success Story

In the mid 1970s, an average Bangladeshi woman had more than six children, which—in combination with poor nutrition and lack of access to quality health services—jeopardized the health of both the woman and her children. Beyond the health impact of this situation, high fertility and rapid population growth represented major constraints to the country's economic development and social progress.

The Bangladeshi family planning program, initiated to reach demographic goals, had four elements. The first element was the deployment of young, married women who were hired as outreach workers and trained to conduct home visits with women, offering contraceptive services and information. The number of these outreach workers, referred to as family welfare assistants, eventually reached about 25,000 in the public sector and another 12,000 in NGOs. The program also recruited 4,500 male outreach workers.

Each family welfare assistant was expected to cover three to five villages, or 850 rural women, visiting each household once every two months (Hossain and Phillips 1996). The program's reach was dramatic: family welfare assistants contacted virtually all Bangladeshi women at least once and reached more than one-third every six months. The family welfare assistants were well-recognized village visitors and constituted the main link between the government program and rural women.

A second element of the program was the provision of as wide a range of methods as possible to meet a variety of reproductive needs. This so-called cafeteria approach offered temporary methods as well as sterilization services for individuals with two living children where the youngest child was at least two years old (Rob and Cernada 1992). A well-managed distribution system provided family planning commodities to outreach workers to support their work.

A third element of the program was the family planning clinics established in rural areas to which outreach workers could refer clients who wished to use long-term or permanent methods such as sterilization. Eventually, about 4,000 government facilities and 200 NGO clinics were established.

A fourth element was the information, education, and communication activities that were intended to change norms about family size and provide information about contraceptive options. State-of-the-art use of mass media proved to be particularly effective.

As a result of the program, virtually all women in Bangladesh are aware of modern family planning methods. Contraceptive use by married women increased from 8 percent in the mid 1970s to about 50 percent in 2000, and fertility decreased from more than 6.0 children per woman in 1975 to about 3.3 in 2000. Even though social and economic improvements have played a major role in increasing the demand for contraception, investigators have shown that the provision of services and information has had an independent effect on attitudes and behavior.

The program is estimated to cost about US$100 million to US$150 million per year, with about one-half to two-thirds of the funding coming from external donors. Cost-effectiveness has been estimated at about US$13 to US$18 per birth averted, a standard measure for family planning programs.

Despite its achievements, the Bangladesh family planning program is far from perfect. Since about 1995, declines in fertility have slowed greatly. Many observers have noted opportunities to increase the program's efficiency, to respond more effectively to women's needs, and to better link family planning and health. Nevertheless, Bangladesh has done something few other countries at its level of social and economic development have been able to accomplish: it has complemented efforts to change attitudes about

(Continued on the following page.)

family size with the provision of family planning services to realize a sustained and dramatic decrease in fertility. Although the original motivation for the program was to achieve demographic aims, the government was able to create a program that responded to couples' needs rather than employing coercive measures.

Source: Authors.

Thirteen countries—Afghanistan, Angola, Bangladesh, China, Democratic Republic of Congo, Ethiopia, India, Indonesia, Kenya, Nigeria, Pakistan, Tanzania, and Uganda—account for 70 percent of all maternal deaths because of varying effects of population size, low incomes, and poor health care. Together South Asia and Sub-Saharan Africa account for 74 percent of the global burden of maternal conditions. Complications experienced by mothers also lead directly to many stillbirths and neonatal deaths each year, and several studies have shown that the survival prospects for a baby whose mother dies are low.

Just five conditions account for three-quarters of maternal deaths: hemorrhage, sepsis, hypertensive disorder, obstructed labor, and unsafe abortion. Many of these conditions can be effectively mitigated through prenatal screening and skilled attendants, and differences in access to such care explain a large part of the regional disparities. For example, fewer than 30 percent of women in the poorest countries have access to skilled birth attendants, compared with more than 98 percent of women in the world's richest countries. Yet progress on this front is frustratingly slow: the regional average for birth attendants in Sub-Saharan Africa has increased by only 0.2 percent per year in the past decade (figure 4.2).

Given the nature of pregnancy and childbirth, no single intervention or approach can fully address their associated disease burden. The only relevant analysis is to compare alternative packages that differ by content and means of distribution. For example, a comprehensive safe motherhood strategy might include the following range of interventions:

- adolescent reproductive health education and services
- community education on safe motherhood and newborn care
- prenatal care and counseling, including nutritional supplements, blood pressure screening, STI screening, treatment for syphilis, breastfeeding advice, tetanus toxoid immunization, and treatment of urinary tract infections
- skilled assistance at delivery

"... the regional average for birth attendants in Sub-Saharan Africa has increased by only 0.2 percent per year in the past decade"

Figure 4.2 Levels of Antenatal Care Coverage, 1990 and 2000

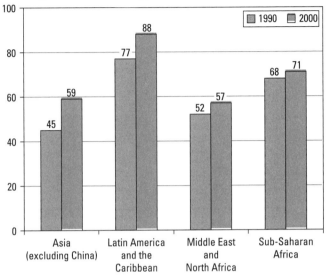

Percentage of live births receiving prenatal care

Source: Adapted from WHO 2003.

- care for obstetric complications and emergencies
- postpartum care.

Other than avoiding unwanted pregnancies, averting problems in maternity involves ensuring general good health, especially adequate nutrition. Complications should be prevented or treated if they occur. Interventions can be population-based or personal; can occur during pregnancy, labor and delivery, or postpartum; and may vary by level of care, whether in the home, at a primary health care facility, or in a hospital.

Population-based interventions address two major risk factors: lack of contraception and maternal undernutrition. Undernutrition is manifested in two ways: being underweight and/or stunted and being deficient in micronutrients, principally iron and vitamin A. Because undernutrition is often chronic, long term, and intergenerational, when and how interventions will be most effective is not clear. Efforts can concentrate on women when they are young, during pregnancy, or while they are of reproductive age. Personal interventions cover a wide range of services that share one important characteristic: they need to be integrated in a continuum. That continuum ranges over time, that is, from conception to the postpartum period; over space, encompassing the home, primary health services, and referral for sophisticated care when necessary; and across caregivers, potentially including outreach workers, public health workers, midwives, nurse-attendants, doctors, and surgeons.

Studies have shown that four prenatal visits with a health care provider can be cost-effective. Training for such providers should include how to recognize danger signs and arrange for rapid transfer to an appropriate facility in the event of an emergency, and should also emphasize the use of skilled attendants during childbirth. Other essential elements of prenatal care include prevention and treatment of malaria and anemia, screening and treatment for syphilis, and immunization against tetanus. Nutritional supplementation is often included, but its effectiveness and cost-effectiveness are not conclusively established.

Women and infants run the greatest risks of disability and death during and just after delivery. In this period, skilled attendants with the possibility of referral to a more sophisticated level of care can be critical. The exact definition of skilled attendants is itself a subject of debate, but the MDGs propose the proportion of deliveries attended by a health professional (doctor, nurse, or trained midwife) as a proxy indicator. The rate of skilled attendants at birth varies substantially across developing regions and across socioeconomic groups within countries, ranging from 48 percent in Sub-Saharan Africa to 59 percent in South Asia and 82 percent in Latin America and the Caribbean.

DCP2 evaluates several different proposed packages of care that would improve the coverage and/or the quality of routine maternal care. The three most cost-effective packages, all of which include nutritional supplementation, range in cost from US$77 to US$104 per DALY averted in Sub-Saharan Africa to US$150 per DALY averted in South Asia. Direct costs are higher in Sub-Saharan Africa but are offset by greater effectiveness because of the higher prevalence of maternal problems (box 4.4).

Neonatal Conditions

The risk of death is greatest during the first 28 days of life (neonatal mortality).[13] About 1 million infants die during their first day of life, another 2 million die during the subsequent week, and a further 1 million die before reaching one month of age. These figures are showing little improvement. In 1980, the infant mortality rate (deaths occurring

[13] This section is based on *DCP2*, chapter 27.

Box 4.4 Implementation Case Study: Indonesia

An intense effort by the government of Indonesia to increase the number of births attended by skilled health providers began in 1993 with the introduction of three-year nursing training followed by a year of training in midwifery. From 1996, this was supplemented by a further package of training interventions, including an in-service course; a supervisory system with peer review and continuing education; a maternal and perinatal audit system; and an information, education, and communication strategy aimed at the community.

Data were collected in three districts of South Kalimantan from 1996, before and after the additional package of training, which permitted measurement of its added value. Before the additional training, 90 percent of births took place at home and only 37 percent were attended by a skilled attendant. By 1998–99, 510 midwives were posted in the districts and skilled attendants at delivery had increased to 59 percent. The training package allowed the midwives to gain confidence and skills in the management of obstetric complications, but despite this, the proportion of women admitted to a hospital for a cesarean section declined from 1.7 percent to 1.4 percent. The proportion admitted to hospital with a complication requiring a life-saving intervention also declined from 1.1 percent to 0.7 percent (Ronsmans and others 2001). Significantly more of the midwives who had participated in the training programs were competent in five key skills than those who had not participated.

Walker and others (2002) undertook an economic analysis of the training programs, distinguishing between those programs run for facilities-based midwives and those run for village-based midwives, which included residential internship at district hospitals. They assessed the incremental cost-effectiveness of these programs from the standpoint of the health care provider. Walker and others estimated that the first scheme could be expanded to increase the number of competent midwives based in facilities and villages in South Kalimantan by 1 percent at incremental costs of US$765 and US$1,176, respectively. Replication in other regions would cost between 50 and 60 percent extra.

Source: Authors.

from birth to one year, including the postneonatal period) in low- and middle-income countries was approximately 88 per 1,000 live births (figure 4.3). Of these, 28 deaths occurred in the early neonatal period, the first week of life. By 2000, the infant mortality rate had fallen to 62 per 1,000 live births; however, almost all the progress was in the late neonatal or postneonatal periods. The rate of early neonatal deaths hardly diminished, declining only to 25 per 1,000 live births in 2000. The MDG of reducing mortality among children under five by two-thirds by 2015 cannot be achieved without addressing mortality in the first 28 days of life.

Appropriate interventions are not highly complex. Up to 40 percent of neonatal deaths could be averted with home- and community-based solutions. Sometimes they require no more than keeping an infant

Figure 4.3 Time Trends in Infant Mortality

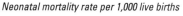

Neonatal mortality rate per 1,000 live births

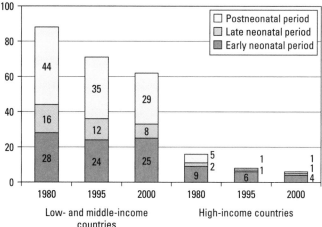

Source: Authors' calculations, based on UNICEF, WHO, various years. (*DCP2,* chapter 27, figure 27.2).

warm, breastfeeding regularly, and protecting against infection by means of proper hygiene and/or timely treatment with antibiotics (box 4.5). In many cases appropriate care is available, but gaps occur in the quality or continuity of care. The difference between obtaining care and obtaining adequate care can mean the difference between life and death (boxes 4.6 and 4.7). Delays in access to care are also an important factor contributing to maternal and neonatal deaths. Such delays occur for many different reasons, for example, failure to recognize the need for clinical attention, cultural norms that inhibit the use of medical services, limited physical or financial access to health care facilities, and delays in receiving care once at a facility.

Strategies to improve neonatal survival that focus only on the supply of health care within facilities will therefore fail unless they are integrated

---

Box 4.5 Successful Strategies for Neonatal Survival

In South Asia and Sub-Saharan Africa, the decline in late neonatal deaths was influenced by the halving of neonatal tetanus deaths that occurred during the 1990s as a result of increased tetanus toxoid protection and clean delivery practices. By 2000, two-thirds of low- and middle-income countries had eliminated neonatal tetanus and an additional 22 countries were nearing this goal.

Source: Adapted from *DCP2,* chapter 27.

with efforts to improve families' practices and to encourage people to
make use of health care services. In many cases, this requires appropriate attention to addressing cultural barriers to care, such as training
female birth attendants when having male attendants assist at a birth is
culturally improper or allowing new mothers and their babies to leave
the home in the first weeks of life if an emergency arises, and financial
barriers, including service fees and transportation costs.

   DCP2 reviews several packages of services that address care of the
newborn in the first 28 days of life. Some of these interventions are

". . . several packages of
services that address care
of the newborn in the first
28 days of life. . . . are
universally applicable and
are feasible even without
skilled health care
professionals."

universally applicable and are feasible even without skilled health care professionals. Others require skilled attention, are more complex, or rely on critical medical supplies. Packages of interventions that have a high impact and are feasible in most contexts can be divided into five groups: family care of the newborn, essential newborn care, resuscitation of the newborn, care for low birthweight babies, and emergency care. The first two emphasize maintaining warmth, breastfeeding, and employing hygiene (including proper care of the umbilical cord and hand washing). The latter three require some training, although resuscitation can often be accomplished with simple equipment costing less than US$5.

Creating a separate program for newborn care does not make sense. Rather, the best way to improve newborn care is to fill the gap in what should be a continuum of care that includes prenatal services, skilled birth attendance, and follow-up support through the first month of life. Adding newborn interventions to existing services (*DCP2*, chapter 63) or introducing them along with basic services where these are lacking would be more cost-effective than trying to introduce neonatal interventions in isolation.

Interventions to improve neonatal health and mortality rates are often simple, but require a functioning network of health services capable of providing continuity during the prenatal, birthing, and postpartum periods. Extending these services into marginalized urban and rural areas is the biggest challenge. As a first step, simple approaches can be implemented in even the poorest settings to improve family practices, particularly with regard to cleanliness, warmth, and breastfeeding. Where basic health care services are available, introducing training and equipment for well-tested interventions such as neonatal resuscitation and case management of infections is feasible, but fully addressing the problem of neonatal survival requires plugging the gaps in the continuity of care and strengthening the network of health care services and outreach. This means assuring that professional midwives can attend births and provide follow-up attention, that families learn when to seek health care, and that health care is readily accessible.

DCP2 finds that modest expenditures can have a significant effect on neonatal survival. For example, in Sub-Saharan Africa, providing basic maternal and child health services that would reduce neonatal mortality by 6 percent to as much as 41 percent, depending on the preexisting coverage of primary services and the baseline neonatal mortality rate, would cost between US$2 and US$10 per capita. An additional US$0.21 to US$0.95 in spending per capita could reduce neonatal deaths by as much as 71 percent. Estimates put the specific costs of adding neonatal resuscitation training, equipment, refresher courses, and supervision at less than US$0.02 per capita for an anticipated reduction in neonatal mortality of around 5 percent in Africa and South Asia.

While some resource-poor countries have demonstrated success, the process of building a functional system, especially for clinical care, takes time. Even though the costs appear small relative to spending in middle- and high-income countries, they are large relative to current spending on health care in low-income countries. Spending in India would have to be doubled and in Africa would have to be tripled to provide the basic maternal and child health care package along with the special interventions related to neonatal survival. International funding is therefore necessary to reduce the disease burden in low-income countries associated with neonatal conditions.

"Spending in India would have to be doubled and in Africa would have to be tripled to provide the basic maternal and child health care package along with the special interventions related to neonatal survival."

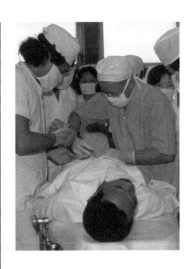

Chapter 5

Cost-Effective Strategies for Noncommunicable Diseases, Risk Factors, and Behaviors

Public health specialists concerned with low- and middle-income countries have devoted considerable attention to communicable diseases and maternal and child health for some time. Recently, however, their attention has turned to noncommunicable diseases such as cardiovascular disease (CVD), diabetes, and various cancers and intentional and unintentional injuries. This shift is due to the recognition that the burden of noncommunicable disease in low- and middle-income countries not only is growing rapidly but is already astoundingly large. Indeed, by 2001, CVD had become the leading cause of death worldwide in both developing and developed countries. Noncommunicable diseases are now dominant sources of morbidity and mortality around the globe.

The profile of some noncommunicable diseases in low- and middle-income countries is similar to that in high-income countries. In all regions of the world, for example, at least 80 percent of the burden of CVD comes from ischemic heart disease, congestive heart failure, and stroke. These conditions share many risk factors—obesity, high blood pressure, physical inactivity, and salt intake—and hence are susceptible to the same interventions.

Other noncommunicable diseases exhibit different profiles in developing and developed countries. Cancer, for example, displays considerable geographic variation. The types of cancers that predominate in the high-income countries—lung, colorectal, breast, and prostate cancer—can be traced to such factors as the earlier beginnings of the tobacco epidemic, earlier exposure to carcinogens, and diet and lifestyle. By contrast, the cancers that predominate in low- and middle-income countries—cervical, liver, and stomach cancer—are associated with chronic infections with human papillomavirus, hepatitis B, and *Helicobacter pylori*. Cancer causes a large and increasing disease burden worldwide, but its epidemiology, and consequently the relevant interventions, differ significantly in low- and middle-income countries and high-income countries.

The burden of noncommunicable disease is growing, but many low- and middle-income countries have not yet experienced the full demands that these conditions will place on their health systems. Ironically, part of that burden will result from successes in preventing or treating communicable diseases and reducing childhood mortality: with improved public health, individuals who would have died in childhood will now survive and become susceptible to noncommunicable disease.

Some of the burden of noncommunicable disease and injury is avoidable. By adopting policies that promote healthy eating and discourage smoking, for example, low- and middle-income countries may escape the risk profiles that wealthier countries acquired as they developed. Implementing proper road safety measures would also permit low- and middle-income countries to avoid a substantial burden of road traffic injuries, which increase as motorized traffic increases. As loss of life from communicable disease is reduced, it need not be replaced by an equal loss of life from noncommunicable disease.

"As loss of life from communicable disease is reduced, it need not be replaced by an equal loss of life from noncommunicable disease."

CARDIOVASCULAR DISEASE, DIABETES, HIGH BLOOD PRESSURE, CHOLESTEROL, AND BODYWEIGHT

The disease burdens from CVD, diabetes, and related conditions of high blood pressure, high cholesterol, and excessive bodyweight are increasing worldwide.[1] Once considered diseases of industrialized countries or of the affluent in developing countries, they are now recognized as global problems.

In 2001, CVD became the world's leading cause of death and now accounts for 28 percent of all deaths worldwide, with 80 percent of the burden in low- and middle-income countries. Most of that burden falls in Asia and Eastern Europe because of the large populations in these regions and the high incidence of coronary artery disease in Eastern Europe and Central Asia. Diabetes is also on the rise around the world, reaching a prevalence of 5.1 percent in 2003. The prevalence of diabetes is greatest in high-income countries at 7.8 percent, and in developing

[1] This section is based on *DCP2*, chapters 30, 33, 44, and 45.

regions ranges from a low of 2.4 percent in Sub-Saharan Africa to a high of 7.6 percent in Eastern Europe and Central Asia. Despite the higher prevalence of diabetes in high-income countries, the majority of the disease burden from diabetes, more than 70 percent, is in the developing regions because of their larger populations.[2]

Another way of looking at the burden of CVD, diabetes, and related conditions is to classify them by risk factor. The *World Health Report 2002* (WHO 2002) estimated that globally, 7.1 million deaths could be attributed to high blood pressure, 4.4 million deaths to high cholesterol, and 2.6 million deaths to excessive weight. Excessive weight is a growing problem in almost every country, even the poorest. It is increasing so rapidly that in middle-income countries the disease burden associated with having a body mass index greater than 25 is now equal to or greater than the disease burden resulting from undernutrition.

These diseases are not inevitable consequences of modern life. Low rates can be achieved with moderate changes in lifestyles that are fully compatible with life in the 21st century. Nevertheless, the requisite changes in smoking habits, physical activity, and diet may not be easy and will require support and encouragement through investments in education, changes in food policies, and sometimes even changes in urban infrastructure. Whereas the required behavioral changes are the same everywhere, the ways to achieve them will necessarily vary across countries and regions, with different approaches corresponding to cultural, social, and economic features.

Lifestyle Interventions

The key risk factors for CVD and diabetes—obesity, physical inactivity, and unhealthy diets—require interventions to change unhealthy lifestyles. These changes are most likely to occur with implementation of a coordinated range of interventions to encourage individuals to maintain a healthy weight, participate in daily physical activity, and consume a healthy diet. A healthy diet replaces saturated and trans fat with unsaturated fat; increases consumption of fruits, vegetables, and

"Despite the higher prevalence of diabetes in high-income countries, the majority of the disease burden from diabetes, more than 70 percent, is in the developing regions because of their larger populations."

". . . in middle-income countries the disease burden associated with . . . a body mass index greater than 25 is now equal to or greater than the disease burden . . . from undernutrition."

---

[2] Diabetes data combine both type 1 (an autoimmune disease that results from destruction of the pancreatic cells, leading to an absolute insulin deficiency) and type 2 (characterized by insulin resistance, in which target tissues do not use insulin properly, and inadequate insulin secretion from the pancreas), plus gestational diabetes. Type 2 diabetes, which has some of the same risk factors as CVD, now accounts for approximately 85 to 95 percent of all diagnosed cases of diabetes.

whole grains; and limits sodium intake and excessive calories from any source, but especially from sugar-based beverages.

Education is key to implementing such changes. It appears to be more effective when provided through multiple methods and sites, such as schools, workplaces, mass media, and health centers. Educational messages are also more effective if they are reinforced by action. Schools, for example, should provide not only curricula on good nutrition but also healthy meals; worksites should not only inform workers about the role of physical activity but facilitate the use of nonmotorized transportation.

Urban design and transportation policy are other key elements of lifestyle interventions. People can be encouraged to increase their physical activity by using public and nonmotorized transport, especially walking and bicycling. Although not normally considered an instrument for improving health, national transportation policies can strongly influence automobile use and dependency. Low taxes on gasoline, free parking, and wide street design encourage the use of automobiles (as in the United States), while narrow streets, limited parking, and high gasoline costs discourage their use (as in Western Europe). Because using an automobile is twice as costly in Europe as in the United States, Europeans walk or bicycle more and use their cars approximately 50 percent less than Americans. The same trends in public policy are played out in low- and middle-income countries. Singapore has been a leader in discouraging private automobile use and encouraging use of public transport, walking, or bicycling. By contrast, China has explicitly encouraged families to buy automobiles by lowering taxes, simplifying registration procedures, and allowing foreign financing.

Food policy is another important area for encouraging lifestyle change. Policy tools include how food is processed by fortifying foods with micronutrients and limiting advertising for unhealthy foods. One of the most effective ways to improve diets is to regulate or provide incentives for food manufacturers to replace unhealthy ingredients or products with healthier ones. Changes in types of fats, for example, can be almost imperceptible to consumers and relatively inexpensive. Many European manufacturers have greatly reduced foods' trans-fatty acid content by changing production methods. In this way, the Netherlands reduced the trans fat content of the food supply from about 6 percent of the energy content to approximately 1 percent in a single decade. In Mauritius, government policies replaced commonly used palm oils for cooking with soybean oil, which reduced the intake of fatty acids and

"Because using an automobile is twice as costly in Europe as in the United States, Europeans walk or bicycle more and use their cars approximately 50 percent less than Americans."

". . . the Netherlands reduced the trans fat content of the food supply from about 6 percent of the energy content to approximately 1 percent in a single decade."

lowered serum cholesterol levels. Other easily targeted changes in food processing include reducing salt and fortifying foods with micronutrients such as vitamin A, vitamin B12, iodine, iron, and folic acid.

Experience has provided some lessons for implementing successful lifestyle interventions across populations:

- Interventions should be long term with multiyear time frames.
- Credible agencies should be responsible for such interventions.
- Collaboration between the health sector, other government agencies, schools, workplaces, and the voluntary sector is important.
- Cooperation with the food industry is essential to ensure the availability of reasonably priced healthier food options with food labeling that presents relevant information in a clear, reliable, and standardized way.

Several lines of evidence indicate that most coronary artery disease, stroke, and diabetes and some cancers can be prevented or delayed by realistic changes in diet and lifestyle. One line of evidence is based on declines in coronary artery disease in countries that have implemented preventive programs. A dramatic example is that of Finland, which had the highest rates of CVD in the world, and where a comprehensive program focused on diet and lifestyle modification reduced the mortality rate by approximately 75 percent between 1972 and 1992 (box 5.1).

Box 5.1 Community Response to CVD in Finland

In 1972, Finland had the world's highest mortality rate from CVD. Planners examined policy and environmental factors contributing to CVD and sought appropriate changes, such as increased availability of low-fat dairy products, antismoking legislation, and improved school meals. They used the media, schools, worksites, and spokespersons from sports, education, and agriculture to educate residents. After five years, significant improvements were documented in smoking, cholesterol, and blood pressure. By 1992, CVD mortality rates for men age 35 to 64 had dropped by 57 percent. The program was so successful that it was expanded to include other lifestyle-related diseases and was used as a model for public health planners throughout the country and elsewhere. Twenty years later, major reductions in CVD risk factor levels, morbidity, and mortality were attributed to the project. Recent data show a 75 percent decrease in CVD mortality (Puska and others 1998).

Source: DCP2, chapter 44, p. 837.

DCP2 estimates the cost-effectiveness of several of these interventions. Replacing saturated fat with monounsaturated fat in manufactured products, accompanied by a community media campaign, can reduce coronary artery disease events by 4 percent. The total cost of these changes would range from US$1.80 to US$4.50 per person per year depending on the region. The incremental cost-effectiveness ratio would range from US$1,865 per DALY averted in South Asia to US$4,012 per DALY averted in the Middle East and North Africa.

Replacing the 2 percent of energy that comes from trans fat with polyunsaturated fat would reduce CVD by 7 to 40 percent and would also reduce type 2 diabetes. The effect would vary by region. Trans fat consumption is already low in China, so replacing it with polyunsaturated fat would not avert as much disease as in South Asia, where commonly used cooking fats have an extremely high trans fat content. Because partially hydrogenated fat could be eliminated or significantly reduced by voluntary industry action as done in the Netherlands or regulation as in Denmark, this intervention requires no consumer education, and the cost amounts to no more than US$0.50 per person per year. The cost-effectiveness ratio for this intervention ranges from US$25 to US$73 per DALY averted depending on the region. The intervention is cost saving in all regions.

Legislation that mandates reducing the salt content of manufactured foods, accompanied by an educational campaign, can reduce blood pressure and would cost US$6 per person per year. This intervention would cost US$1,325 per DALY averted in South Asia and US$3,056 per DALY averted in the Middle East and North Africa.

"Legislation that mandates reducing the salt content of manufactured foods, accompanied by an educational campaign, can reduce blood pressure and would cost US$6 per person per year."

Medical Interventions

When lifestyle changes are insufficient to avert CVD or diabetes, a variety of medical interventions exist. Many of these are sophisticated and expensive, such as grafting new arteries around the heart or opening a blockage with angioplasty, but relatively inexpensive treatments for chronic CVD are also available. For individuals who have suffered heart attacks, medications such as beta-blockers and aspirin can reduce the chance of a recurrence. The essential treatment for averting death from type 1 diabetes is insulin injections to maintain proper blood glucose levels. For type 2 diabetes, treatment requires changes in diet and physical activity, which are also needed for type 1 disease, and oral glucose-lowering agents, with insulin required only in severe cases. Blood pressure and lipids can also be controlled with pharmaceuticals. Other effective interventions for diabetes include early detection and screening followed by treatment for retinopathy, microalbuminuria, and foot disease.

Glucose levels of those with both type 1 and type 2 diabetes are currently poorly controlled in low- and middle-income countries. A 1997 survey by the International Diabetes Federation showed that no country in Africa had universal access to insulin for those who needed it. In the Democratic Republic of Congo, those with type 1 diabetes had access to insulin less than 25 percent of the time, implying a high mortality rate. Even in middle-income countries, such as El Salvador and Peru, diabetics requiring glycemic control had access to insulin only 26 to 49 percent of the time.

Most of the evidence regarding the cost-effectiveness of medical treatments for CVD and diabetes is from high-income countries. Medical interventions for CVD that are likely to be cost-effective in low- and middle-income countries include the following:

- anticlotting agents such as aspirin and heparin to prevent venous thromboembolism
- benzathine penicillin injections as secondary prevention, usually for five years, for those whose who have had rheumatic fever
- angiotensin-converting enzyme inhibitors for congestive heart failure
- anticoagulants for mitral stenosis and atrial fibrillation
- various drugs, including beta-blockers and off-patent statins, for long-term care of postmyocardial infarction.

Having defibrillators in emergency vehicles is highly cost-effective in high-income countries but is unlikely to be cost-effective in most lower-income countries. Nevertheless, having them available in hospitals may be cost-effective.

Medical researchers are pinning great hopes on the development of a so-called polypill to prevent CVD. The hypothetical polypill would combine several medications, including generic aspirin, a beta-blocker, a thiazide diuretic, an angiotensin-converting enzyme inhibitor, and a statin. When taken by a population with a 35 percent risk of CVD, the incremental cost-effectiveness ratio of such a polypill ranges from US$721 per DALY averted in the Middle East and North Africa to US$1,065 per DALY averted in East Asia and the Pacific. The cost-effectiveness is understandably lower in populations where the prevalence of CVD is lower.

"Even in middle-income countries . . . diabetics requiring glycemic control had access to insulin only 26 to 49 percent of the time."

"Medical researchers are pinning great hopes on the development of a so-called polypill to prevent CVD . . ."

" . . . for diabetes . . . glycemic control, blood pressure control, and foot care are all cost-effective and feasible."

The cost-effectiveness of medical interventions for diabetes varies greatly. Some are cost saving; others can cost more than US$73,000 per quality-adjusted life year gained. *DCP2* estimates of the cost-effectiveness of these interventions explicitly incorporate differences in implementation, including the ease of reaching the targeted population and interventions' technical complexity, capital intensity, and cultural acceptability. Using this framework, glycemic control, blood pressure control, and foot care are all cost-effective and feasible.

Glycemic control costs less than managing the complications that arise in its absence. Ensuring adequate access to insulin is an important, cost-effective approach for people with type 1 diabetes, for whom insulin is essential. Blood pressure control for those with hypertension is also cost-effective and cost saving. Because many of the medications that control blood pressure are generic drugs, the drug cost in low- and middle-income countries is quite low. Furthermore, many people with diabetes in these countries also have poor control of their blood pressure. The combination makes these medications highly cost-effective.

Thus the cost-effectiveness of medical interventions varies considerably across contexts, depending on the availability of skilled personnel, the prices of drug, and the prevalence of risks. By contrast, lifestyle interventions are often cost saving because they avert conditions that can be costly to treat.

CANCER

"By 2020, unless cancer prevention and screening interventions effectively reduce . . . incidence . . . the number of new cancer cases will increase from . . . 10 million cases in 2000 to an estimated 15 million . . ."

Cancer is another noncommunicable disease long considered a health threat primarily for high-income countries, but now imposing a considerable disease burden worldwide.[3] In 2001, cancer caused more than 7 million deaths, of which 5 million were in low- and middle-income countries. That year, cancer resulted in the loss of more than 100 million DALYs, with nearly 75 million lost in low- and middle-income countries. By 2020, unless cancer prevention and screening interventions effectively reduce the incidence of cancer, the number of new cancer cases will increase from an estimated 10 million cases in 2000 to an estimated 15 million per year, and 9 million of them will occur in developing countries.

While cancer is a problem everywhere, it is not manifested in the same way worldwide. A substantial portion of cancers in developing

[3] This section is based on *DCP2*, chapter 29.

countries, up to 25 percent, are associated with chronic infection. Liver cancer is causally associated with hepatitis B infection, cervical cancer with infection by certain types of human papillomavirus, and stomach cancer with *Helicobacter pylori* infection. The incidence of these cancers is also related to the absence of a well-developed public health infrastructure for the control of cancer-causing infectious agents.

In 2000, seven types of cancer accounted for approximately 60 percent of all newly diagnosed cancer cases and cancer deaths in developing countries: cervical, liver, stomach, esophageal, lung, colorectal, and breast. The first four exhibit elevated incidence and mortality rates in developing countries. The last three have a lower but increasing incidence because of demographic and industrial transitions. Developing regions also exhibit considerable variation in their cancer burdens. Deaths from liver cancer are relatively high in East Asia and Africa because of the high prevalence of chronic hepatitis B infection and inadequate food storage and preservation in those regions. Deaths from colorectal and breast cancer are relatively high in Eastern Europe as people in those regions have adopted less healthy, high-fat diets and more sedentary lifestyles. Deaths from oral cancer are particularly high in South Asia, where chewing betel quid is common. These different types of cancer call for different intervention strategies.

Interventions fall into several categories. Primary prevention eliminates exposure to cancer-causing agents; secondary prevention involves detecting and treating precancerous lesions; treatment includes surgery, chemotherapy, and radiotherapy; and palliative care addresses patients' physical and psychological comfort from diagnosis through death.

Primary prevention for the types of cancer that are of greatest concern in developing countries include immunizing against and treating infectious agents, implementing dietary interventions, introducing tobacco control programs, reducing excessive alcohol consumption, and using chemoprophylaxis. Cost-effectiveness studies of these interventions are relatively rare and are concentrated in high-income countries. For example, studies in the United Kingdom and the United States find that the costs of screening and treating individuals for *helicobacter* infections to reduce the risk of stomach cancer run between US$25,000 and US$50,000 per life year saved, but another study found that this intervention would be much more cost-effective in Colombia, where health care costs are lower and the prevalence of stomach cancer is higher.

Secondary prevention consists of screening programs to detect and treat precursors of cancer, which can prevent or reduce the incidence of highly invasive cancers, such as cervical or colorectal cancers. Effective screening can also detect invasive cancers, such as breast and lung cancers, at an earlier stage than would otherwise be possible and thus improve the likelihood that treatments will be successful. The cost-effectiveness of secondary prevention depends on many factors, including the costs of diagnostic tests, the prevalence of the disease, and the availability of effective treatments.

Cancer treatment includes surgical removal of tumors, chemotherapy, and radiation therapy. Treatment cost-effectiveness for cervical, breast, oral, and colorectal cancer ranges from US$1,300 to US$6,200 per year of life saved. For cancers that are more difficult to treat, such as liver, lung, stomach, and esophageal cancer, the cost-effectiveness is much worse, ranging from US$53,000 to US$163,000 per year of life saved.

The availability of cost-effective methods of prevention and treatment for cancers in low- and middle-income countries varies significantly depending on the type of cancer, with a consequent substantial effect on the equity of outcomes. In the case of cancers for which effective detection and treatment are not available, that is, esophageal, liver, lung, and pancreatic cancer, survival rates are similar in rich and poor countries. For cancers with proven methods of treatment, such as large bowel, breast, ovarian, and cervical cancer, a substantial gap is apparent between the better survival rates in high-income countries and the worse survival rates in low- and middle-income countries. A third group of cancers requires treatments that are complex and multimodal, including testicular cancer, leukemia, and lymphoma. The challenges to providing appropriate care for these cancers are particularly large in settings without specialized medical staff and good health care infrastructure.

CONGENITAL AND DEVELOPMENTAL DISORDERS

Another component of the burden of noncommunicable disease comes from congenital and developmental disorders.[4] As low- and middle-income countries make progress in controlling the major childhood illnesses, a number of congenital and developmental disorders are likely to be revealed.

[4] This section is based on *DCP2*, chapter 34.

Figure 5.1 Global Distribution of Hemoglobinopathies

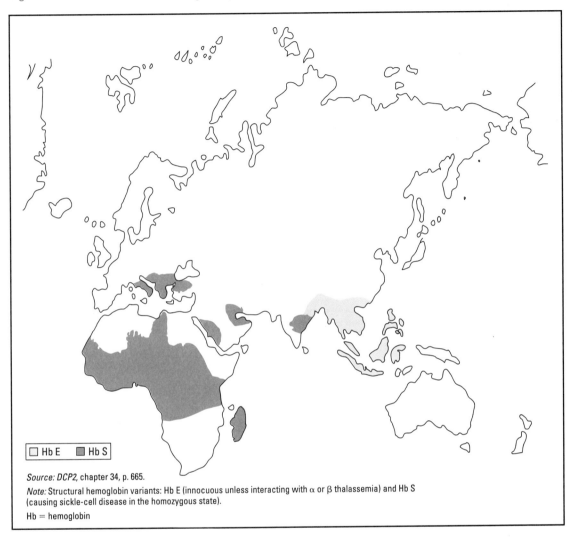

Source: DCP2, chapter 34, p. 665.

Note: Structural hemoglobin variants: Hb E (innocuous unless interacting with α or β thalassemia) and Hb S (causing sickle-cell disease in the homozygous state).

Hb = hemoglobin

In Africa, 2 percent of infants have sickle cell disease, one of the inherited conditions, or hemoglobinopathies, that affects the normal functioning of hemoglobin in the red blood cells (figure 5.1). The condition is largely absent among adolescents and adults because of the high mortality rates among children. As countries control malaria and improve the diagnosis and treatment of infections with antibiotics, more infants with this condition will survive into adulthood.

The prevalence of learning and developmental disabilities (functional limitations that result from damage to the nervous system) is at

"In Africa, 2 percent of infants have sickle cell disease . . ."

least 10 to 20 percent in high-income countries. Infants and children with these disabilities are less likely to survive and come to the attention of the health system until countries are better able to control common infectious diseases and the coverage of their health systems becomes more complete.

Congenital and developmental disorders arise from a variety of conditions. Many of these disorders are strictly genetic: sickle cell anemia occurs in one out of four children whose parents carry the recessive gene for this condition, and Down syndrome is caused by the presence of a third chromosome. Other disorders arise when fetal development is harmed, as occurs with fetal alcohol syndrome, iodine deficiency, and congenital rubella. A third class of disorders arises from adverse environmental exposure, for example, neurological damage caused by cerebral malaria, bacterial meningitis, or lead poisoning.

These disorders account for a significant share of the world's disease burden. Some 7 percent of the world's population carries genes that can cause hemoglobin disorders, and each year between 300,000 and 500,000 babies are born with severe forms of these disorders. Mild mental retardation from lead ingestion accounts for 1 percent of the global disease burden, about 9.8 million DALYs, and lead ingestion is only one of many causes of mental retardation.

The consequences of these disorders vary widely and depend both on the severity of the condition and on the context. When a health system can assure proper diagnosis and penicillin prophylaxis, many children can live normal lives despite carrying sickle cell. Hyperactivity disorders and dyslexia are problematic in school settings that do not have resources to address them. Stigmatization may prevent individuals from participating in social activities even when their functional limitations are not a constraint. In places where public policy promotes the construction of ramps for wheel chairs or Braille signs, functional limitations are less restrictive.

Some health interventions address congenital and developmental disorders by preventing them. These include measures like offering genetic screening and counseling for couples when serious congenital disorders are detected, vaccinating against Hib and meningitis to avert neurological damage, implementing behavioral interventions to stop alcohol use during pregnancy to avert fetal alcohol syndrome, eliminating environmental exposure to toxins such as lead that cause mental retardation, and redressing nutritional deficiencies among pregnant women.

"... 7 percent of the world's population carries genes that can cause hemoglobin disorders, and each year between 300,000 and 500,000 babies are born with severe forms of these disorders. Mild mental retardation from lead ingestion accounts for 1 percent of the global disease burden ..."

Other interventions are available to prevent disorders from progressing to disability:

- Screening for metabolic disorders identifies individuals who will develop neurological damage after ingesting certain foods. Children at risk for such disorders and their parents can be counseled to restrict the identified children's diets accordingly.
- Screening for sickle cell anemia can be followed by penicillin prophylaxis to reduce the risk of death and morbidity from infections.
- Screening and treatment for congenital hypothyroidism can avert developmental damage that results in severe cognitive disabilities.
- Prompt treatment for cerebral malaria can avert long-term neurological damage.

When disorders cannot be prevented, in some cases treatments are available to mitigate their impact on an individual's health. People with conditions caused by severe thalassemias, genetic disorders involving defective hemoglobin production in the blood, may require blood transfusions with washed red blood cells adequately screened for blood-borne diseases; individuals with sickle cell disease can be hospitalized and treated with analgesics when they develop severe bone pain; and nutritional fortification, surgery, rehabilitation, or special education may be able to reduce the severity of impairments.

Finally, when disorders cannot be prevented or treated, mitigating the impact of the disability on a person's quality of life might be possible. Many interventions are directed at associated health conditions; for example, people born with Down syndrome are likely to require treatment or therapy for poor hearing and vision, congenital heart defects, and low mental capacities. Other interventions address environmental constraints on an individual's participation in family and social life, whether by improving physical mobility through appropriate investments in public infrastructure, such as wheelchair accessible mass transit, buildings, and restrooms; building social support networks; or addressing social stigma and educating the public to be more inclusive of people with disabilities.

DCP2 finds that many interventions for addressing congenital and developmental disorders are cost-effective. Chapter 34 highlights penicillin prophylaxis for newborns with sickle cell anemia, which costs between US$7,000 and US$12,000 per death averted and US$250 to US$600 per DALY averted. It also notes that screening for sickle cell

"... many interventions for addressing congenital and developmental disorders are cost-effective."

anemia among people of African descent costs about US$6,700 per death averted, but that universal screening in other populations with low prevalence is not cost-effective. Chapter 49 finds that folic acid fortification of grains to prevent birth defects is cost-effective, costing an average of US$36 per DALY averted in Latin America and the Caribbean, US$40 per DALY averted in Sub-Saharan Africa, US$58 per DALY averted in South Asia, and US$160 per DALY averted in East Asia and the Pacific. Prenatal screening and selective pregnancy termination to prevent Down syndrome, spina bifida, and other frequently fatal congenital disorders can be highly cost-effective, but raise ethical, social, and cultural concerns that have to be addressed in ways that respect the gravity of such decisions and assure the protection of human rights.

In addressing congenital and developmental disorders, the evidence in *DCP2* demonstrates the strong relationships between diseases. Immunization programs aimed at preventing rubella reduce the likelihood of congenital deformities in newborns, and better control of malaria would reduce the prevalence of neurological disorders resulting from cerebral malaria. Better nourishment for pregnant women, with particular attention to micronutrients such as vitamin A, folic acid, and iodine, not only would be beneficial to women's own health and reduce the risk of maternal mortality, but would also reduce the chances of their children being born with a congenital disorder.

UNINTENTIONAL INJURIES

Unintentional injuries, particularly road traffic injuries, are another component of the burden of noncommunicable disease.[5] Worldwide, unintentional injuries accounted for 3.5 million deaths in 2001, of which more than 90 percent occurred in low- and middle-income countries and accounted for about 7 percent of all deaths in these countries. Of these, road traffic injuries accounted for about 34 percent of deaths from unintentional injuries. While men account for 66 percent of all deaths from unintentional injuries, they account for 73 percent of road and traffic injuries.

Road traffic injuries increase when the volume of travel and the use of motorized vehicles, especially two-wheeled vehicles, increase. They also occur more frequently with increasing speed and in places where

[5] This section is based on *DCP2*, chapter 39.

roads cannot handle the increasing volume and speed of traffic. Injuries also result when pedestrians must share roadways with motorized and nonmotorized vehicles.

Road traffic injuries tend to increase as countries industrialize and grow economically. Later, as wealth increases and public institutions strengthen, countries invest in safety measures, but waiting for incomes to rise before implementing preventive measures results in the needless loss of millions of lives. Awareness of this historical pattern of rising traffic accidents may help low- and middle-income countries recognize the need to incorporate safer designs when building roads and highways and to promote safe driving.

Many effective interventions are available to reduce the risk of road traffic injuries. The first set of interventions manages exposure to risk. Examples include substituting safer modes of transportation for more dangerous ones and minimizing high-risk scenarios, for example, by raising the legal minimum age for driving a motorcycle. A second set of interventions involves constructing safer roads. This can include placing speed bumps to slow traffic, separating vehicular lanes from paths used by pedestrians and bicycles, constructing median barriers, providing passing lanes, and improving street lighting. A third set of interventions focuses on encouraging people to adopt safer behaviors. These include introducing legislation and enforcing it with respect to speed limits, blood alcohol levels, driving hours for commercial drivers, provision and use of seatbelts, and use of bicycle and motorcycle helmets along with providing education for pedestrians.

DCP2 assesses the cost-effectiveness of several different interventions aimed at reducing traffic accidents, including increased penalties for violating road safety regulations paired with enforcement, speed bumps, and requirements for using bicycle and motorcycle helmets along with enforcement.

Evidence for the effectiveness of stronger road safety laws is available from Brazil, where a package of three interventions that included legislative changes to increase penalties, broadcast of messages in the media to inform the public about the changes, and better enforcement achieved a 25 percent reduction in traffic fatalities between 1997 and 1998. Even though education about road safety alone can have an impact, studies in Malaysia and Thailand demonstrated that education has a much greater impact when it is part of a package that includes strong legislation and increased enforcement because the interventions reinforce one another.

"Brazil . . . achieved a 25 percent reduction in traffic fatalities between 1997 and 1998 . . ."

". . . education has a much greater impact when it is part of a package that includes strong legislation and increased enforcement because the interventions reinforce one another."

Speed bumps installed at dangerous intersections or near pedestrian crossings are a simple way to reduce speed and the risk of accidents. Prior surveillance and data collection are required, because to be effective, speed bumps must be installed at the most dangerous locations. Ghana introduced speed bumps in hazardous places and reduced road traffic fatalities at these locations by more than 50 percent.

Bicycle helmets are extremely effective at preventing head injuries; motorcycle helmets are somewhat less so. In China, bicycle-related deaths kill 22 people per million inhabitants each year, while motorcycle accidents kill 16 people per million inhabitants. Case-control studies indicate that bicycle helmets can reduce injuries by 85 percent.

In modeling the cost-effectiveness of these interventions, *DCP2* finds that all of them cost less than US$1,000 per DALY averted. For traffic safety legislation and enforcement, cost-effectiveness ranged from US$14 per DALY averted in South Asia to US$584 per DALY averted in Eastern Europe and Central Asia. Putting speed bumps in the 10 percent of intersections that are the most lethal in a city of 1 million would cost only US$2 per DALY averted in Latin America and the Caribbean to US$9 per DALY averted in East Asia and the Pacific. Increasing bicycle helmet use in China would cost US$107 per DALY averted, while increasing motorcycle helmet use would cost US$467 per DALY averted (table 5.1).

Thus interventions to reduce the risk of traffic injuries are reasonably simple and cost-effective. Nonetheless, investments in such interventions are low. In 1998, Uganda spent only US$0.09 per capita and Pakistan US$0.07 per capita on road safety, or less than 1 percent of public spending on health in each country. Reviews of road safety initiatives found similar underinvestment in road safety in Benin, Côte d'Ivoire, Kenya, Tanzania, and Zimbabwe.

Implementing road safety measures does not require new knowledge: the risk factors are well known. Implementation often fails, however, because of conflicts between government ministries, inefficient civil services, and corruption. While the costs are not negligible, the interventions are cost-effective.

TOBACCO USE

While some diseases—HIV/AIDS, TB, cancer—seem to stalk people, some behaviors seem to seek out disease.[6] Addictive behaviors put people into the latter category.

[6] This section is based on *DCP2,* chapters 44 and 46.

> "Putting speed bumps in the 10 percent of intersections that are the most lethal in a city of 1 million would cost only US$2 per DALY averted in Latin America and the Caribbean to US$9 per DALY averted in East Asia and the Pacific."

Table 5.1 Key Findings: Cost-Effective Interventions to Prevent Unintentional Injuries in Low- and Middle-Income Countries

Injury	Promising interventions	Interventions shown to be effective in low- and middle-income countries (references)
Road traffic injuries (RTIs)	Reducing motor vehicle traffic: efficient fuel taxes, changes in land-use policy, safety impact assessment of transportation and land-use plans, provision of shorter and safer routes, trip reduction measures	Increasing the legal age of motorcyclists from 16 to 18 years (Norghani and others 1998)
	Making greater use of safer modes of transport	
	Minimizing exposure to high-risk scenarios: restricting access to different parts of the road network, giving priority to higher occupancy vehicles or to vulnerable road users, restricting the speed and engine performance of motorized two-wheelers, increasing the legal age for operating a motorcycle, using graduated driver's licensing systems	
	Safer roads	
	Safety awareness in planning road networks, safety features in road design, and remedial action in high-risk crash sites: making provisions for slow-moving traffic and vulnerable road users; providing passing lanes, median barriers, and street lighting	
	Traffic calming measures, such as speed bumps	
	Speed cameras	Speed bumps in reducing pedestrian injuries (Afukaar, Antwi, and Ofusu-Amah 2003)
	Safer vehicles	
	Improving the visibility of vehicles, including requiring automatic daytime running lights	Daytime running lights on motorcycles (Radin Umar, Mackay, and Hills 1996; Yuan 2000)
	Incorporating crash protective design into vehicles, including installing seat belts	
	Mandating vehicle licensing and inspection	Increases in fines and suspension of driver's licenses (Poli de Figueiredo and others 2001)
	Safer people	
	Legislating strategies and increasing enforcement of, for example, speed limits, alcohol-related limits, hours of driving for commercial drivers, seat belt use, bicycle and motorcycle helmet use	Legislation and enforcement of motorcycle helmets (Ichikawa, Chadbunchachai, and Marui 2003; Supramaniam, Belle, and Sung 1984).
Poisonings	Better storage, including positioning and nature of storage vessels	Free distribution of child-resistant containers (Krug and others 1994)
	Use of child-resistant containers	
	Warning labels	
	First-aid education	
	Poison control centers	
Fall-related injuries	*Older people*	
	Muscle strengthening and balance retraining, individually prescribed	
	Tai chi group exercise	
	Home hazard assessment and modification for high-risk individuals	
	Multidisciplinary, multifactorial screening for health and environmental risk factors	
	Younger people	
	Multifaceted community programs of the Children Can't Fly type	

(Continued on the following page.)

Table 5.1 (*Continued*)

Injury	Promising interventions	Interventions shown to be effective in low- and middle-income countries (references)
Burn-related injuries	*Fire-related injuries*	
	Introducing programs to install smoke alarms	
	Separating cooking areas from living areas	
	Locating cooking surfaces at heights	
	Reducing the storage of flammable substances in households	
	Supervising children more effectively	
	Introducing, monitoring, and enforcing standards and codes for fire-resistant garments	
	Scald-related injuries	
	Separating cooking areas from play areas	
	Improving the design of cooking vessels	
	Fire- and scald-related injuries	
	Increasing awareness of burns prevention	
	Providing first-aid education	
Drowning	Limiting exposure to bodies of water close to dwellings, such as by fencing	
	Providing learn-to-swim programs	
	Providing education about risks for drowning	
	Increasing supervision and providing lifeguards at recreational facilities	
	Equipping boats with flotation devices and ensuring their use	
	Legislating and enforcing rules about the numbers of individuals carried on boats	
	Having trained and responsive coast guard services	

Source: DCP2, chapter 39, table 39.3.

> "Worldwide, tobacco use accounts for 1 of every 5 deaths among men and 1 of every 20 deaths among women over the age of 30."

Worldwide, tobacco use accounts for 1 of every 5 deaths among men and 1 of every 20 deaths among women over the age of 30. In 2000, 4.8 million premature deaths could be attributed to diseases caused by tobacco, including CVD, lung cancer, and chronic obstructive pulmonary disease. In low- and middle-income countries, smoking is also associated with respiratory illnesses such as asthma and TB. Among men in China, smoking was responsible for an estimated 12 percent of deaths from TB. In India, TB was four times more likely in smokers than nonsmokers, suggesting that smoking is a contributory factor in about half of all TB deaths among men. The eventual risk of death from smoking is high: about one-half to two-thirds of long-term smokers will die from diseases caused by their addiction. Smokers also impose health risks on others, with passive smoking being a significant risk factor for children in developing asthma, throat inflammations, and respiratory illnesses.

An estimated 1.1 billion people currently smoke, and four-fifths of these smokers reside in low- and middle-income countries. Smoking prevalence is highest in Eastern Europe and Central Asia, where 35 percent of all adults smoke. However, East Asia and the Pacific currently accounts for most tobacco-related deaths, about 40 percent. Men smoke more than women, although the gap is smaller in high-income countries.

The global trends in smoking are worrisome. If the proportion of young people taking up smoking continues its current pattern—about half of men and 1 in 10 women—each year will see some 30 million new long-term smokers. As a result, by 2030 the number of tobacco-related premature deaths will rise to 10 million per year (figure 5.2).

Yet these deaths are avoidable, as demonstrated by experiences in countries where quitting has become common. Serious tobacco control efforts first began in the United Kingdom and the United States in the 1960s. Their sustained impact has discouraged young people from smoking and helped millions of smokers to quit. As a direct result,

> "... one-half to two-thirds of long-term smokers will die from diseases caused by their addiction."

Figure 5.2 Projected Rise in Tobacco-Related Deaths of Smokers Who Fail to Quit

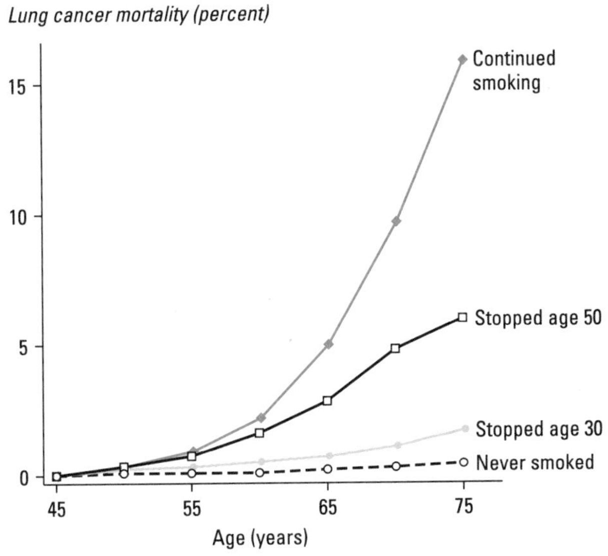

Lung cancer mortality (percent)

Continued smoking
Stopped age 50
Stopped age 30
Never smoked

Age (years)

Source: DCP2, chapter 46, p. 5.

Figure 5.3 Trends in Deaths Attributed to Smoking

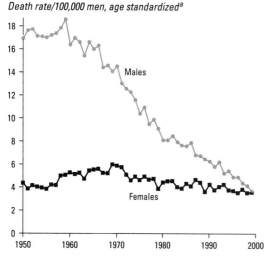

a. United Kingdom

Death rate/100,000 men, age standardized[a]

Males

Females

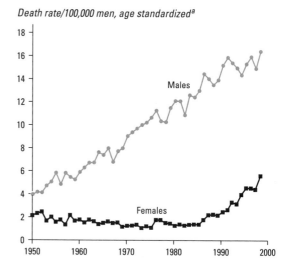

b. France

Death rate/100,000 men, age standardized[a]

Males

Females

Source: DCP2, chapter 46, p. 4.

a. Mean of annual rates in component five-year age groups.

"In the United Kingdom . . . , the incidence of lung cancer among men age 35 to 44 fell from 18 cases per 100,000 people in 1950 to 4 cases per 100,000 in 2000."

lung cancer rates in the United Kingdom and the United States have dropped rapidly. In the United Kingdom, where the main increase in smoking began before World War II, the incidence of lung cancer among men age 35 to 44 fell from 18 cases per 100,000 people in 1950 to 4 cases per 100,000 in 2000 (figure 5.3a). By contrast, smoking became common in France much later, efforts to discourage smoking did not have an impact until the 1990s, and the incidence of lung cancer among French men has continued to climb (figure 5.3b).

The addictive substance in tobacco is nicotine, a psychoactive drug. Inhalation is the most effective way of getting nicotine to receptors in the brain. Nicotine creates positive sensations when it is administered and leads to unpleasant sensations when it is withdrawn. In this regard, it is on a par with such other powerfully addictive drugs as heroin and cocaine.

Behavioral influences strengthen the biochemically addictive nature of tobacco. Unlike illicit drugs that entail risks of incarceration and social disapproval, social mores and licit commercial interests have favored tobacco. Tobacco companies and governments have encouraged smoking through advertising and other forms of promotion. Mass marketing also presents smokers with many opportunities and frequent cues to both purchase and use tobacco, making cessation that much more difficult.

Prevention is the best way to address diseases caused by tobacco. Anything that reduces smoking, whether reducing the number of people who start smoking, increasing the number who quit, reducing the number who relapse, or decreasing smoking among those who continue, will ultimately reduce the burden from tobacco-related illnesses such as CVD, cancer, and TB. The addictive nature of tobacco has implications for discouraging its use. Educating consumers that tobacco is an addiction and causes health problems is insufficient, because people regularly underestimate their future health risks and because young people are more prone to adopting risky behaviors. Once people are addicted, cessation is difficult. Interventions proven effective at reducing smoking include increasing tobacco taxes, disseminating information about tobacco's health risks, restricting smoking in public places and workplaces, banning advertising, and increasing access to cessation therapies.

Nearly all governments tax tobacco to generate revenue, but as awareness of the dangers of smoking has grown, governments are increasingly using tobacco tax policy to raise the cost of the habit and discourage the use of tobacco. In some cases, countries have even earmarked tobacco taxes to finance health programs aimed at reducing exposure to tobacco.

Tobacco taxes have a greater effect on reducing consumption among lower-income groups, youths, and those who are less educated. Taxes are also more effective in the long run than in the short run, because addicted consumers change their habits slowly. Higher tobacco prices appear to be particularly effective in preventing young smokers from moving beyond experimentation to becoming regular smokers. Studies have estimated that the effect of raising tobacco prices may be twice as high in low- and middle-income countries than in higher-income countries, implying that significant increases in tobacco taxes in the former would be effective in reducing tobacco use. Taxes account for more than two-thirds of the retail price in most high-income countries but less than one-half in low- and middle-income countries.

In addition to raising the price of tobacco, many countries have effectively discouraged smoking by restricting it in public areas. The

"... governments are increasingly using tobacco tax policy to raise the cost of the habit and discourage the use of tobacco."

justification for such measures is to protect nonsmokers from harm caused by inhaling secondhand smoke, but such measures also create a hindrance to smokers, forcing them to change their habits and seek out special smoking areas. This can help raise barriers to smoking and also stigmatize the practice, thereby inducing changes in social norms. To have an impact, such regulations require enforcement, particularly when they are first introduced.

Interventions that affect people's attitudes toward and knowledge about the dangers of smoking can also be extremely helpful. Cigarettes are among the most heavily advertised and promoted products in the world. Information and education campaigns can counter the impact of this marketing by publicizing reports about the dangers of smoking, putting warning labels on packages, and broadcasting antismoking messages in the media. Comprehensive bans on advertising and promoting tobacco may reduce smoking and make public awareness campaigns more effective.

While the dangers of smoking have become widely known in most high-income countries, awareness of the risks of mortality and disease posed by smoking is still not widespread in low- and middle-income countries. The key messages that need to be transmitted are that addiction will eventually kill one-half to two-thirds of all smokers; that, on average, smokers will lose 20 to 25 years of life and will die between the ages of 35 and 69; and that quitting raises the chances of survival no matter how long an individual has smoked.

"... quitting raises the chances of survival no matter how long an individual has smoked."

The recent development of drugs that counter the effects of nicotine improve the chances that smokers who would like to quit can succeed. Ironically, nicotine-containing tobacco products are often cheaper and easier to purchase than nicotine replacement therapies. Policies that redress this imbalance by decreasing the costs of nicotine replacement therapies and increasing their availability can help smokers quit. These therapies become more effective when coupled with counseling and peer support. Promoting cessation is particularly important, because the bulk of tobacco-related deaths between now and 2050 will be among current smokers. By contrast, policies aimed at preventing young people from taking up smoking will have their main impact after 2050.

Interventions aimed at reducing the supply of tobacco do not seem to be particularly effective. Some of these programs, such as prohibiting the sale of tobacco products to young people, are difficult and costly to enforce. Restrictions on the importation of tobacco products might raise domestic prices, but also violate international trade agreements. Programs aimed at encouraging farmers to stop growing tobacco are ineffective because other farmers can expand their production to fill the gap. Hence, low- and middle-income countries would be well advised to concentrate their efforts on reducing demand.

Fortunately, most demand-side interventions are cost-effective, and even cost saving. Tobacco taxes aimed at raising the cost of smoking are the most cost-effective way to reduce smoking. A 70 percent increase in the price of tobacco could avert 10 to 26 percent of all smoking-related deaths worldwide. The effect would be particularly strong in low- and middle-income countries, among young people, and for men. Using a base-case scenario of a 33 percent price increase yields a cost-effectiveness ratio of US$3 to US$42 per DALY averted in low- and middle-income countries and US$85 to US$1,773 per DALY averted in high-income countries. Successful interventions in Poland and South Africa went well beyond such a modest price increase, almost doubling cigarette prices over a short time (*DCP2*, chapter 8; Levine and others 2004). Despite price increases being the most cost-effective approach to controlling tobacco consumption, this public health measure is grossly underutilized. Indeed, when adjusted for purchasing power, the price of tobacco products actually fell in most developing countries between 1990 and 2000.

Increasing access to nicotine replacement therapies to assist smokers who want to quit is more expensive, costing between US$75 and US$1,250 per DALY averted, but is still relatively cost-effective, especially where the direct cost of therapies is low. Other nonprice interventions could be implemented for between US$233 and US$2,916 per DALY averted. The cost-effectiveness of nonprice measures is extremely sensitive to context. In countries where the public readily absorbs public health messages, the costs could be low.

Tobacco-related deaths are the fastest growing cause of death in low- and middle-income countries, on par with the HIV/AIDS epidemic. The availability of cost-effective control measures eliminates any excuse for inaction. The obstacles to forestalling a rapid increase in tobacco-related deaths, which requires strong and skillful responses to those who market tobacco products and lobby against reform, lie squarely in the political realm.

"A 70 percent increase in the price of tobacco could avert 10 to 26 percent of all smoking-related deaths worldwide."

". . . when adjusted for purchasing power, the price of tobacco products actually fell in most developing countries between 1990 and 2000."

"Tobacco-related deaths are the fastest growing cause of death in low- and middle-income countries, on a par with the HIV/AIDS epidemic."

ALCOHOL ABUSE

High-risk alcohol use[7] is a serious public health problem.[8] It directly harms the health of those who drink excessively and contributes to risky behaviors that cause injury and impairment to themselves and others. Alcohol consumption is linked to long-term health and social consequences through three intermediate mechanisms: intoxication, dependence, and direct biological effects (figure 5.4).

Alcohol-related diseases account for about 4 percent of global DALYs each year and range from a low of 0.5 percent in the Middle East and North Africa, where alcohol consumption is low, to between 1.5 and 2.0 percent in South Asia and Sub-Saharan Africa, 4.3 percent in East Asia and the Pacific, 8.8 percent in Latin America and the Caribbean, and 10.7 percent in Eastern Europe and Central Asia. About 75 percent of this disease burden is manifested in chronic illnesses such as alcohol

Figure 5.4 Model of Alcohol Consumption, Intermediate Outcomes, and Long-term Consequences

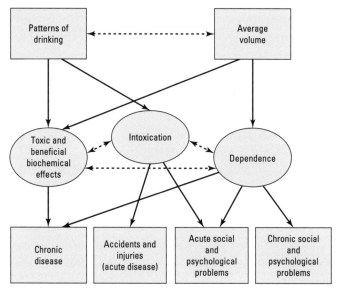

Source: DCP2, chapter 47, figure 47.1.

[7] High-risk alcohol use is defined differently for men and women. For men it is defined as consuming an average of more than 40 grams per day of pure alcohol, and for women the figure is more than 20 grams per day. This gender-specific difference reflects biological differences in metabolizing alcohol.
[8] This section is based on *DCP2*, chapter 47.

dependence, vascular disease, cirrhosis of the liver, and cancer, with unintentional and intentional injuries (particularly road traffic accidents) accounting for the remaining 25 percent.

High-risk drinking is particularly problematic in Europe and Central Asia, where as many as 1 in 5 men and 1 in 10 women between the ages of 15 and 29 engage in high-risk drinking. Even though high-risk drinking in Europe and Central Asia is only marginally more prevalent than in high-income countries, it accounts for double the disease burden because more of that drinking is in the hazardous, higher volume part of the high-risk range.

Interventions may be designed to prevent high-risk drinking or to mitigate its effects. Some of these interventions operate at the population level, such as legislative measures and taxes, improved law enforcement, and mass media campaigns. Other measures aim specifically at high-risk drinkers to encourage behavior modifications.

As in the case of tobacco, public policy can have a substantial effect on alcohol abuse. Taxing alcohol raises the price and thereby reduces consumption. Estimates indicate that a 10 percent increase in the price of alcohol reduces consumption of beer by about 3 percent, wine by 10 percent, and distilled spirits by as much as 15 percent. Restricting sales to a limited number of licensed retail outlets or restricting the hours when alcohol can be sold can make obtaining alcohol more difficult. Strict drunk driving laws also discourage excessive consumption, prevent traffic accidents, and can reduce traffic fatalities by 7 percent. When enforcement through random breath testing is included, fatalities and nonfatal injuries from accidents may fall an additional 15 percent. Making these kinds of public policy measures effective requires enforcing regulations and laws, whether by means of additional policing to reduce smuggling and tax evasion or by mounting random breath testing of drivers to discourage drunk driving (box 5.2).

When they are effective, bans or restrictions on advertising alcoholic products remove cues that encourage alcohol consumption; however, manufacturers often substitute other methods of marketing, such as sponsoring sporting events. Consequently, restricting advertising may only reduce high-risk drinking by 1 to 3 percent.

Many countries engage in mass media campaigns and school-based education about the risks of drinking. Studies show that such efforts do increase knowledge about and attitudes toward alcohol and its risks to health, but they have not shown sustained reductions in the rate of alcohol consumption or reductions in alcohol-related harm.

"... a 10 percent increase in the price of alcohol reduces consumption of beer by about 3 percent, wine by 10 percent, and distilled spirits by as much as 15 percent."

"Strict drunk driving laws ... can reduce traffic fatalities by 7 percent."

Box 5.2 Tax Rate Reduction and the Resulting Disease Burden in Mauritius

Mauritius, an island nation in the Indian Ocean, has a population of about 1 million. Tourism is the third-ranked industry in terms of hard currency earnings. In June 1994, the government drastically lowered customs duties on imported alcoholic beverages to 80 percent from rates that had ranged from 200 percent for wine to 600 percent for whisky and other spirits (Abdool 1998). The government made the change under pressure from the hotel industry, which claimed that tourists were not purchasing enough alcohol because of its high prices (Lee 2001). Other reasons given for the change were to reduce unofficial imports from abroad and to make better, more refined alcoholic beverages available to the local population. Despite little evidence to support the view, there were claims in the public discussion that better-quality alcohol would result in fewer health problems.

The effects of the change were felt mainly by Mauritians rather than tourists, as follows:

- Arrests for driving with blood alcohol over the legal limit made primarily in connection with traffic crashes increased by 23 percent between 1993 and 1997.
- Admissions of alcoholism cases to the island's psychiatric hospital shot up in 1994. The 1995 rate was more than twice the 1993 rate, and the rate rose again slightly in 1996 and 1997. Medical specialists in Mauritius agree that patients with alcohol problems account for an increasing portion of admissions in general medical wards and now represent between 40 and 50 percent of bed occupancy (Abdool 1998).
- Age-adjusted death rates per 100,000 population for chronic liver disease and cirrhosis rose from 32.8 for males and 4.0 for females in 1993 to 42.7 for males and 5.3 for females in 1996 (WHO 1999, 2000).

Even though available statistics are limited, the reduction in alcohol import taxes clearly had a substantial negative effect on the health of Mauritians. Thus, the government's 1997 call for control measures for alcohol—specifically, new permits for licensed premises, increased excise duties on alcohol, and limitations on bars' opening hours—was not surprising. Alcohol taxes were increased somewhat in the 1999/2000 budget (U.S. Department of State 1999). However, an analysis by World Bank staff that did not take health effects into account called for further reductions in maximum tariff rates, identifying Mauritius as having an antitrade bias on the basis of the structure of its alcohol and tobacco taxes (Hinkle and Herrou-Aragon 2001).

Source: Adapted from *DCP2*, chapter 47, p. 900.

Brief interventions to reduce high-risk drinking at the personal level through educational sessions and psychosocial counseling in primary health care settings reduce alcohol consumption among high-risk drinkers by 13 to 34 percent, but poor adherence and low coverage can offset these gains substantially.

In the three regions where high-risk alcohol use is found among more than 5 percent of the population—Europe and Central Asia, Latin America and the Caribbean, and Sub-Saharan Africa—the most effective interventions are taxation and brief interventions, averting more than 500 DALYs per 1 million total population per year. The remaining control strategies, random breath testing, reduced hours of sale at the weekend, and a comprehensive advertising ban, produced effects in the range of 200 to 400 DALYs averted per 1 million population per year. In the two remaining regions with lower rates of high-risk drinking, particularly among the female population, the burden that is avertable via taxation is significantly reduced: 10 to 100 DALYs averted per 1 million population per year. In South Asia, the most effective intervention appears to be enforcement of drinking and driving laws given the combination of the higher prevalence of traffic-related injuries and lower levels of high-risk drinking.

The cost-effectiveness of interventions also varies substantially between regions. Whereas taxation, limitations on retail sales, and advertising bans are the most cost-effective interventions in the three regions with a higher prevalence of high-risk drinking, these same interventions are among the least cost-effective in the other two developing regions.

In Europe and Central Asia, Latin America and the Caribbean, and Sub-Saharan Africa, raising excise taxes by 25 percent costs between US$100 and US$200 per DALY averted, reducing access to retail outlets costs between US$152 and US$340 per DALY averted, and enforcing advertising bans cost between US$134 and US$380 per DALY averted. Random breath testing of drivers is much more costly, ranging from US$973 per DALY averted in Sub-Saharan Africa to US$1,856 per DALY averted in Europe and Central Asia. By contrast, in South Asia, the cost-effectiveness ranking of these interventions is inverted: enforcing a 25 percent increase in taxes on alcoholic beverages costs US$3,654 per DALY averted, whereas random breath testing of drivers costs US$531 per DALY averted.

In general, countries with a high prevalence of high-risk drinking should begin with taxation because in such contexts it appears to have the largest effect for the fewest resources. In places where high-risk drinking is less of a public health burden, other intervention strategies that restrict the supply or promotion of alcoholic beverages appear to be promising and relatively cost-effective.

"... where high-risk alcohol use is found among more than 5 percent of the population . . . . the most effective interventions are taxation and brief interventions . . ."

"High-risk alcohol use, along with tobacco use . . . demonstrate[s] that . . . public policy measures can be substantially more cost-effective than individualized medical treatment."

High-risk alcohol use, along with tobacco use, accounts for a sizable and growing portion of the disease burden in low- and middle-income countries. They both demonstrate that for some risk factors and conditions public policy measures can be substantially more cost-effective than individualized medical treatment. They also show that good health policies may also be good tax policies. The value of such multisectoral interventions is a common theme in *DCP2* chapters dealing with addictions and recurs in discussion of interventions to reduce CVD, diabetes, and road traffic injuries.

MENTAL HEALTH

"About 13 percent of all DALYs are due to neurological and psychiatric disorders."

By looking beyond mortality figures to consider the burden of disability in developing countries, the first edition of *Disease Control Priorities in Developing Countries* (Jamison and others 1993) revealed that mental health accounts for a substantial amount of the disease burden in these countries.[9] Depression, schizophrenia, bipolar disorder, anxiety disorders, dementias, and epilepsy are conditions that do not appear as significant causes of mortality, but they seriously reduce the quality of life for individuals and their families. Disease burden estimates in *DCP2* confirm that mental health contributes significantly to the global burden of disease. *DCP2* also presents what is known about cost-effective interventions while emphasizing the need for further research to develop better ways to address the mental health burden.

About 13 percent of all DALYs are due to neurological and psychiatric disorders. Alzheimer's disease and other dementias account for 17.1 million DALYs and are twice as common among women as men, while epilepsy accounts for another 6.2 million DALYs and Parkinson's disease for 2.3 million DALYs. Depression is the most common psychiatric disorder, accounting for 51.9 million DALYs or 3.4 percent of the global burden of disease. It is ranked fourth among all causes of DALYs and is the leading nonfatal condition globally. It is also more common among women than among men. Schizophrenia, bipolar disorder, and panic disorder account for another 11.6 million DALYs, 9.7 million DALYs, and 4.5 million DALYs, respectively. Mental health conditions are common in developing countries, but are less frequently recognized, diagnosed, and treated than in developed countries.

"Depression is the most common psychiatric disorder, . . . ranked fourth among all causes of DALYs and . . . the leading nonfatal condition globally."

[9] This section is based on *DCP2*, chapters 31 and 32.

The interventions available for preventing and treating mental health problems in developing countries are relatively limited. Many neurological conditions, such as Alzheimer's disease and Parkinson's disease, have no cure, and preventive measures are also lacking. The major exception is stroke, for which preventive measures were discussed earlier. For other mental health problems, large advances have been made in both pharmacological treatments and psychosocial therapies, but many interventions are still focused on mitigating symptoms or easing the burden on families caring for members with mental health problems.

Some pharmacological treatments are available for Alzheimer's disease and other dementias, but most interventions for this disease aim to reduce stress and depression among patients' caregivers. For example, training caregivers about proper diet or establishing bowel and bladder routines can make caring for someone with Alzheimer's less stressful. For Parkinson's disease, treatments aim at symptomatic relief by means of pharmaceuticals, physical therapy, and traditional medicines. For schizophrenia, depression, bipolar disorder, and panic disorders, a variety of pharmacological treatments are available, including older mood stabilizers, for instance, lithium; antipsychotics, for example, haloperidol; and antidepressants such as tricyclic medications, which are also used to treat anxiety disorders. Psychosocial treatments, which consist largely of cognitive-behavioral approaches, have also proven to be effective.

While it is necessary to generate a wider range of interventions to address mental health problems, the quality of life for a large number of people in low- and middle-income countries could be substantially enhanced by applying interventions already demonstrated to be cost-effective. For people suffering from epilepsy, administering phenobarbitol helps avert seizures at a cost of US$89 per DALY averted. For Parkinson's disease, two interventions are reasonably cost-effective: l-dopa and carbidopa at US$1,500 per DALY averted and ayurvedic treatments at US$750 per DALY averted. Treatment of acute stroke because of vascular occlusion using aspirin costs only US$150 per DALY averted. Interventions to prevent the recurrence of stroke are cost-effective in part because they are easily targeted to a population that is known to face higher risks, costing US$70 per DALY averted for aspirin treatment, US$932 per DALY averted for dipyridamole and aspirin, and US$1,458 per DALY averted for carotid endarterectomy.

The variations in labor, transportation, and service delivery costs across regions generate significant differences in the cost-effectiveness of these treatments. For example, aspirin is the most cost-effective

"For schizophrenia, depression, bipolar disorder, and panic disorders, a variety of pharmacological treatments are available . . ."

"Treatment of acute stroke because of vascular occlusion using aspirin costs only US$150 per DALY averted."

intervention for acute stroke in South Asia and Sub-Saharan Africa, whereas aspirin plus dipyridamole treatment is more cost-effective in the other developing regions.

For psychiatric disorders, combining drugs with psychosocial treatment is generally the most cost-effective intervention (table 5.2). For example, treating schizophrenia with older antipsychotic medications such as haloperidol along with family psycho-education is the most cost-effective intervention available, ranging between US$5,000 and US$8,000 per DALY averted in the Middle East and North Africa, South Asia, and Sub-Saharan Africa and between US$10,000 and US$17,000 per DALY averted in the other regions. Treating depression with new antidepressants such as Fluoxetine and group psychotherapy costs between US$2,000 and US$3,000 per DALY averted in all the regions. Treating panic disorders with newer antidepressant drugs such as Fluoxetine costs between US$1,000 and US$1,500 per DALY averted.

Addressing the burden of mental health in developing countries requires closing a treatment gap between what can be done for people with neurological and psychiatric disorders compared with what is currently being done. *DCP2* identifies the available cost-effective measures, but closing this gap also relies heavily on general improvements in health systems. Cost-effective treatment largely involves outpatient care, but depends significantly on the ability of health professionals at the primary level to recognize symptoms and refer patients to appropriate care. It also requires better management of drug supplies to assure the availability and potency of drugs, along with counseling for patients and their families to encourage adherence. Research is needed to widen the range of available interventions, reduce the cost of current interventions, discover more cost-effective treatments, and, if possible, find ways to prevent or cure these debilitating conditions.

CONCLUSION

Addressing noncommunicable diseases and injuries is not something that low- and middle-income countries can leave to the future. These conditions already account for a substantial share of the disease burden in most countries and are likely to increase further as these countries make progress in controlling infectious diseases and reducing the high rates of mortality and morbidity associated with childbearing and infancy.

Table 5.2 Costs and Effects of a Specified Mental Health Care Package

	World Bank region					
	Sub-Saharan Africa	Latin America and the Caribbean	Middle East and North Africa	Europe and Central Asia	South Asia	East Asia and the Pacific
Total effect (DALYs averted per year per 1 million population)						
Schizophrenia: older antipsychotic drug plus psychosocial treatment	254	373	364	353	300	392
Bipolar disorder: older mood-stabilizing drug plus psychosocial treatment	312	365	322	413	346	422
Depression: proactive care with newer antidepressant drug (SSRI; generic)	1,174	1,953	1,806	1,789	1,937	1,747
Panic disorder: newer antidepressant drug (SSRI; generic)	245	307	287	307	284	330
Total effect of interventions	1,985	2,998	2,779	2,862	2,867	2,891
Total cost (US$ million per year per 1 million population)						
Schizophrenia: older antipsychotic drug plus psychosocial treatment	0.47	1.81	1.61	1.32	0.52	0.75
Bipolar disorder: older mood-stabilizing drug plus psychosocial treatment	0.48	1.80	1.23	1.39	0.62	0.95
Depression: proactive care with newer antidepressant drug (SSRI; generic)	1.80	4.80	3.99	3.56	2.81	2.59
Panic disorder: newer antidepressant drug (SSRI; generic)	0.15	0.27	0.21	0.23	0.16	0.20
Total cost of interventions	2.9	8.7	7.0	6.5	4.1	4.5
Cost-effectiveness (DALYs averted per US$1 million expenditure)						
Schizophrenia: older antipsychotic drug plus psychosocial treatment	544	206	226	267	574	522
Bipolar disorder: older mood-stabilizing drug plus psychosocial treatment	647	203	262	298	560	446
Depression: proactive care with newer antidepressant drug (SSRI; generic)	652	407	452	502	690	675
Panic disorder: newer antidepressant drug (SSRI; generic)	1,588	1,155	1,339	1,350	1,765	1,649

Source: DCP2, chapter 31, p. 622.

Note: SSRI = selective serotonin reuptake inhibitor.

Prevention, often through multisectoral public policies, is key, whether it involves educational efforts to promote healthier lifestyles, food regulations that discourage the use of unhealthy fats and oils by food manufacturers, urban transportation policies that encourage bicycling and wearing helmets, fiscal policies that tax tobacco and alcohol products, or cultural activities aimed at reducing social stigma attached to developmental disabilities. For the burden that remains, many cost-effective interventions are available and should be promoted. Where treatments are unavailable or not cost-effective, research is needed.

Prevention, care and treatment, and research are all activities that are facilitated by the presence of a strong and functioning health care system. If countries can successfully strengthen their health systems to improve the coverage of interventions that reduce infectious disease and maternal and neonatal conditions, building further capacity to address the demands that noncommunicable diseases will impose should be possible. The next two chapters address the range of policies available to build and strengthen health care systems so that they can meet these challenges.

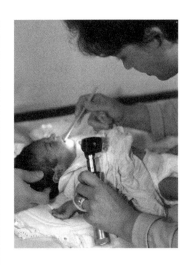

Chapter 6
Providing Interventions

No matter how thoroughly they are researched and how carefully they are designed, interventions are useless without mechanisms for delivering them. Delivery mechanisms are critical to both the effectiveness and the cost of any intervention. They vary considerably from one country to the next depending on broad factors like a country's economy, politics, and culture, but also on the presence of a well-functioning health system.

While conducting public health interventions in isolation is occasionally possible, for the most part, health interventions form a web of services that work best when they are coordinated. Screening provides no benefits without subsequent treatment, referrals are no help without access to the required care, and treatment centers will be overwhelmed if essential preventive care is neglected.

In a static world, any decisions about health system structure would involve a trade-off between specialization and integration, between care at one level versus that at another. However, the world is dynamic, and the key to progress is to think of health system development as a phased process, beginning with use of the institutions, resources, and staffing currently available to establish a platform for health care delivery that through time fills in, expands, and deepens the web of services and interventions offered.

This chapter discusses the challenge of implementing and delivering health interventions. It describes and assesses approaches to delivering care at different levels and then highlights a few elements of the health system that need to function across all these levels. It also discusses ways to integrate care for people in different parts of the life cycle.

LEVELS OF CARE

Health interventions need to reach people either by being provided at their homes, schools, and workplaces or by encouraging them to visit health facilities. Programs based in communities can reduce the costs and barriers that impede people's access to services, while general primary care can act as an interface between community health programs and individual clinical care, whether ambulatory or inpatient. District and referral hospitals are needed to provide more specialized or costly care to reinforce community and primary care services with interventions that are required when these levels cannot bring the specialized equipment or skills to bear.

Community Level

Many countries have attempted to construct links between community-based health care resources and households for a range of health programs.[1] These programs do not substitute for a health system, but they provide a channel for reaching families with information and resources. They also mobilize additional resources, such as volunteers' time, local knowledge, and community confidence and trust.

Community-level programs can include a range of interventions but generally focus on services related to safe motherhood, nutrition, and simple prevention and treatments. They commonly include the following services:

- prenatal care
- reproductive health and maternal nutrition
- breastfeeding
- complementary feeding
- growth monitoring and promotion
- micronutrient supplementation
- supplementary feeding with either external supplies or local supplies
- ORT
- immunization
- deworming.

These interventions collectively reduce such risk factors as malnutrition that account for as much as 40 percent of the disease burden in low- and middle-income countries.

[1] This section is based on *DCP2*, chapter 56.

Community programs are organized in a variety of ways, particularly with respect to the status and number of community workers. At one end of the spectrum are community-based programs that rely heavily on local resources and volunteer time. For example, Thailand recruited and trained 60,000 village health volunteers who were responsible for mobilizing and supervising 600,000 village health communicators, who in turn attended an average of 20 children each (box 6.1). At the other end of the spectrum, some countries recruit workers from target communities but then hire and supervise them as part of the public health workforce. In Costa Rica, for example, health workers were full-time employees, recruited and managed by the government's rural health program. Costa Rica hired two full-time health workers for every 350 children. *DCP2* assesses the evidence and concludes that an effective ratio of health workers to children is in the range of 1 to 500 for full-time, paid community workers and 1 to 10 or 20 for local, part-time volunteers.

In addition to developing staffing strategies, community programs must decide whether to include food supplementation to address malnutrition. Food supplementation can help a community health program achieve its goals when integrated with other services or it can become the program's primary focus to the exclusion of other health services. In some communities, food supplementation is part of a broader program that also addresses micronutrient supplements, preschool education, growth monitoring, and sometimes improvements in local food supplies. At the other end of the continuum, the food distribution component has dominated some community programs, as occurred with India's Integrated Child Development Services Program.

Community programs also need to find a balance between health promotion activities and curative care. When primary facilities are distant or poorly supplied, community workers may be pressured into providing direct curative care, distracting them from other health promotion activities. When this happens, community systems may be coopted and "medicalized" with the addition of diagnostic and treatment modules. While such additions may succeed in giving people access to services that would otherwise be absent, they also divert community programs from the initial purpose of general health promotion. Community health workers not only can promote healthy behaviors and preventive action but can mobilize demand for appropriate services at other levels.

"... an effective ratio of health workers to children is in the range of 1 to 500 for full-time, paid community workers and 1 to 10 or 20 for local, part-time volunteers."

"Community health workers not only can promote healthy behaviors and preventive action but can mobilize demand for appropriate services at other levels."

A sense of the potential effect of community-based programs can be seen in the prevalence of children age 2 who are underweight in Indonesia, the Philippines, and Thailand. Of
the three countries, Thailand has been the most successful in implementing a community-
based health program. Thailand's Ministry of Public Health spent approximately US$11 per
beneficiary per year mobilizing a network of volunteer supervisors and volunteer community workers that included about 1 percent of the population. While the proportion of
underweight children is influenced by a variety of societal and individual factors, the rapid
reduction in the share of underweight children in Thailand that coincided with the introduction of this community-based program shows that it contributed to this effect. By contrast,
Indonesia's national village program spent somewhat less (about US$2 to US$11 per child
per year) and depended heavily on supplementing food. It had some impact, but it was
slower and less consistent. Finally, the Philippines started a national program that was not
fully implemented, spending only US$0.40 per child per year in targeted areas.
Underweight prevalence among children showed little improvement during this period.

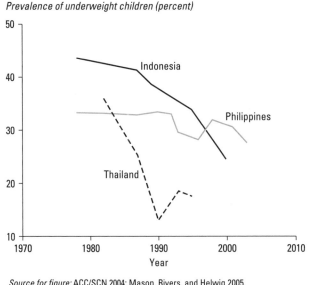

Prevalence of underweight children (percent)

Source for figure: ACC/SCN 2004; Mason, Rivers, and Helwig 2005.
Source for text: DCP2, chapter 56.
a. −2 standard deviations.

Finally, community-based programs must seek to maintain a balance between extensive coverage and adequate supervision. A program
that supervises tens of thousands of volunteers needs hundreds of
supervisors. *DCP2* finds that supervision ratios in effective programs
are approximately 1 supervisor for every 20 community health workers. If this supervisory responsibility is laid on primary care facilities, it

can become an excessive burden. If it is managed well, however, it can be the difference between ineffective and effective programs.

Effective health programs build on established community practices. Hence in Thailand, health services are combined with religious organizations at the village level. In Indonesia, social organizations have played an important role. In Bangladesh, NGOs that had been successful in other areas, such as food security and education, became active in health. In Costa Rica, Honduras, and Jamaica, national heath services already had a sufficient local presence to initiate community-based health programs.

Organization at the local level can accomplish a good deal, but only with adequate guidance and resources from more central levels. Training, supervision, and supplies must be sustained to have a lasting effect. Generally this means linking community health workers with primary care facilities.

Thus the success of community health efforts depends critically on the context, including level of development of infrastructure, services, and socioeconomic resources. For example, in Indonesia, the weakness of the primary health care system encouraged community programs to shift toward providing individual clinical services. In Costa Rica, by contrast, community health programs could focus on prevention and health promotion as a complement to a stronger primary care system.

General Primary Care

The term primary care denotes several different, yet related, aspects of health systems.[2] In some contexts it refers to certain activities, such as immunization and prenatal care. In others it denotes a level of care with relatively low technical and skill requirements. For some countries it is a strategy for structuring and managing health care. For others it is a perspective or philosophy. The broad concept of primary care includes a range of initiatives that are associated with the Alma Ata Declaration on Primary Health Care approved by WHO in 1978. More recently, the WHO Commission on Macroeconomics and Health described the need for developing services that are close to the client. Despite the variations in the specific use of the term *primary care*, the basic notion is a common one: recognition that a certain range of health care services must act as an interface between families and community programs on the one hand, and hospitals and national health policies on the other.

Since the 1978 Alma Ata Declaration, WHO, the World Bank, and specific countries have refined and constructed alternative packages of

"Effective health programs build on established community practices."

". . . primary care . . . must act as an interface between families and community programs on the one hand, and hospitals and national health policies on the other."

[2] This section is based on *DCP2*, chapter 64.

services under the umbrella of general primary care. *DCP2* notes substantial convergence in the content of general primary care over time: maternity-related care (for instance, prenatal care, skilled birth attendance, and family planning), interventions to address childhood diseases (such as vaccine-preventable diseases, acute respiratory infections, diarrhea, and malnutrition), and prevention and treatment of major infectious diseases. The list is familiar from numerous studies of cost-effective packages and priorities for the global disease burden (table 6.1).

Table 6.1 Package of Cost-Effective Interventions *(US$)*

	Cost per DALY	
Interventions	**Low-income countries**	**Middle-income countries**
Public health		
Expanded program of immunization plus (that is, including vaccine against hepatitis B and vitamin A supplementation)	15–22	32–38
School health program	25–32	48–54
Tobacco and alcohol control program	44–70	57–70
AIDS prevention program	4–6[a]	16–23[a]
Other public health interventions (includes information, communication, and education on selected risk factors and health behaviors, plus vector control and disease surveillance)	—	—
Total	18	—
Clinical services		
Chemotherapy against tuberculosis	4–6	6–9
Integrated management of the sick child	38–63	63–127
Family planning	25–38	127–190
Sexually transmitted disease treatment	1–4	13–19
Prenatal and delivery care	38–63	76–139
Limited care (includes treatment of infection and minor trauma; for more complicated condition, includes diagnosis, advice, and pain relief, and treatment as resources permit)	253–380	507–760
Total	—	168

Source: DCP2, chapter 64, table 64.2.
Note: — = not available, presumably because the authors were not able to aggregate data to country level.
a. Understates cost-effectiveness because the analysis examined the probability of transmission to others in the first year only.

Nevertheless, local health facilities that are equipped exclusively to carry out these kinds of functions may not meet local demand for other kinds of curative care or may miss important local health threats altogether. Consequently, public health experts stress the importance of having a local management team to plan local care and support services for a defined population, ranging from 10,000 to 50,000 people. With a local management team responsible for a specific population, that team can set priorities and monitor progress, as well as ensure a good fit between national priorities and local needs and demand for health promotion and treatment.

In practice, achieving this kind of planned, local effort is difficult in low- and middle-income countries for several reasons:

- Primary care facilities frequently lack the resources they need to function.
- Staff positions may remain unfilled or staff members may be absent.
- Supplies may not be delivered or may have expired.
- Facilities may not be properly maintained.
- People often seek health care from a variety of traditional healers, pharmacists, and private medical professionals in addition to public services. This fragmentation can make proper surveillance and planning difficult to manage.

With effective use of adequate financial, institutional, and human resources, general primary care can potentially address up to 90 percent of health care demand in developing countries. The direct effect of general primary care is well documented. For example, local reductions of 5 to 32 percent in mortality among children in Liberia, Niger, and the Democratic Republic of the Congo are attributed to the provision of general primary care in these locations. A well-functioning general primary care system is also integral to the success of a health system overall, because it acts as the bridge between local care and care at the next levels, such as district and referral hospitals.

District Hospitals

In most countries, district hospitals account for the largest share of inpatient services.[3] They are generally designed to serve from 100,000 to as many as 1 million people with services that are more sophisticated, technically demanding, and specialized than those available at a primary care facility, but not as specialized as those provided by referral hospitals.

[3] This section is based on *DCP2*, chapter 65.

> ". . . general primary care can potentially address up to 90 percent of health care demand in developing countries."

The range of services district hospitals offer includes diagnostics, treatment, care, counseling, and rehabilitation. The technical demands of these services require professionals with training and experience spanning the fields of family medicine and primary health care, obstetrics, mental illness, eye health, rehabilitation services, surgery, pediatrics, and geriatrics. They require substantial capital investment in facilities, equipment, and management. District hospitals may also provide health information, training, and administrative and logistical support to primary and community health care programs. When a district hospital's service area coincides with a local government administrative unit, it may be responsible for other public health functions throughout the district.

The strength of a district hospital is that it concentrates skills and resources in one place for conditions that are either uncommon or difficult to treat. It is also a repository of knowledge and diagnostic tools for assessing whether referral to an even more specialized facility is indicated. A district hospital can only realize these strengths if it is properly integrated with other levels of care that are also functioning well. If primary care facilities are not meeting local needs, for example, then people will bypass them and overwhelm hospitals with demands for services that could be provided more effectively and efficiently in other settings. Primary care facilities must also screen patients to identify those who do require hospital attention. Timeliness and adequate transportation are essential, as no amount of screening or referral can make a difference to a patient stranded in a distant village.

At the same time, district hospitals' concentration of resources give rise to their potential weakness. Too often, district hospitals benefit those who live nearby and are not readily accessible to the poor or to those dispersed in rural areas. District hospitals can serve populations most equitably when their concentration of resources is accessible to all, that is, when barriers created by poverty, low service quality, costly transportation, or remote geography are addressed.

Costs of care in district hospitals are sensitive to the salaries paid to their staff, the utilization rates, and the inclusion of additional health functions. Staff salaries generally account for the bulk of hospitals' recurrent costs even when salaries are low. When utilization rates are high, the average fixed cost per patient day will be lower. In some places, hospital utilization rates are below 50 percent and the unused capacity represents a substantial economic loss for the health system. In other cases, hospitals are overutilized, and even though this reduces average

"Too often, district hospitals . . . are not readily accessible to the poor or to those dispersed in rural areas."

costs, it results in more rapid depreciation of facilities. Additional functions also raise hospitals' costs. These functions might include training new health professionals and providing continuing education for them; supervising, supporting, or managing primary-level services; and designing and implementing district-wide public health campaigns.

Cost studies indicate the potential range of hospital costs in low- and middle-income countries. A Tanzanian hospital spent approximately US$4 per patient per day, but the study argued that it was underfinanced and that a little more than US$12 per patient per day would be necessary to provide care according to the provider's own standards. Researchers estimated that inpatient care in Kenya cost about US$9 per patient per day and in Bangladesh cost almost US$16 per patient per day. Costs for South African hospitals in five districts ranged from US$40 to US$97 per patient per day.

DCP2 includes an exercise to estimate the cost-effectiveness of district hospital care. Despite the exercise's admitted roughness, it gives a sense of the possible order of magnitude. Using data from a study of a Kenyan district hospital in a rural community with reasonably good access to health care, it finds that the hospital served 2,223 children, spent about US$10 per patient, and saved an estimated 215 lives at an average cost per life saved of US$104, implying a cost per DALY averted of only about US$4 to US$5.

Strategies for improving district hospital care vary. In many countries, district hospitals have been turned over to local governments as part of a decentralization of public services. In others, hospitals are given greater decision-making, or even financial, autonomy. In parts of Central Asia and East Asia, particularly in the former Soviet republics and in China, public hospitals have become so dependent on fees paid by patients that they effectively function as private institutions. Most public hospitals receive budgets that are based on their staffing and size, but reforms in some places have introduced reimbursement based on the number and complexity of services provided, with mixed results. In other places, efforts focus on improving the quality of care in hospitals. One goal is to reduce hospital-acquired diseases, a serious problem in resource-constrained Sub-Saharan African countries, where blood transfusions and the re-use of needles can transmit HIV, hepatitis, and other infections. Improving blood safety would cost less than US$8 per DALY averted.

District hospitals are subject to various pressures that affect how well they carry out their role. Some of these pressures force district

"... a Kenyan district hospital in a rural community ... served 2,223 children, spent about US$10 per patient, and saved an estimated 215 lives at an average cost per life saved of US$104 ..."

"... in the former Soviet republics and in China, public hospitals have become so dependent on fees paid by patients that they effectively function as private institutions."

hospitals to intervene as if they were primary centers, while others push them toward functioning as public health management centers. The appropriate mix will result from balancing investments in district hospitals with investments in other levels of care.

Referral Hospitals

The next level of care is the referral hospital, which provides complex clinical care to patients referred from the community, primary, or district levels.[4] Referrals explicitly link the different levels of health care in both directions. Community, primary, or district facilities direct patients to a specialized hospital for care. The referral hospital, in turn, provides support and information to assist the other levels and refers patients back to them when appropriate. For the full benefits of linkages between levels of care to be realized, referral hospitals need to provide many forms of support, including advice on which patients to refer, proper postdischarge care, and long-term management of chronic conditions. Coordinated training in the use of shared protocols is also necessary, as is technology support by skilled technicians and scientists.

Referral hospitals can also provide important managerial and administrative support to other facilities, serving as gateways for drugs and medical supplies, laboratory testing services, general procurement, data collection from health information systems, and epidemiological surveillance. Sometimes they take on the role of managing transportation for medical supplies and staff, or even financial, payroll, and human resource management for lower-level facilities.

Other important functions of referral hospitals are research and training. In industrial countries, referral hospitals may be developing new technologies, but in developing countries they are more likely to be involved in research for piloting and introducing technologies that have been developed elsewhere, that is, assessing these technologies for their effectiveness and adaptability to a new context. Referral hospitals become the vehicle for disseminating such technologies by training new staff and providing continuing professional education for existing staff at different facilities. Research that is responsive to local disease burdens and local technology constraints fills a critical gap, because industrial countries and pharmaceutical companies do

"For the full benefits of linkages between levels of care to be realized, referral hospitals need to provide many forms of support . . ."

[4] This section is based on *DCP2*, chapter 66.

not generally undertake such research if they do not foresee sufficient returns to their investments. Research activities also help attract and retain the specialists needed to treat complex cases and train new specialists.

As with district hospitals, referral hospitals in low- and middle-income countries frequently end up offering a full range of services, from the most specialized to basic ambulatory treatment. The demand for basic care results from people bypassing poorly equipped or inadequately staffed lower-level facilities.

The costs and effectiveness of referral hospitals are highly sensitive to the range of services they provide, to staff wages, and to utilization rates. In general, they tend to be more expensive than district hospitals because they treat more complex cases, have more expensive inputs, and are also engaged in teaching and research. Studies indicate that per bed day, referral hospitals can be two to five times as costly as district hospitals.

Referral hospitals tend to be located in large urban areas, exacerbating unequal access to specialized care for rural and generally poorer citizens. Because referral hospitals are by definition specialized, redressing such inequities by constructing more facilities is not feasible. Rather, equitable access to referral hospital services requires improving referral from other levels of care and reducing transportation costs and other financial barriers for the poor.

Investments in and functions assigned to referral hospitals need to be properly balanced and coordinated with investments and functional assignments to district hospitals, primary care centers, and community health workers. Just as referral hospitals cannot function efficiently without the other levels fulfilling their roles, so too community, primary, and district hospital levels cannot function effectively without the ability to refer complex cases to specialized hospitals. Lower levels of care certainly require strengthening, but this is more likely to reflect inadequate financing of the entire public health system than a grossly excessive allocation to referral hospitals.

CROSS-LEVEL SERVICES AND INPUTS

Even though different levels of the health care system are associated with distinct types of services, each level requires some capacity for common services. *DCP2* discusses a wide range of these cross-level services and related issues, three of which are discussed here.

Surgery

Surgery has often been associated with technology-intensive interventions that can be extremely costly.[5] Furthermore, surgery is neither specific to a particular disease or risk factor nor is it exclusive to a particular level of health care. Consequently, its public health potential has often been overlooked by health policy makers. *DCP2* gives renewed attention to surgery as a cost-effective health care service for a range of common conditions.

DCP2 estimates that about 12 percent of the world's disease burden is associated with conditions that could benefit from surgery. These conditions cause losses of 21 DALYs per 1,000 people in the Americas and 38 DALYs per 1,000 people in Africa. Injuries account for about 38 percent of these surgical conditions, followed by malignancies and congenital anomalies.

Surgically treatable conditions fall into four general categories:

- surgical care to avert death or dysfunction among injury survivors
- obstetrical complications
- treatment of emergent and life-threatening abdominal conditions
- elective care of simple conditions, including hernias, club feet, and cataracts.

DCP2 defines surgery as services involving sutures, incisions, excisions, manipulation, and other invasive procedures that require local, regional, or general anesthesia. This definition focuses explicitly on the procedures and not on those who perform the surgery or the facility in which it takes place. This permits recognizing that many different kinds of health care workers can perform surgery if properly trained and that it can be done in different places if they are properly equipped. For conditions like cataracts or trachoma, surgery can be conducted via campaigns in which a cadre of workers is trained to screen, identify, and perform simple procedures using mobile facilities (box 6.2). Simple surgery can also be provided at the primary level for injuries, obstetrical complications, or congenital anomalies. District hospitals and referral hospitals can be configured to provide more complex surgical procedures as required.

DCP2 estimates the cost-effectiveness of surgeries conducted at a hypothetical community clinic serving a population of 20,000 people. Such a facility would treat approximately 4,000 surgical cases per year and be staffed by a nurse, a skilled birth attendant, and an orderly. The

[5] This section is based on *DCP2*, chapter 67.

procedures would include treating simple cuts and bruises, removing
foreign materials from the body, draining abscesses, treating basic
burns, assisting normal deliveries, and treating simple trauma. Such
services would cost an estimated US$150 to US$350 per DALY averted.
More complicated surgeries, including abdominal and thoracic surgery,
head injuries, obstetrical complications, and burn care, would be
handled by district hospitals at an estimated cost of US$40 per DALY
averted in South Asia and Sub-Saharan Africa, US$70 per DALY averted
in East Asia and the Pacific, and close to US$100 per DALY averted in
the remaining regions. The cost per DALY averted of surgical services in
district hospitals is lower than in primary care facilities because of
economies of scale. The fixed costs of district hospital surgeries are
higher, but the hospital can be configured to handle a disproportionately larger number of surgeries. Whether these economies are realized
in practice depends on reaching appropriate utilization rates.

Surgery can clearly be a significant component of any public health
strategy. Surgery can prevent death and chronic disability in injured
patients if it is timely and appropriate; it can reduce the risk of mortality
and disability from obstructed labor, prepartum and postpartum hemorrhage, and other obstetrical complications; it can resolve a wide range
of emergency conditions; and it can have a substantial impact on quality
of life through elective surgery for such conditions as cataracts, ear infections, club feet, hernias, and hydroceles. If the right facility is appropriately staffed and equipped, surgery can be a cost-effective and important
element of a functioning health system and of a public health policy.

Emergency Medical Services

Like surgery, emergency medical services represent a cluster of interventions that are not exclusive to any particular medical condition or level
of health care.[6] The defining feature is that outcomes are extremely

"... surgery can be a
cost-effective and
important element of a
functioning health system
and of a public health
policy."

---

[6] This section is based on *DCP2*, chapter 68.

time dependent. Emergency medical services address sudden medical conditions that require immediate intervention to avoid death or disability. While emergency services are often equated with ambulances, hospital emergency rooms, advanced technology, and high costs, in practice, emergency medical services are not exclusively focused on rapid transportation and invasive procedures. Rather, good emergency care can often be achieved through improved planning, appropriate training of first responders, effective communication, and innovative approaches to transportation.

Emergencies commonly arise from sudden injuries, obstetric complications, and infections, as well as from neglecting slow and chronic conditions. Thus the disease burden that is relevant to emergency medical services overlaps considerably with conditions that have already been discussed in previous chapters, such as maternal conditions and road traffic injuries. In total, such conditions account for 36 percent of the disease burden when measured in DALYs. About one-third of these DALYs are due to injuries; another one-third are related to chronic illnesses like diabetes, CVD, and asthma; and the final one-third are associated with communicable diseases and maternal conditions.

Emergency medical services comprise a continuum of care from first contact with patients until their conditions are stabilized. This includes making a rapid assessment to determine which interventions are most appropriate, arranging for prompt transportation to a facility best suited for treating the condition, and providing immediate emergency care. Once a patient arrives at a facility, emergency care services continue until the patient's condition has been stabilized.

The character of emergency medical services varies considerably across countries and regions. In many rural, low-income contexts, traditional healers such as bone setters may provide first aid, and transportation could be by canoe or animal-pulled cart. In high-income cities, by contrast, it is often characterized by the arrival of paramedical personnel in an ambulance. The key is not to emulate some ideal technology but to improve the organization and planning for emergency care, which can be done at a reasonable cost and would improve the utilization of resources, the care received, and the outcomes.

DCP2 highlights a range of issues that hinder low- and middle-income countries from providing adequate emergency care along with some innovative approaches to dealing with these obstacles. First, emergency care requires investments be made in facilities that can treat patients once they have been stabilized. Arranging for rapid transportation to a health facility that is ill-equipped or overburdened serves little purpose. Hence, as with so many other matters, the presence of an effective health care system is important.

Second, rapid forms of communication can make a big difference to survival. In places where traditional telephones are not available, simple radio phones or, increasingly, cell phones can be used. Communication is important for coordinating care between the site of initial care and the facility where the patient will receive treatment, and it also serves to support first responders by allowing them to consult with other medical personnel and receive expert advice at the emergency site.

Third, proper planning can reduce response times and improve care. Sometimes this is as simple as assuring that accurate maps are available and that houses are numbered and streets have signs. One study in Kuala Lumpur found that emergency response teams could not find the patient in 20 percent of emergency calls.

Fourth, transportation has to be accessible at short notice. Vehicles with stretchers are the ideal, but many other means will do. In Malawi, a bicycle ambulance originally aimed at improving emergency obstetric care found regular use in transporting patients with all kinds of emergencies, including injuries.

Studies have found that the primary factor in survival has less to do with the speed of transport than with the effectiveness of life-saving care provided by the responding team. Emergency response systems require skilled and motivated personnel with appropriate supplies, pharmaceuticals, equipment, and support staff for coordination and management. Where resources are available, such systems can rely on full-time personnel with motorized transportation. Where resources are limited, a great deal can still be done with simple, sustainable approaches. For example, recruiting and training motivated citizens who often confront emergencies, such as public transport drivers, can greatly speed responses to emergencies (box 6.3).

DCP2 reviews information on the use of trained lay responders in combination with trained volunteers. Such a program would require 7,500 lay first responders and 150 volunteer paramedics to serve a population of 1 million. The lay first responders could be trained in half a day whereas the volunteer paramedics would undergo 25 days of training. In each case, refresher courses would be required every three years to keep skills and motivation high. Such a program might be highly cost-effective, costing between US$73 and US$706 per death averted or between US$3 and US$27 per life year saved.

"... in Kuala Lumpur ... emergency response teams could not find the patient in 20 percent of emergency calls."

"... the use of trained lay responders in combination with trained volunteers ... might be highly cost-effective, costing between US$73 and US$706 per death averted or between US$3 and US$27 per life year saved."

Background: The efficacy of a program that builds upon the existing, although informal, system of prehospital transport in Ghana was assessed. In Ghana, the majority of injured persons are transported to the hospital by some type of commercial vehicle, such as a taxi or bus.

Methods: A total of 335 commercial drivers were trained using a six-hour basic first aid course. The efficacy of this course was assessed by comparing the process of prehospital trauma care provided before and after the course, as determined by self-reporting from the drivers.

Results: Follow-up interviews were conducted on 71 of the drivers, a mean of 10.6 months after the course. Sixty-one percent indicated that they had provided first aid since taking the course. There was considerable improvement in the provision of the components of first aid in comparison to what was reported prior to the course (see table 1).

Table 1 Provision of Emergency Medical Care Before and After First Aid Course

Type of care	Provided before course (%)	Provided after course (%)
Crash scene management	7	35
Airway management	2	35
Bleeding control	4	42
Splint application	1	16
Triage	7	21

Source: Mock and others 2002.

The course was conducted with moderate amounts of volunteer labor and gifts-in-kind, such as transportation to the course. The actual cost of the course amounted to US$3 per participant.

Conclusions: Even in the absence of formal emergency medical services, improvements in the process of prehospital trauma care are possible by building upon existing, although informal, prehospital transport.

Source: DCP2, chapter 68, box 68.1.

When an ambulance is added, costs are substantially higher. The level of cost-effectiveness is nonetheless still within reason. In urban areas, the increased costs are offset by greater utilization. *DCP2* estimates that in urban areas, relying on ambulances would cost as little as US$60 per life year saved in South Asia, to about US$111 per life year saved in Latin America and the Caribbean, and US$176 per life year saved in the Middle East and North Africa. In rural areas, ambulance services would cost between two and three times more per life year saved because of lower utilization rates.

Countries should not neglect emergency medical services. At a minimum, improved planning and communications and additional training of volunteers can make a substantial difference to survival in emergency situations. Emergency medical services are another element requiring coordination in the health care service system, linking trauma scenes and other emergency sites to appropriate interventions at various levels of care. To be cost-effective, strategies must be appropriate to local conditions, whether this involves training bus drivers in first response care, engaging bicycle taxis, or equipping professional paramedics.

Drugs

In the last 50 years, the number of effective medications for preventing and treating diseases has grown enormously.[7] Some have prevented millions of people from contracting diphtheria, tetanus, polio, and measles. Others have treated bacterial and viral infections, such as pneumonia, TB, and HIV/AIDS. A large class of drugs is now available for dealing with chronic illnesses such as diabetes, CVD, and depression. Others are essential for palliative care.

The supply of drugs is critical for effective health care interventions. Policies to ensure that appropriate drugs are available to those who need them must address a range of issues:

- financial issues include funding for carrying out basic research and commercial development, defining and protecting intellectual property rights, and assuring affordability
- logistical issues relate to procurement, storage, and distribution
- clinical issues pertain to ensuring appropriate prescription practices and adherence to prescribed drug regimens
- incentive issues affect the involvement of pharmaceutical companies, private health care providers, pharmacies, and publicly financed or managed health services in drug research, development, and marketing.

The availability of drugs is highly uneven and exacerbates the inequitable distribution of health care around the world. Some 30 percent of the world's population lacks regular access to essential medications, ranging from 26 percent of Southeast Asians (excluding India), 29 percent of those in the WHO Eastern Mediterranean, Region, and

[7] This section is based on *DCP2,* chapters 4, 6, 55, and 72.

"In the last 50 years, the number of effective medications for preventing and treating diseases has grown enormously."

"Some 30 percent of the world's population lacks regular access to essential medications . . ."

47 percent of Africans, to 65 percent of Indians. Meanwhile, the 15 percent of people who live in high-income countries consume approximately 90 percent of all medications (as measured by value).

Private pharmaceutical companies and governments in high-income countries have focused on developing drugs that address the disease burden in their own countries. Of 1,325 new medicines that became available between 1975 and 1997, only 11 were specifically developed for tropical diseases. In the past decade, a few international initiatives have sought to redress this uneven distribution of benefits from medications. Some aim to improve access to essential medications that are already available, as is the case with GAVI and the Global Fund to Fight AIDS, Tuberculosis and Malaria. The goal of others is to promote research and development of new vaccines, treatments, or easier-to-administer drug regimens. These include Doctors Without Borders' Drugs for Neglected Diseases initiative, public research into developing vaccines for malaria, and new therapies for drug-resistant TB.

The key objectives of drug policies are to increase access to effective medications, improve and ensure their quality, and promote rational prescription practices by providers and rational use by patients. WHO has assisted numerous low- and middle-income countries to adopt national drug policies that include selecting a list of essential medications, assuring their affordability, regulating their quality, encouraging regular supplies, and promoting rational use.

The essential drug list is an important element of drug policy, because it focuses attention on the least expensive alternatives for treating priority categories of disease. In this way it simplifies the process of procurement, purchase, training, and use. WHO's guidelines include a list of 320 drugs in 559 formulations. Most of the countries that have used these guidelines list fewer than 300 drugs, ranging from a low of 180 drugs in Liberia to a high of 389 in the state of Karnataka, India. Like the drug list, the list of recommended vaccines has also increased through time as new ones have become available. Most countries still adhere to the original vaccines that were promoted as EPI (against TB, diphtheria, tetanus, pertussis, polio, and measles), but since these were first promoted, WHO has recommended adding new vaccines, such as those for hepatitis B, Hib, and yellow fever in countries where it is endemic.

Procurement processes must pay attention not only to obtaining the best price but also to assuring the quality of the drugs and the reliability of the supply. For this reason, countries have been switching from open

"The essential drug list . . . focuses attention on the least expensive alternatives for treating priority categories of disease."

tender methods, which use price as the primary selection criterion and only secondarily consider quality and reliability, to restricted tender methods, which require bidders to submit information about their companies' reliability, financial stability, production quality, and past performance. Only manufacturers who are prequalified can enter the next stage at which bids are sought and the lowest bid is selected.

In general, drug prices have tended downward. This is due, in part, to the natural cycle of drug development. A new drug is usually protected by a patent, which restricts supply and keeps prices high until the patent protection expires or compulsory licensing is enacted and generic manufacturers can enter and compete. Some prices have declined dramatically as a consequence of collective negotiations, international advocacy, and public pressure, notably those of drugs to treat TB and HIV/AIDS, some of which have fallen by more than 90 percent in recent years.

Purchasing generic drugs in bulk is by far the easiest way for a country to get the most from a limited budget. When available in the appropriate forms and quality, generics are substantially cheaper than brand name drugs. A study in Malaysia found that 13 brand name drugs were from 4 to 45 times more expensive than the generic equivalents that were included in that country's essential drug list. To facilitate better negotiation and pricing, information on prices is now available internationally via Web sites. A variety of international programs have aimed to improve the affordability of essential drugs for low- and middle-income countries: the United Nations Children's Fund has a vaccine procurement program that handles 40 percent of the global demand, the Pan American Health Organization manages a revolving fund for the Latin American and Caribbean region, and the Gulf Cooperation Council Group Purchasing Program assists with tenders and logistics for six Persian Gulf states.

Procurement is only one element of the cost of supplying drugs, and the local component of drug prices can represent a sizable markup. In Sri Lanka, local costs add 64 percent to the imported price of drugs. In Kenya, the local component is more than 100 percent of the import price. Surveys suggest these levels of markups between import and retail are common. Public policy aimed at reducing this price wedge includes changing tax policies, such as granting exemptions from import duties or value added tax; implementing policies that reduce transportation costs; and introducing marketing regulations.

Once drugs have been selected and purchased, they must be appropriately stored and distributed. When drugs are distributed through public providers, the government must manage the logistics of forecasting demand, moving drugs effectively to where they are needed, making certain that they are stored in appropriate packaging at the proper humidity and temperature, and assuring the disposal of expired medications. To this end, countries have employed various methods, including distributing predefined kits of drugs on a schedule to more flexible and complex systems whereby health facilities place orders. Vaccines present their own challenges, especially the management of a cold chain to ensure that vaccines are kept at proper temperatures until used. When drugs are distributed through private pharmacies, the government's role focuses on monitoring distribution channels to ensure that packaging information is accurate, that appropriate storage is being used to maintain quality, and that expired medications are disposed.

Proper prescription and use are the next steps. To be effective, the correct drug needs to be prescribed for the patient's condition with appropriate adherence to the correct dosage and duration of treatment. *DCP2* estimates that as many as half of failures in drug therapies occur because patients do not comply with the prescribed regimen. Ensuring patient adherence is an element of the quality of health care services. It is best achieved where the health care system is sensitive and responsive to local attitudes, education, and culture; where health care workers communicate respectfully and clearly with patients; and where community support and information are available.

Errors by medical staff or pharmacists account for the other half of failures in drug therapies. Ironically, overprescribing drugs is just as common in low- and middle-income countries, which can ill afford to waste medications, as it is in high-income countries. Studies of IMCI programs in various countries found that better training of health care workers resulted in health outcomes that were similar to or better than average and that costs were often lower because the training led to more rational use of drugs and reduced unnecessary prescriptions (box 6.4). Doctors who also dispense drugs regularly appear to prescribe more drugs than nondispensing doctors, confirming the general recommendation that prescribing and dispensing should be separated whenever possible.

Overuse of drugs for infectious diseases and improper adherence can both be devastating to the effectiveness of health care, because they accelerate the emergence of drug-resistant strains. Cheaper drugs for malaria are already becoming ineffective, requiring recourse to costlier ACT. Drug-resistant strains of TB have emerged, requiring more frequent recourse to multidrug therapies and second-line drug regimens.

Many of the increasingly resistant infections are common in low- and middle-income countries but not in high-income countries, which reduces the effective demand for research into new treatments to replace the old ones.

To delay the emergence of drug-resistant strains of illnesses requires actions that, concomitantly, improve the quality of health care. Appropriate prescriptions and adherence improve cure rates and inhibit the further spread of an infection. This can be achieved through a range of educational programs for public and private providers and dispensaries. It also requires ensuring a reliable drug supply, reducing financial barriers for people in low-income households, and improving communication with patients to support better compliance. Eliminating the routine addition of antimicrobial supplements to animal feed, as recommended by WHO, is another important component of this strategy.

INTEGRATION OF SERVICES ACROSS THE LIFE CYCLE

In addition to analyzing health care by level and function, *DCP2* presents information about efforts to integrate care by stages in the life cycle. Newborns, children, adolescents, and women of reproductive age all have clusters of risks and conditions that can be addressed most

"Integrating the management of childhood illnesses involves . . . improving health workers' performance, . . . health systems, and . . . family and community practices."

". . . in Tanzania, . . . districts that implemented IMCI spent the same or less per child as districts with traditional health care programs but achieved better care and a 13 percent reduction in mortality."

effectively through access to an appropriate range of preventive measures and treatments. Chapter 4 addressed maternal and neonatal conditions. This chapter focuses on some of the *DCP2* chapters that address integrated care for specific age groups.

Integrated Management of Childhood Illness

Following the neonatal period, deaths among children to age five are concentrated among those who suffer from diarrhea, pneumonia, malaria, and other infectious diseases and from malnutrition.[8] Because comorbidity is highly prevalent and effective interventions are available, efforts have been made to integrate attention to children. The foremost initiative for this is the IMCI program, launched by WHO and the United Nations Children's Fund in the mid 1990s and implemented in dozens of countries since that time.

Integrating the management of childhood illnesses involves three components: improving health workers' performance, improving health systems, and improving family and community practices. The first of these includes training in the use of a treatment guide that instructs staff to look for danger signs, make thorough assessments, and then implement the appropriate case management interventions. The training also instructs health workers to integrate preventive and curative care by, for example, checking that children who are brought to a facility with a respiratory illness are current with their vaccinations and are adequately nourished. Second, integrated care of the child requires improvements in the health system to ensure that drugs are available, supervision and training are effective, referral services are functioning, and health information systems are in place. Third, improving family and community practices requires support for good breastfeeding practices, better nutrition, attention to hygiene, use of bednets, administration of fluids during an illness, and appropriate and timely care-seeking behaviors (figure 6.1).

Evaluations of the IMCI program demonstrate, above all, the difficulties of implementing an integrated strategy of training, health system strengthening, and community involvement in countries with limited resources and weak public institutions. Most of the countries that have formally adopted IMCI have not fully implemented it. Of its three components, the one most successfully implemented is training workers. One of the better implementations was in Tanzania, where

[8] This section is based on *DCP2*, chapter 63.

Figure 6.1 Schematic Outline of IMCI Case Management

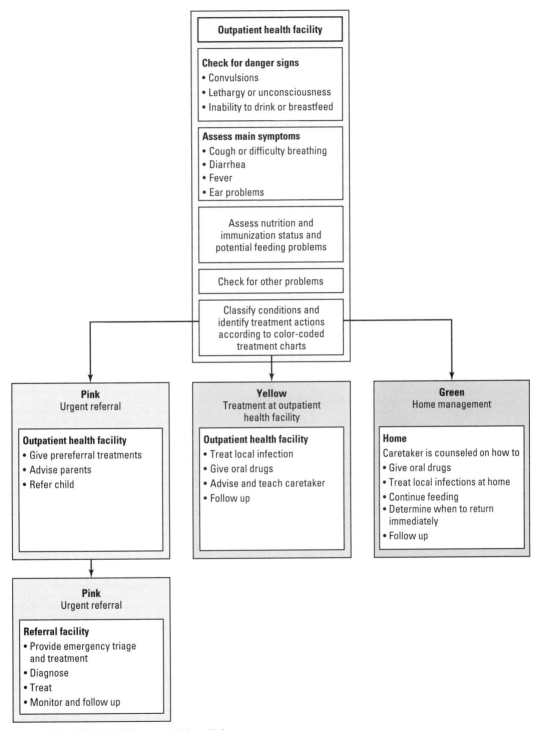

Source: WHO, UNICEF 2001. (*DCP2*, chapter 63, figure 63.1).

districts that implemented IMCI spent the same or less per child as districts with traditional health care programs but achieved better care and a 13 percent reduction in mortality (see box 6.4). However, the promise of integrated care has not been realized in most places because insufficient resources have been applied to implementing the strategy; health systems have been unable to provide the required personnel and managerial support; and no country has fully succeeded at linking IMCI to changes in family behaviors related to caring for illnesses at home, seeking care when appropriate, and improving nutrition practices.

School Health and Nutrition Programs

Schoolchildren are another well-defined subgroup whose health conditions cluster around a manageable number of illnesses and risk factors.[9] Their school attendance creates a simple opportunity for reaching children through preexisting infrastructure. Furthermore, most low-income countries have more teachers than nurses. Thus the incremental cost per child of health interventions at schools is exceptionally low, amounting to less than US$1 per year for the simplest package. Targeting schoolchildren can be a cost-effective approach to delivering health interventions.

Health interventions at schools also complement their educational mission because good health and nutrition are prerequisites for effective learning. For example, deworming programs have been successfully implemented through schools and have subsequently improved attendance and educational achievement. Concomitantly, education is an important component of many preventive health programs, such as teaching children the importance of proper hygiene, road safety, use of bednets, and nutrition along with messages about sexuality and associated health risks.

An important element of this approach is a focus on minimizing the need for clinical diagnosis. While traditional medical practice emphasizes treatment after diagnosis, the new approach suggests that mass delivery of services, such as deworming and micronutrient supplementation, is often preferable on technical, economic, and equity grounds to approaches that require diagnostic screening.

"While traditional medical practice emphasizes treatment after diagnosis . . . mass delivery of services, such as deworming and micronutrient supplementation, is often preferable on technical, economic, and equity grounds . . ."

[9] This section is based on *DCP2*, chapter 58.

Adolescents and Young Adults

Mortality rates among adolescents tend to be low relative to those for other age groups.[10] Most of the disease burden is associated with depression, road injuries, and falls. Nevertheless, adolescence is a critical period for adopting or avoiding behaviors that increase the risk of illnesses in later years. Risk factors that often begin in adolescence include smoking, excessive use of alcohol, poor eating habits, subjection to sexual abuse, and unprotected sex.

In Sub-Saharan Africa, the HIV/AIDS epidemic makes intervention in this age group particularly important. In this region, 63 percent of DALYs for young women age 15 to 29 are related to sexual and reproductive illnesses. Patterns of early marriage to older men and unprotected sex greatly increase a girl's chances of contracting HIV/AIDS and other sexually transmitted infections.

Interventions for adolescents are often difficult, because most risks at this age are not simple to address with preventive or curative care. They involve changing risky behaviors that may actually be encouraged by either traditional or modern mores. Generally, interventions need to give young people the information and skills for making good decisions; provide them with a range of health services that help them act on those decisions, such as contraceptives; and construct a social, legal, and regulatory environment that supports healthy behaviors and protects young people from harm, such as banning tobacco advertising.

Relatively few programs focused on adolescents and young adults have been implemented on a large scale. The most widespread programs focus on sexual and reproductive health, including prevention of HIV/AIDS. Of these, school-based programs are the most common. Nutrition, mental health, and tobacco prevention programs aimed at adolescents are more common in high-income countries. Services are often divided among various programs. For example, teen pregnancy may be addressed as part of an NGO's family planning program, while the ministry of transportation promotes road safety and a maternal health intervention promotes good nutrition.

As yet, little has been documented regarding the costs or effectiveness of national health initiatives for adolescents and young adults. In Bangladesh, the Newlyweds Program has encouraged low fertility among recently married young people. New Zealand has established a

---

[10] This section is based on *DCP2*, chapter 59.

"Risk factors that often begin in adolescence include smoking, excessive use of alcohol, poor eating habits, subjection to sexual abuse, and unprotected sex."

"Interventions for adolescents are often difficult, because . . . [t]hey involve changing risky behaviors that may actually be encouraged by either traditional or modern mores."

program for preventing suicide among adolescents. Mongolia has introduced sex education after the third grade in response to rising STI rates attributed to early debut of sex, sexual violence, and exploitative messages in the media. South Africa's Love Life initiative has promoted sexual health and healthy lifestyles among 12- to 17-year-olds. Assessments of the South Africa program have found raised awareness of health risks, delayed debut of sex, fewer partners, more assertive behavior regarding condom use, and better communication with parents about sex.

Implementing such programs requires coordinating a complex range of interventions. In addition, the responses to the risky behaviors that are targeted may conflict with the goals of the government and the views of religious leaders, parents, or teachers. Some of the key principles in developing an integrated approach to this age group are to involve them in the process of program design, engage them as peer educators, make health services appealing and welcoming, and confront gender inequalities.

In sum, interventions are more cost-effective if they are implemented by a functioning health system and no interventions are helpful unless they are delivered. This section has discussed some of the issues that arise in organizing health care services by level, function, or around the needs of particular age groups. In general, *DCP2* shows that these facets of the health care system function best when they are linked and can provide a continuum of care with appropriate staff and in appropriate locations. This in turn requires systems for generating and exchanging information, managing quality and staff, and mobilizing and allocating funds.

Chapter **7**
Pillars of the Health System

A health system is more than a mix of facilities and medical consultations. It is a structure within which people, institutions, and organizations interact to mobilize and allocate resources for preventing and treating diseases and injuries. This structure has to rest on certain fundamental pillars if it is going to work. These pillars are essential elements that enable the health care system to function. They include everything from a well-managed civil service to an extensive communications system. This section highlights four of these pillars: information, management, human resources, and financing.

INFORMATION, SURVEILLANCE, AND RESEARCH

The importance of collecting, processing, and using data in the campaign to improve health cannot be stressed enough.[1] As noted in chapter 1, much of the progress in extending and improving the quality of human life is due to technical progress, including advances in knowledge about diseases and about appropriate, cost-effective responses. To the extent that the generation and application of information and knowledge can be facilitated and become more systematic, accelerating progress in improving human health and eliminating health inequities should be possible.

Information and Surveillance

Health sector decision makers—whether health care workers in small clinics, managers of major hospitals, directors of drug safety, local

[1] This section is based on *DCP2*, chapters 4, 5, 6, 53, and 54.

political officeholders, or ministers of health—ask a number of questions that must serve as the starting point for any discussion of information. For example, is the recent surge in flu cases the beginning of a new epidemic? Are we reaching 90 percent of children under five with the recommended vaccines? What are likely to be the major causes of death in the next 10 to 20 years? What social behaviors are contributing the most to the spread of STIs? Where is the public sector's health expenditure going? What interventions are effective against a particular disease? Are more cost-effective methods available?

The information for answering such questions generally comes from the following six major sources:

- *Vital events registration* provides data on births and deaths, as well as on marriages, divorces, and migrations. The data on births, deaths, and migration are particularly critical for good health policy analysis, as without them tracking the population and calculating such basic indicators as disease incidence rates are impossible. However, these basic data are poorly recorded in most of the world: fewer than half of all births and only a third of all deaths are reported to national registration systems.

- *Health service statistics* comprise information on consultations by patients, services provided, and diagnoses. Health facilities routinely gather much of this information for local use, but it is rarely collected in standardized formats or reported to a national health database. Health service statistics are fundamental to managing public health services, identifying health trends, and allocating resources efficiently.

- *Public health surveillance* comprises a wide range of efforts to track and respond to disease trends. One common approach is to identify a list of notifiable diseases that health care providers are required to report to national authorities, generally infectious diseases that might be rare, but that require an immediate response. In another kind of surveillance known as sentinel surveillance, samples of health care providers or facilities agree to report all cases of particular conditions. This kind of arrangement is good for large public health programs, but is not effective at detecting rare or new health threats. Surveillance can be based on health care providers reporting cases with particular symptoms or laboratory tests with particular diagnoses. In general, surveillance works best when a wide range of sources are integrated in a system that includes detection, monitoring, analysis, and response.

- *Census data* that are accurate and collected regularly provide the basis for calculating important ratios and designing reliable samples.
- *Household surveys* are an effective way to obtain information about population demographics, social characteristics, and dynamics on a regular basis between censuses. They can also be expanded to gather important information about behaviors or particular health conditions.
- *Resource tracking* involves measuring and managing human resources, facilities, commodities, and finances. It relies on a variety of reporting methods and data collection efforts. Collecting information about health care professionals generally requires more than tracking public health sector employment to include activities by health care professionals with private practices. Similarly, financial flows in the health system cannot be fully understood without combining public budget information with data on private health spending, including out-of-pocket spending on consultations and drugs, health insurance premiums, and pharmaceutical research and development expenditures.

Timeliness and appropriate reporting intervals are important for all data collection systems. Surveillance for outbreaks of infectious epidemics needs to be rapid and constant to provide early warning. By contrast, surveillance for changes in behavioral risk factors may merit longer intervals.

When building health information systems, seeking highly detailed information on health status and health services at every possible site is tempting, but this does not necessarily yield data that are reliable and amenable to analysis. A sample of preselected sites that are reliable in relation to the accuracy and completeness of the information gathered can often provide better data than haphazard attempts at universal reporting. If an appropriate sampling method has been used to select these sites, the information they provide will permit accurate extrapolations to the population at large. Many countries have therefore started to improve their vital registration systems by focusing on a sample of preselected districts to provide good quality data for national analyses and decision making, while at the same time working to expand and improve vital event registration in other districts so that the system will eventually be universal.

Standardization will also enhance the value of data collection efforts. Setting common standards for data collection facilitates recording,

"Surveillance for outbreaks of infectious epidemics needs to be rapid and constant . . . [but] surveillance for changes in behavioral risk factors may merit longer intervals."

communicating, and analyzing information. It also permits more efficient training and hardware and software development. For example, the U.S. Centers for Disease Control and Prevention developed standards for automatic reporting of diagnostic laboratory results for notifiable diseases and disseminated related software that is used in many countries. The key in such initiatives is to develop standards in an open process, engaging other countries and international agencies both to improve the standards and to encourage widespread adoption.

Technology is reshaping and expanding methods for collecting, storing, and processing information. For example, cheaper, faster, and simpler techniques for obtaining and analyzing tissue samples permit diagnosing diseases and collecting epidemiological information in a much wider range of places and circumstances than was previously possible, and new communication technologies allow the rapid transmission of newly collected data if the requisite hardware and skilled staff are available to use them properly.

Indeed, *DCP2* argues that the principal barriers to improving information systems in low- and middle-income countries have less to do with the technologies and more to do with the required investments in training and coordinating people. The expertise required to operate and use an effective health information system goes beyond knowledge of survey design, sampling, hardware, and software to include skills required for management, medical research, and field epidemiology and knowledge of such fields as economics and sociology. International initiatives can play a valuable role in developing such expertise. For example, the U.S. Centers for Disease Control and Prevention and WHO coordinate a program to train field epidemiologists in more than 30 countries.

In controlling disease, examples of specific instances underscore the importance of having skilled people supported by good communication. The severe acute respiratory syndrome (SARS) epidemic broke out in China in November 2002 and spread to Canada, Hong Kong (China), Vietnam, Singapore, and other countries within five months. Success in controlling this first new pandemic disease of the 21st century depended on a combination of open collaboration among scientists and politicians of many countries and the rapid and accurate communication of surveillance data within and among countries. The global pandemic ended in July 2003 after more than 8,000 patients in 26 countries and 5 continents had been affected and 774 deaths had been confirmed. The successful containment of SARS, for which no cure or vaccine is yet available, is attributable to the organized work of

"The successful containment of SARS, for which no cure or vaccine is yet available, is attributable to the organized work of competent, dedicated health workers with access to good communications . . ."

competent, dedicated health workers with access to good communications (see *DCP2*, chapter 53, for more details).

To be effective, health information has to be integrated in ways that facilitate analysis and are linked to responses and actions. For example, WHO's Regional Office in Africa is working with a number of countries to link epidemiological and laboratory data to decision making under an integrated disease population surveillance strategy that successfully responded to the health threat of Ebola in Uganda (box 7.1). Surveillance in the Philippines regularly detects outbreaks including cholera and typhoid (box 7.2). More recently, the type A H5N1 avian influenza threat in Southeast Asia is under very close scrutiny by several countries and the WHO and plans are being developed for its containment of a new pandemic should inter-human spread begin.

Finally, health information systems cannot be established and operated without funds. A good, comprehensive information system can cost as little as US$3 per person in certain countries, but even these limited financial resource requirements may be prohibitive in low-income countries where the entire public health budget is of a similar order of magnitude (table 7.1). Fortunately, many international programs have recognized this problem and are financing health information activities as components of loans and grants.

"A good, comprehensive information system can cost as little as US$3 per person . . ."

Box 7.1 Controlling Ebola in Uganda

In October 2000, an outbreak of Ebola hemorrhagic fever was identified in Gulu district in northern Uganda. Rapid reporting and recognition of the problem and the subsequent response led to successful containment of the epidemic. Public health surveillance was difficult because Gulu was a politically unstable area and because people reacted to infection by seeking traditional healers or fleeing, which spread the epidemic further. Hospitals were also desperately short of supplies to control the spread of infection from so many patients simultaneously affected. The Ugandan government mobilized the military to help with locating cases and invited WHO, the U.S. Centers for Disease Control and Prevention, and other international teams to assist. Ugandan health workers cared for the sick at great risk to themselves. With 425 cases identified, it was the largest Ebola outbreak ever recorded. Only 53 percent of the patients died, a proportion far less than the 88 percent reported in previous epidemics.

The successful containment of the epidemic testifies to the Ugandan Ministry of Health's investment in developing competent, motivated health workers through its Public Health School Without Walls, an active partnership with Makerere University, the Rockefeller Foundation, the U.S. Centers for Disease Control and Prevention, and WHO, along with the successful implementation of an integrated strategy for disease surveillance strategy.

Source: Adapted from *DCP2*, chapter 53.

Box 7.2 The Philippines National Epidemic Surveillance System

In the late 1980s, the Philippines Department of Health (PDOH), relying on its integrated management information system, detected less than one outbreak per year in a population of more than 60 million people. In 1989, the PDOH designed the National Epidemic Surveillance System, a hospital-based sentinel surveillance system that encompasses both the flow of data and the personnel requirements needed to make the surveillance system work effectively. After the pilot study demonstrated promising results, the PDOH created personnel positions and a supervisory structure for sentinel physicians, nurses, and clerks in regional epidemiology and surveillance units (RESUs) integrated into the public health system. In 1995 alone, the system detected and formally investigated about 80 outbreaks, including 25 bacteriologically confirmed outbreaks of typhoid and 5 of cholera. As the Philippines developed HIV serological and behavioral risk surveillance, the RESU staff members conducted surveys in their communities. By integrating surveillance functions based on the skills of the workforce, PDOH was able to avoid the duplications, inefficiencies, and sustainability problems of multiple vertical systems (White and McDonnell 2000).

Source: DCP2, chapter 53, p. 1004.

Table 7.1 Cost of Essential Health Information System Subsystems

Health information system subsystem	Total cost (US$ million)		Per capita cost (US$)	
	Low-income countries	High-income countries	Low-income countries	High-income countries
Health service statistics	4.8	25.9	0.16	1.66
Public health surveillance (included with health service statistics)	0	0	0	0
Census	7.5	30.0	0.25	1.0
Household surveys	0.6	1.0	0.02	0.03
Vital events surveillance	1.5	6.0	0.05	0.20
Resource tracking	1.5	3.0	0.05	0.10
Total	15.9	65.9	0.53	2.99

Source: DCP2, chapter 54, p. 1024.
Note: Table is based on a population of 30 million. Household survey costs are based on the experience of the demographic and health surveys during 2001–2003 (Macro International, personal communications). Costs vary by sample size and by length of the survey instrument; Macro International estimates an average cost of US$100 per survey participant. A sample of 6,000 is assumed for the low-income setting, and a sample size of 10,000 is assumed for the high-income setting. Cost estimates for vital events monitoring are based on demographic surveillance sites. In the high-income setting, the annual costs are assumed to quadruple. Resource-tracking costs are based on the experience of national health accounts (Abt Associates, personal communications) and the Egyptian Budget Tracking system. Similar costs are estimated for human resources and commodities.

Health information is also valuable in improving the efficiency of health services. For example, a study in rural Mali found that the cost of childhood immunization programs in areas covered by community-based information systems was only US$1.47 per child, compared with US$2.79 per child for areas without such systems. Similarly, in South Africa's Eastern Cape Province, improved pharmaceutical tracking and management reduced situations where facilities ran out of essential drugs by 39 percent, improving treatment for thousands of patients by improving access to required medications.

The Tanzania Essential Health Interventions Program (TEHIP) provides evidence on the cost-effectiveness of health information systems. This program provided training to health care workers and managers in the use of information to determine priorities and better manage existing interventions (box 7.3). TEHIP cost approximately US$0.80 per person in the districts where it was implemented. Looking only at the resulting reduction in mortality among children under five, the program cost US$68.50 per DALY averted. Because adults' health also improved and morbidity declined, a fuller accounting would have shown the health information system initiative to be even more cost-effective.

Research and Development

Health information systems must be useful to decision makers if they are to influence clinical choices, health system management, and public

"... in rural Mali ... the cost of childhood immunization programs in areas covered by community-based information systems was only US$1.47 per child, compared with US$2.79 per child for areas without such systems."

policy. However, they also need to furnish information and generate questions for the fundamental research that generates new understanding of disease; improved techniques for prevention, diagnosis, and treatment; and better methods for delivering and organizing health care services.

Health research is a global endeavor. Countries are increasingly recognizing that their own health research efforts are enhanced through more interaction with researchers in other countries, studies with multiple sites, and teamwork and joint training. There are five chapters in *DCP2* devoted to the fact that science, new product development, and analytic capacity are essential for economic and social progress. *DCP2* argues that thinking of research as a national or local function makes little sense, and that a global health research system with a global agenda should be conceived instead.

DCP2 identifies areas for future research that require a wide range of tools, from field epidemiology to genomics and from the behavioral sciences to biochemistry. The research agendas discussed throughout *DCP2* and summarized in chapter 5 include priorities that are already on the global health agenda and promising topics that should be added to it.

Infectious diseases dominate the priorities that are already on the global health agenda. Many of the research goals address HIV/AIDS, malaria, and TB. These involve research on the epidemiology and risk factors associated with these diseases, with the development of new or better diagnostics, vaccines, and treatments. They also entail research on behavior change and counseling programs and how best to extend effective interventions in low-income and institutionally weak contexts. The absence of a marked departure from previous research priorities for these conditions attests to the complexity of these diseases and their importance in the poorest countries.

Research into the basic science of existing infectious diseases and how they evolve is also necessary to prepare for and respond to emerging infectious diseases. Since 1970, 32 new infectious diseases have been reported, including hepatitis C, Legionnaires' disease, Ebola, Nipah virus, SARS, and particular strains of Avian flu and cholera. Concerns have also arisen about the possible use of infectious diseases for terrorism and warfare.

In addition to infectious diseases, another significant part of the global research agenda focuses on maternal and neonatal conditions, an area that necessarily includes significant attention to extending basic

"Since 1970, 32 new infectious diseases have been reported . . ."

health care services. Research on the financing, provision, management, and delivery of health services is central to extending cost-effective interventions. Without progress in this area, meeting international health targets, such as the MDGs pertaining to reducing maternal and child mortality, will be impossible.

Regarding priorities as they relate to developing countries that do not yet figure prominently on the global health research agenda, *DCP2* emphasizes such conditions as CVD, neuropsychiatric disorders, obesity, diabetes, and cancers, which already cause a large and increasing share of the disease burden in developing regions. *DCP2* identifies research priorities for these conditions that focus on gaining a better understanding of the causes of noncommunicable diseases, particularly the effect of diet, lifestyle, obesity, and consumption of tobacco and alcohol; the transfer of knowledge about effective interventions from one context where they have succeeded to other places; and the development of new approaches for managing chronic conditions such as diabetes and depression in ways that improve patients' quality of life and prevent or mitigate further deterioration of their health.

With the growth of basic knowledge of disease and health interventions, opportunities for studying how to adapt successful programs and policies to new contexts increase. For example, many of the successful interventions against noncommunicable diseases that have been developed in high-income countries appear to be feasible in low- and middle-income countries, yet differences in culture, resources, and institutions complicate the transfer of this knowledge. Research can bridge this gap and bring the benefits of these interventions to new places.

Finally, health care systems themselves are an important object of research. Identifying institutional arrangements that are more efficient at channeling resources into effective health interventions can reduce waste and improve health. Research may indicate better ways to train and motivate health care workers and design policies to retain highly skilled staff. It can also assess different ways of mobilizing and allocating public financial resources for health and enhance understanding of how incentives encourage or discourage medical innovation.

DCP2's broad review of global health problems indicates an increasing convergence of some health problems between rich and poor countries. Some of this convergence is due to today's more interdependent world, where the speed of travel and commerce implies that the outbreak of an infectious epidemic in one place is of concern to everyone, but it is also due to the shared burden of noncommunicable diseases

"Research on the financing, provision, management, and delivery of health services is central to extending cost-effective interventions."

". . . many of the successful interventions against noncommunicable diseases that have been developed in high-income countries appear to be feasible in low- and middle-income countries, yet differences in culture, resources, and institutions complicate the transfer of this knowledge."

and injuries. The benefits of research on these conditions cannot be confined by artificial borders, and findings in poor countries are as valuable as findings in richer ones.

Adoption of this global perspective on health research requires promoting and supporting scientific capacity in all countries, making innovative use of technology and institutions to share and build new knowledge, setting global priorities to guide investments in research and development, and supporting the freedom of scientific inquiry (box 7.4).

MANAGEMENT OF HEALTH SERVICES

"... the quality of health care is not a luxury that only high-income countries can afford, but another pillar of the health service system that has a profound impact on the cost-effectiveness and equity of interventions."

While countries often focus on increasing the quantity of health care—for instance, the number of immunizations or consultations or the rates of coverage—health care can be useless, wasteful, or even harmful if it is not appropriate for the particular condition and consistent with the best medical knowledge.[2] Thus paying attention to the quality of health care is not a luxury that only high-income countries can afford, but another pillar of the health service system that has a profound impact on the cost-effectiveness and equity of interventions. Indeed, quality of care is a key element of the intangible technical progress that explains so many of the health improvements of the past 50 years. While more resources will support improvements in quality, such improvements are possible even with few resources.

Poor quality care is endemic in many health systems, whether in low-, middle-, or high-income countries. In a study of pediatric care in

[2] This section is based on *DCP2,* chapters 70 and 73.

Papua New Guinea, only 24 percent of health center workers were able to indicate correct treatment for malaria, and clinical encounters observed by investigators met minimal examination criteria in only 1 percent of cases. In Pakistan, only 56 percent of providers demonstrated the ability to diagnose viral diarrhea and only 35 percent adhered to treatment standards. In Indonesia, one study attributed 60 percent of infant deaths to poor practices in health care services, compared with 37 percent attributed to economic constraints. In the United States, the Institute of Medicine has documented serious shortcomings in medical care that account for more than 40,000 deaths each year, including large numbers of mistaken diagnoses, cases of improper care, and harmful errors in health care provision.

The problem of poor health care quality is not the fault of isolated health professionals or solely attributable to limited resources. Rather, quality problems are systemic and are consequences of gaps in knowledge and inadequate communication, training, supervision, and incentives. These problems persist when organizations providing healthcare are unable to monitor the quality of care and take corrective action. Sometimes these failures are related to incentives that encourage inappropriate care, as when dispensing drugs is an important source of income for health care providers. At other times, poor quality may be unrelated to incentives and merely reflect practices that do not draw upon modern evidence. Redressing this problem requires attention to measuring health outcomes and relating them to clinical practice so that problems can be identified and strategies for correction implemented. For low- and middle-income countries this is, in some ways, an optimistic finding. In general, quality can be improved much more quickly than other factors that promote good health such as income, education, new technology, or infrastructure.

To assess the quality of health care services, data are generally collected on the structural features of health care delivery, processes, and health outcomes. Structural features that are expected to improve quality include the amount and types of health infrastructure, equipment and supplies, and staffing. Such structural indicators can be relatively easy to collect, but they have also proven to be weak predictors of quality and health outcomes. Although good structural features may be necessary, they are not sufficient for good quality care.

Processes, by contrast, are the ways in which personnel apply modern knowledge to the diagnosis, prevention, and treatment of diseases and disability. The quality of health care processes can be measured by

"In Pakistan, only 56 percent of providers demonstrated the ability to diagnose viral diarrhea and only 35 percent adhered to treatment standards."

". . . quality problems are systemic . . . consequences of gaps in knowledge and inadequate communication, training, supervision, and incentives."

". . . quality can be improved much more quickly than other factors that promote good health such as income, education, new technology, or infrastructure."

observing staff to see whether they respond according to scientifically validated protocols when diagnosing and treating patients. The process of interaction between caregivers and patients can also influence whether patients follow prescribed medication and advice, and thus influences health outcomes. Although processes are often more difficult and costly to measure than structural features, they tend to be more closely related to health outcomes.

The U.S. Institute of Medicine's definition of the concept of quality encompasses the following six elements:

- patient safety
- effectiveness (scientifically proven appropriate care)
- patient centeredness (respect and responsiveness)
- timeliness (minimal delays and barriers to getting access to care)
- efficiency (minimal waste of equipment, supplies, ideas, and energy)
- equity (care provided consistently across genders, ethnic groups, locations, and socioeconomic classes).

A range of policy interventions can affect these six dimensions of good quality care. These interventions include direct efforts to identify appropriate care and verify whether individual providers or groups of providers are following evidence-based standards of practice. Direct interventions have included training with feedback from peers who observe consultations and processes in a health care setting.

Policies aimed at improving the quality of health care have also included indirect interventions to change providers' behavior by altering the structural conditions or financial incentives in the health care system or its organization. Performance-based remuneration is one way that providers can be induced to provide better quality care. Relatively small incentives (3 to 10 percent of a provider's total compensation) appear to have significant effects on providers' behavior in Cambodia, Haiti, and Nicaragua, as well as in the United States. Mexico and Uganda have successfully used performance-based professional recognition without remuneration to promote better processes.

Other indirect measures include setting legal standards for care. Accreditation, periodic recertification of knowledge and competency, and administrative regulations can establish minimum standards by controlling entry into practice and establishing conditions for license renewal. However, despite barring unqualified persons from practice, such measures have not generally had a significant impact on improving the quality of care among those who are permitted into practice. Malpractice litigation can induce better quality care, but uncertainties and perverse incentives in the judicial process make this a blunt and costly mechanism for public policy. Professional oversight, peer review, and inspections are better ways to get information about the quality of care but are more effective at providing information on processes than at improving providers' behavior and practice. Training in the use of evidence-based protocols and guidelines has shown promise in high-income countries. For example, in the Netherlands, implementing patient management guidelines improved health outcomes for people with asthma and chronic obstructive pulmonary disease.

Targeted education and professional training is the most direct way to affect the practice of medicine. Great hopes have been attached to continuing medical education, but it appears to have little impact on health outcomes unless it is attached to strategies that encourage changes in practice based on the knowledge received.

One of the biggest challenges for public policy is to improve the quality of care that private practitioners provide. This is critical in many countries in which private practitioners account for the bulk of primary health care. For example, in India, private health professionals are the first to see most patients with symptoms of TB, and unless the public sector can find ways to improve case identification, screening, and referral among private practitioners, TB control will remain out of reach.

Health sectors have used organizational changes to improve the quality of health care provision, including adopting such modern management techniques as total quality management, collaborative improvement models, and plan-do-study-act cycles from other sectors. When effective, these policies result in increased coverage rates, better prescribing patterns, and increased adherence to clinical guidelines (box 7.5).

Measures that improve the quality of care have costs: the direct costs of human and physical resources and the costs of implementing organizational changes. *DCP2* assesses the cost-effectiveness of improving the quality of care for treating pneumonia and diarrhea. It finds that the cost-effectiveness of improving quality depends substantially on how far current practice is from the optimum and how prevalent the disease is. When current practices are poor and prevalence is high, the cost-effectiveness of improving adherence to good protocols for treating pneumonia is between US$132 and US$800 per life saved. For

". . . continuing medical education . . . appears to have little impact on health outcomes unless it is attached to strategies that encourage changes in practice based on the knowledge received."

". . . the cost-effectiveness of improving adherence to good protocols for treating pneumonia is between US$132 and US$800 per life saved. For improvements in the correct treatment of diarrhea with ORT, the cost-effectiveness ranges from US$14 to US$500 per life saved."

Recognizing the failure of previous training attempts to improve the quality of health
services, the Ministry of Health, with support from the U.S. Agency for International
Development and the participation of local institutions, developed an innovative program
in Peru. The program was implemented by multidisciplinary teams in approximately
2,500 health facilities, including 88 hospitals. The program focused on (a) standardizing
care, (b) assuring the availability of supplies, (c) making better use of existing information
systems, (d) promoting broad staff participation in implementing local action plans, and
(e) measuring patients' satisfaction and addressing complaints. The main training activity
showed how to use a participatory problem-solving technique.

By the end of the three year program (1996–99), demand for health services had
increased considerably, motivation and satisfaction on the part of patients and health
workers had increased, and revenue collected at the facilities had risen. Areas with
the quality improvement program experienced a 25 percent reduction in maternal
mortality rates between 1997 and 1999, but no change occurred in other areas and
the inequitable regional distribution of maternal mortality had not narrowed.

Source: Adapted from *DCP2*, chapter 65.

improvements in the correct treatment of diarrhea with ORT, the cost-
effectiveness ranges from $14 to $500 per life saved. In other cases, interventions are cost saving, for example, reducing overprescription or
avoiding unnecessary treatments (see, for example, box 6.4).

HUMAN RESOURCES

Technical progress is often associated with sophisticated new equipment, such as MRI devices and CT scanners, or with new drugs, such
as vaccines and anticoagulants, but technical progress is also embodied
in improved skills to prevent, diagnose, and treat illnesses and injuries.[3]
Thus investments in the people who provide health care services are
critical for achieving progress against disease and injury. Low- and
middle-income countries face particular challenges in their efforts to
mobilize and retain a skilled workforce in the health sector in all areas,
from recruitment and training to payment policies, retention, rewards,
motivation, and deployment. Unless countries can substantially
increase the number and skills of health care workers, reaching the

*". . . investments in the
people who provide health
care services are critical
for achieving progress
against disease
and injury."*

[3] This section is based on *DCP2*, chapters 3, 71, and 73.

MDGs for health and nutrition will be difficult. Reducing maternal and neonatal mortality, in particular, requires substantial increases in skilled birth attendance; increasing the coverage of immunization programs may require more staff; and preventing and treating TB, HIV/AIDS, and malaria also demand skilled cadres.

Part of the problem facing many low- and middle-income countries is an inadequate supply of health professionals. For example, while high-income countries average 283 physicians per 100,000 people and the global average is 146 physicians per 100,000 people, Peru has 10, Papua New Guinea has 7, and Nepal has 4, and 10 countries in Sub-Saharan Africa have fewer than 3 doctors per 100,000 people. Nurses are also scarce. While high-income countries have an average of 750 nurses per 100,000 people and the global average is 334, Papua New Guinea has 67, Peru has 6, and Nepal has 5 and 11 countries in Sub-Saharan Africa have fewer than 20 nurses per 100,000 people.

The relatively few health care professionals in many low- and middle-income countries are not distributed evenly across the population. In general, deploying doctors, and even nurses, to remote rural areas is difficult and health professionals tend to be concentrated in major urban areas. Public health systems find themselves competing to retain skilled staff against the pull of private practice and hiring by international agencies and aid programs. Many health professionals emigrate to higher-income countries with better pay and working conditions.

Health professionals who remain in their countries use a range of strategies to cope with low-paying jobs and poor working conditions. In many countries, absenteeism is a serious problem, often resulting from health care workers pursuing other remunerative activities within or outside the health sector. Among doctors, in particular, dual employment is common: they receive a salary from the public sector, but also earn fees though private practice. Those who remain at their public jobs may demand informal and illegal charges to supplement their low incomes. In addition, low productivity is compounded by lack of skills, poor supervision, little continuing education, dilapidated facilities, and lack of basic medical supplies.

Countries are grappling with these human resource issues in a variety of ways, including innovative staffing, changes in financial and non-financial incentives, and organizational reforms. *DCP2* observes the great variety of these reforms, assessing the interventions themselves and also their degree of implementation and suitability to context.

Countries that seek to address shortages of skilled health care workers by training more doctors and nurses sometimes find that shortages persist because of high rates of attrition. To discourage health care workers from leaving for private practice or emigrating to countries with better pay, some countries have altered the skill mix in training programs to reduce the portability of professional degrees. Training can be adequate for particular domestic health care needs without necessarily being recognized internationally as an accepted medical program. In this way, countries can reduce the risk of losing trained staff to emigration.

Many innovations in human resource management in low-income countries involve creating new health professions, that is, categories of health care workers who perform a variety of functions that have traditionally been reserved for physicians or nurses. Professional associations often resist this process to protect their standards and positions, yet studies in developing countries have shown that in some cases nurses can perform many functions in primary care settings as safely and effectively as doctors. As a direct response to internal and external migration, Zimbabwe has introduced a new cadre known as primary health care nurses, who have fewer qualifications than general nurses. Malawi has created the profession of clinical officers, who do not receive a full medical education, but still obtain extensive training that permits them to carry out a number of medical procedures, including surgery and anesthesia. Emergency cesarean sections conducted by clinical officers are somewhat riskier than those doctors perform, but the risks are substantially lower than no timely treatment at all. Insisting on fully qualified doctors where they can be hired and retained and perform procedures is clearly preferable, but where no medical services exist, training and deploying less-skilled workers can make a substantial difference.

The creation of new kinds of health care workers is a common theme in *DCP2*. Chapter 68 discusses how emergency care services can be extended to more people, addressing a substantial disease burden from trauma, by recruiting, training, and supporting bus and taxi drivers. Chapter 56 discusses the role that community health workers can play in monitoring children's growth and providing nutritional education and in screening and referral for many common conditions. Chapter 26 discusses the need for skilled birth attendants without full medical degrees. In some places, paying attention to the skills and technical methods that are needed rather than the title of the health care worker can mean the difference between providing a service or not.

"... nurses can perform many functions in primary care settings as safely and effectively as doctors."

Countries have also made changes in financial and nonfinancial incentives. Raising salaries is often costly, as payroll expenses account for 50 to 80 percent of recurrent costs, but when financial incentives are targeted toward specific aims, they can be effective. For example, Thailand improved service provision in rural areas by paying bonuses to doctors willing to work in more remote locations and providing nonfinancial incentives, including different contractual relationships, housing, peer review, and professional recognition.

Other efforts have included increasing salaries by linking pay to performance. Some of these involve public administration reforms in which periodic performance reviews trigger pay raises or bonuses. In other cases, direct payments are linked to the numbers of services provided or the achievement of performance targets. China has had some success with improving treatment of TB patients by paying village doctors for each case identified and treated (box 7.6). In other cases, pay linked to performance may actually be harmful. For example, incentives to generate additional revenue at hospitals in Shandong province succeeded, in part, through the provision of unnecessary care.

> "China has had some success with improving treatment of TB patients by paying village doctors for each case identified and treated . . ."

Box 7.6 Incentive Payments in China

In China, village doctors play an essential role in patient diagnosis, treatment, and surveillance. In the 1980s, most practiced privately because commune-based insurance schemes had collapsed and local governments were not providing salaries. Their reliance on payments for drugs and services made the provision of free TB treatment problematic, even if they received free drugs. An incentive scheme was created, whereby village doctors received US$1 for each patient enrolled in the treatment program, an additional US$2 for each smear examination carried out in the county TB dispensary at 2 months, and a further US$4 for each patient completing treatment. A reporting system monitored performance, and quality of treatment and reported information were checked through random visits and examinations. The program was highly successful, achieving within 2 years a cure rate for new cases of 95 percent.

Incentive payments have also been very widely used in China in hospitals and even public health programs, and research suggests their deleterious effects when their ability to skew behavior is not controlled. In Shandong province, changes in bonus systems for hospital doctors, from a system tied to quantity of services provided to one tied to revenue generated, found that the switch to a revenue-related bonus was associated with a significant increase in hospital revenue, but a separate study found that around 20 percent of hospital revenue was generated by the provision of unnecessary care.

Source: DCP2, chapter 3, box 3.4.

Nonfinancial incentives can be as effective as financial incentives in altering staff behavior. Such incentives include giving productive workers access to special training and promotion opportunities, recognizing good performance publicly, awarding bonuses to be used for improving local working conditions, delegating responsibilities, and providing education for dependents and housing.

Many countries have used organizational reforms to alter the entire framework within which they recruit and employ human resources. Decentralizing health functions to local governments is a major trend worldwide. It is almost always introduced as a general political reform within which the health sector, like other public service sectors, has to find an accommodation. Decentralization can exacerbate problems of paying and retaining health workers unless an adequate assignment of revenues accompanies the assignment of responsibilities to local governments. Countries have also initiated broad civil service reforms to improve the salaries, supervision, and retention of public sector workers. Unfortunately, research has shown that few civil service reforms of this nature have led to decisive improvements. Efforts in Uganda and Zambia to separate health workers from the general civil service encountered substantial political resistance and were not implemented.

Finally, many governments are contracting health services from NGOs or private providers. Some of these efforts have been quite successful, leading to improved service coverage and quality. South Africa had successful experience with contracting out the management of several hospitals to a private company, and Cambodia has successfully used performance contracts with NGOs to provide primary health care services. In other cases, however, the same weaknesses of public administration in supervising public workers have simply transferred to weaknesses in the supervision of contracts, leaving NGOs or private providers to absorb resources without fulfilling their responsibilities.

Traditional planning models for human resources have tended to be mechanistic, assuming that people trained as doctors and nurses could be easily deployed to wherever they were needed. These models have ignored the wide range of opportunities available to health care workers within their own countries as well as overseas. Addressing human resource management requires understanding that it operates in a competitive market. Health care professionals continue to be motivated by their vocation, but are also swayed by financial and nonfinancial incentives, working conditions, and access to opportunities for professional advancement. Innovative staffing arrangements hold promise

"Addressing human resource management requires understanding that it operates in a competitive market."

for meeting some of the need for trained health care workers. Experiments in personnel management and organizational reform may result in better ways to recruit, retain, and deploy health care workers in the future.

FINANCING

Financing is another major challenge facing low- and middle-income countries.[4] The challenge is twofold: to mobilize sufficient funds for operating the health system and to apply those funds well. However, mobilizing funds to finance public health interventions is difficult both because some health care is costly and because raising revenues in low- and middle-income countries is not easy.

Financing health expenditures is expensive. In 2001, the world spent about US$3 trillion on health, but these expenditures were not distributed evenly around the globe. Only 12 percent of the total was spent for people in low- and middle-income countries even though they account for 84 percent of the world's population and 92 percent of the disease burden. Low-income countries spent approximately US$25 per capita in 2001, while middle-income countries spent an average of US$176 per capita and high-income countries spent an average of US$1,527 per capita, but these are only averages. The world's poorest countries, such as Ethiopia and Nepal, spend the least on health, some US$2 or US$3 per capita at best, while Canada, Japan, the United States, and Western Europe spend between US$2,000 and US$5,000 per capita.

Health spending is strongly correlated with national income. Countries that are wealthier not only spend more on health but also spend a greater proportion of their income on health. Thus, on average, countries in Sub-Saharan Africa spend about 4.5 percent of their national income on health compared with average expenditures of 7.7 percent by high-income countries. In addition, countries that are wealthy finance a larger share of their health expenditure through public mechanisms. Tax revenues and social insurance premiums pay for 70 percent of health expenditures in high-income countries, but account for an average of 50 percent of health expenditures in low-income countries. In addition, whereas health insurance finances a substantial share of private health expenditures in high-income countries, such expenditures are overwhelmingly out-of-pocket in low-income countries.

"... mobilizing funds to finance public health interventions is difficult both because some health care is costly and because raising revenues in low- and middle-income countries is not easy."

"... whereas health insurance finances a substantial share of private health expenditures in high-income countries, such expenditures are overwhelmingly out-of-pocket in low-income countries."

[4] This section is based on *DCP2*, chapters 11, 12, and 13.

Raising additional revenues to increase public spending on health is difficult in low- and middle-income countries. Tax revenues account for 14.5 percent of GDP in low-income countries, compared with 26.5 percent in high-income countries. Payroll taxes designated for health and pension benefits, that is, social security taxes, are even more constrained in low-income countries because the share of formal employment tends to be small. Social security taxes represent less than 1 percent of GDP in low-income countries, but amount to 7.2 percent of GDP in high-income countries.

Sales taxes on particular commodities, such as alcohol and tobacco, can be seen both as health interventions and as sources of revenues. DCP2 shows that raising the price of alcohol and tobacco is highly cost-effective for discouraging high-risk drinking and smoking and, consequently, reducing the disease burden associated with these behaviors. At the same time, taxes on alcohol and tobacco can increase government revenues. Some countries earmark these taxes for use in health campaigns to encourage people to stop smoking or to drink more responsibly.

Public financing plays an important role in health services, especially in high-income countries, and even in the United States where public health insurance for the elderly (Medicare), the poor (Medicaid), and the military (Veterans Administration) accounts for more than half of all health expenditures. The rationale for publicly financing health is strong. Economists have shown that markets for health care services do not function well if left to themselves. For example, consumers cannot easily shop around for the best quality and lowest-price health care services as they might do for other kinds of services. Furthermore, private markets are unlikely to allocate sufficient resources to preventive measures that have a large effect on a population's collective health status, such as vaccinating children or controlling environmental risks. Public financing also gives society a public policy tool that can be used to create incentives to improve health care quality, contain costs, redress inequities, or improve access. Notably, public financing is an essential feature of most, if not all, public health successes around the world (see chapter 2 in this volume and DCP2, chapter 8). Public involvement in health care is not a panacea, but it is the main way that many countries have chosen to address health care, and DCP2 argues a case can be made for public financing of at least some health services in all countries.

In low- and middle-income countries, where public spending is low, access to care often depends on a household's ability to pay for it. This is the case when seeking treatment not only from private health care providers, but also in many cases from public health care providers. Public health services sometimes charge fees to recover a portion of their costs, but even in systems where public services are ostensibly free, patients and their families may be coerced into paying informally for access to services or be required to provide their own food, bedding, and even medical supplies.

DCP2 cannot resolve the debate about charging for health care services in low- and middle-income countries. Some chapters argue that the negative consequences of discouraging people from getting treatment offset the benefits of raising revenues through fees. Some chapters even make the case for negative prices, that is, paying people to encourage them to obtain treatment or preventive care and point to a number of successes. For example, in Tajikistan, poor patients with TB were given food supplements if they complied with their drug treatment regimen, resulting in better adherence. In another successful program in Mexico, the government pays a stipend to poor families on the condition that their children are fully immunized, are brought to clinics for regular checkups, and maintain good school attendance. However, fees also have an impact on the productivity of health care services in those places where they work to assure drug availability or reduce absenteeism, and in such cases may help sustain services that the poor use. Overall, *DCP2* takes a pragmatic stance, encouraging countries to eliminate financial barriers to care wherever possible and to assure that when fees are charged, they demonstrably improve the productivity and quality of health care available to the poor.

DCP2's prescriptions for financing health vary considerably between low- and middle-income countries. In low-income countries, the absolute levels of income and tax revenues severely constrain the possibilities for financing adequate and universal health care. In the past decade, a variety of studies have estimated the costs of providing basic health care. These exercises have estimated that providing a basket of health care services that could make a substantial difference to a population's health costs between US$12 and US$50 per capita per year. While these sums are within reach of most middle-income countries, they are not feasible in low-income countries without large amounts of external assistance.

Thus the problem low-income countries face is multifaceted. On the one hand, they need to raise domestic revenues, an approach that can at most generate an additional 1 or 2 percent of GDP. On the other

"... where public services are ostensibly free, patients and their families may be coerced into paying informally for access to services or be required to provide their own food, bedding, and even medical supplies."

"... providing a basket of health care services that could make a substantial difference to a population's health costs between US$12 and US$50 per capita per year."

hand, low-income countries need to use what resources they have from both domestic and foreign sources as effectively as possible. It is this latter strategy—deriving the greatest health gain from new and current health expenditures—that motivated the Disease Control Priorities Project.

In middle-income countries, the problems of financing are different and the economic and institutional resources for addressing them are stronger. Middle-income countries can finance most of their health expenditures with domestic sources, but they face a range of options for shaping the structure of health care financing, with important implications for equity and productivity. Choices of different financing mechanisms also have important implications for who will bear the costs of health care: the population at large may share spending, thereby providing effective insurance to those unlucky enough to become ill, or it may fall most heavily on those who are sick.

Some countries are choosing to finance health services with general tax revenues, while others are relying on payroll taxes and social insurance schemes. Middle-income countries often use both approaches for different population groups. Initiatives to promote health insurance coverage through voluntary schemes are also under way. Strong arguments can be made in favor of pooling the financial risk associated with paying for health care among the widest population possible, effectively paying for the health care of the poor and the sick with taxes and premiums paid by those who are healthier and wealthier. *DCP2*, chapter 12, appraises these different approaches.

Development assistance plays a much larger role in the health policy of low-income than of middle-income countries. In low-income countries, development assistance to the health sector accounted for an average of 20 percent of all health spending, compared with about 3 percent in middle-income countries. In 13 Sub-Saharan African countries, external financing represented more than 30 percent of all health spending. Overall, international development assistance declined in the 1990s and represented only 0.25 percent of the gross national income of the world's wealthy countries despite their public commitments to contribute 0.70 percent of their total income to international development assistance.

Despite this overall trend, development assistance to the health sector has increased during the past decade, though it is still too low to reach international health targets. International aid to health grew from an estimated US$6.7 billion in 1997–99 to around US$9.3 billion in 2002.

"In low-income countries, development assistance to the health sector accounted for an average of 20 percent of all health spending, compared with about 3 percent in middle-income countries."

This includes funds from bilateral development agencies and multilateral development banks, but also increasingly from private foundations, such as the Bill & Melinda Gates Foundation, and from new global initiatives, such as the Global Fund to Fight AIDS, Tuberculosis and Malaria and GAVI. However, between US$60 billion and US$70 billion of development assistance for health is needed each year to meet the health targets set by the MDGs, significantly more than current levels.

As with domestic resources, much of the debate about international development assistance is how to make it effective. *DCP2* discusses a range of initiatives aimed at making development assistance more effective by redirecting it toward cost-effective measures, but also by reducing transaction costs, improving coordination, and increasing country ownership. Some of the more promising innovations involve performance-based programs that disburse funds against results, such as reaching immunization coverage targets. Other initiatives have engaged host country governments with international agencies and domestic stakeholders in developing and following coordinated sectorwide plans tied to poverty reduction and improved health status targets. The new funds created by global initiatives concentrate attention on particular diseases and challenges in low-income countries. Global action is also being taken to encourage research and development of vaccines and drugs not only through direct funding, but also by establishing advance purchase commitments.

Decisions about how to finance health care strongly influence how the health system will function in any country, but low- and middle-income countries can do more with the funds they have by allocating resources to cost-effective interventions and by mobilizing additional funds to support health improvements. In the case of low-income countries, meeting today's health challenges requires wealthy countries to fulfill their commitments to increase international development assistance to health, even as it requires low-income countries to face the challenges of absorbing these funds and using them in ways that will effectively improve the health of their populations.

Chapter **8**
The Way Forward: A Blueprint for Action

Vast progress is needed in health, and vast progress is possible. *DCP2* recounts substantial successes that have been achieved in human health during the course of the past century. Public health interventions have reduced infant deaths, prevented epidemics, and managed chronic illnesses. From studies that look at historical trends to those that analyze particular cases, *DCP2* makes clear that these achievements are largely the consequence of technical progress, understood broadly to include not only innovative medical interventions but also public health initiatives, improvements in organizing and financing the delivery of care, and beneficial changes in other sectors. Waiting for economic growth to improve health would be a mistake when developing and applying knowledge can achieve so much.

Appreciating past success, however, should not hinder recognition of the extent and gravity of the challenges that still lie ahead. Many of these challenges involve infectious diseases that are disproportionately concentrated among the poor. HIV/AIDS is prominent in terms of the social disruption it has caused in countries with high prevalence and the urgent need for multipronged actions to prevent and treat it. The disease burden of malaria is obstinately high despite decades of work to reduce it, and the emergence of drug-resistant strains makes controlling infectious diseases like malaria and TB a continually moving target.

Some challenges direct attention directly to the weaknesses of health systems. *DCP2* points out that the gap between high- and low-income countries in the risk of death during childbirth is 500 to 1—the most extreme contrast among all health indicators—and reducing maternal mortality requires that a continuum of services be available to address risk factors and complications. The challenge of reducing infant mortality, particularly during the neonatal period, also depends strongly on public action to assure that a range of good quality, basic health care services be made available equitably.

The developed and developing countries share much of the burden of noncommunicable diseases, such as the high burden of CVD and diabetes. Responding to the resultant challenges requires collaborative efforts to learn the best ways to prevent and treat such diseases. Low- and middle-income countries can also anticipate trends that high-income countries have already experienced, such as rising mortality from traffic injuries or environmental contaminants, and need to take cost-effective actions today to avoid unnecessary deaths tomorrow.

Ultimately, the uneven application of knowledge and resources results in unjustifiable health gaps between rich and poor, whether within or between countries. Assuring that the benefits of scientific and technical progress are shared quickly and effectively on a global scale is perhaps the biggest challenge of all.

Even though the selection and design of interventions is not something that can be characterized in a single universal plan, some common features do emerge from *DCP2*:

- Assuring that cost-effective interventions to address the major burdens of disease are delivered and available to everyone is the only way to close the health gap between the haves and the have-nots.
- Having adequate public financing is a critical ingredient for successful public health interventions.
- Bridging the current large gaps in health requires increased and more effective international financial and technical assistance.
- Improving health often requires collaboration with other sectors, such as transportation, education, agriculture, law enforcement, and finance.
- Strengthening health systems multiplies the effect of expenditures by making health interventions more cost-effective and permitting greater integration of services.
- Building knowledge in basic sciences, applied sciences, and management is necessary for research and product development that will feed progress in the future.

Thus the research and analysis in *DCP2* yields two overarching messages. First, more resources are needed for effective health interventions in low-income countries if the glaring inequities in health are to be narrowed. With more resources, highly cost-effective interventions—such as basic vaccines, deworming drugs, and ORT—that improve health can be brought to places that lack them. With more resources, coverage of basic health care services can be extended and become more equitable. More resources can also be channeled into research, with the priorities being diseases for which cost-effective interventions are not yet available and obstacles to effective health care delivery where existing institutions are failing.

The second message is that much more could be done to improve health with existing resources if knowledge of cost-effective interventions were applied more fully. *DCP2* demonstrates that current resources can yield substantial health gains when knowledge of cost-effective interventions is acted upon. Resources are wasted when the wrong interventions are selected or low-quality care becomes an accepted norm. By documenting the scale of the disease burden, the cost-effectiveness of different interventions, and the practical solutions available to assure implementation, *DCP2* provides blueprints for doing better, even under trying circumstances.

Applying the information, analysis, and strategies set out in *DCP2* requires a careful assessment of the local situation, including patterns of disease, institutional capacity, and resources. Combining insights from *DCP2* and knowledge of their local situation, actors at many levels—from parliamentarians and health ministers to hospital administrators, health care workers, and concerned citizens—will be able to set priorities, select appropriate interventions, devise better means of delivery, improve management, and be more effective in mobilizing resources. In this manner, the benefits of technical progress in improving health can be extended and shared by all.

". . . much more could be done to improve health with existing resources if knowledge of cost-effective interventions were applied more fully."

References

Abdool, R. 1998. "Alcohol Policy and Problems in Mauritius." Paper prepared for the World Health Organization Alcohol Policy in Developing Societies Project, World Health Organization, Geneva.

Afukaar, F. K. 2003. "Speed Control in LMICs: Issues, Challenges, and Opportunities in Reducing Road Traffic Injuries." *Injury Control and Safety Promotion* 10 (1–2): 77–81.

Breman, J. G., M. S. Alilo, and A. Mills. 2004. "Conquering the Intolerable Burden of Malaria: What's New, What's Needed: A Summary." *American Journal of Tropical Medicine and Hygiene* 71 (2 suppl.): 1–15.

Hinkle, L. E., and A. Herrou-Aragon. 2001. "How Far Did Africa's First Generation Trade Reforms Go?" World Bank, Washington, DC.

Holding, P. A., and P. K. Kitsao-Wekulo. 2004. "Describing the Burden of Malaria on Child Development: What Should We Be Measuring and How Should We Be Measuring It?" *American Journal of Tropical Medicine and Hygiene* 71 (2 suppl.): 71–79.

Hossain, M. B., and J. F. Phillips. 1996. "The Impact of Outreach on the Continuity of Contraceptive Use in Rural Bangladesh." *Studies in Family Planning* 27 (2): 98–106.

Ichikawa, M., W. Chadbunchachai, and E. Marui. 2003. "Effect of the Helmet Act for Motorcyclists in Thailand." *Accident Analysis and Prevention* 35 (2): 83–89.

Jamison, D. T. 2002. "Cost-Effectiveness Analysis: Concepts and Applications." In *Oxford Textbook of Public Health*, 4th ed., ed. R. G. Detels, J. McEwen, R. Beaglehole, and H. Tanaka, 903–19. Oxford, U.K.: Oxford University Press.

Jamison, D. T., J. G. Breman, A. R. Measham, G. Alleyne, M. Claeson, D. B. Evans, P. Jha, A. Mills, and P. Musgrove, eds. 2006. *Disease Control Priorities in Developing Countries,* 2nd ed. New York: Oxford University Press.

Jamison, D. T., H. W. Mosley, A. R. Measham, and J. L. Bobadilla, eds. 1993. *Disease Control Priorities in Developing Countries.* Washington, DC: World Bank.

Krug, A., J. B. Ellis, I. T. Hay, N. F. Mokgabudi, and J. Robertson. 1994. "The Impact of Child-Resistant Containers on the Incidence of Paraffin (Kerosene) Ingestion in Children." *South African Medical Journal* 84 (11): 730–34.

Lee, V. J. 2001. *Tourism and Alcohol in the Developing World: Potential Effects on Alcohol Policies and Local Drinking Problems.* Stockholm: Stockholm University, Centre for Social Research on Alcohol and Drugs.

Levine, R., and the What Works Working Group, with M. Kinder. 2004. *Millions Saved: Proven Successes in Global Health.* Washington, DC: Center for Global Development.

Lopez, A. D., M. Ezzati, C. D. Mathers, D. T. Jamison, and C. J. L. Murray, eds. 2006. *Global Burden of Disease and Risk Factors.* New York: Oxford University Press.

Low-Beer, D. and R. Stoneburner. 2003. "Behavior and Communication Change in Reducing HIV: Is Uganda Unique?" *African Journal of AIDS Research* 2 (1): 9–21.

Murray, C. J. L., and A. D. Lopez, eds. 1996. *The Global Burden of Disease,* vol. 1. Cambridge, MA: Harvard University Press.

Norghani, M., A. Zainuddin, R. S. Radin Umar, and H. Hussain. 1998. *Use of Exposure Control Methods to Tackle Motorcycle Accidents in Malaysia.* Research Report 3/98. Serdong, Malaysia: Road Safety Research Center, University Putra, Malaysia.

Oeppen, J. 1999. "The Health and Wealth of Nations Since 1820." Paper presented at 1999 Social Science History Conference, Fort North, Texas.

Poli de Figueiredo, L. F., S. Rasslon, V. Bruscagin, R. Cruz and M. Rochee Silva. 2001. "Increases in Fines and Driver License Withdrawal Have Effectively Reduced Immediate Deaths from Trauma on Brazilian Roads: First-Year Report on the New Traffic Code." *Injury* 32 (2): 91–94.

Puska, P., K. Vartiainen, J. Tuomitento, V. Saloman, and A. Nissinen. 1998. "Changes in Premature Deaths in Finland: Successful Long-

Term Prevention of Cardiovascular Diseases." *Bulletin of the World Health Organization* 76: 419–25.

Radin Umar, R. S. G. M. Mackay, and B. L. Hills. 1996. "Modelling of Conspicuity-Related Motorcycle Accidents in Seremban and Shah Alam, Malaysia." *Accident Analysis and Prevention* 28 (3): 325–32.

Rob, U., and G. Cernada. 1992. "Fertility and Family Planning in Bangladesh." *Journal of Family Planning* 38 (4): 53–64.

Ronsmans, C., A. Endang, S. Gunawan, A. Zazri, J. McDermott, M. Koblinsky, and T. Marshall. 2001. "Evaluation of a Comprehensive Home-Based Midwifery Programme in South Kalimantan, Indonesia." *Tropical Medicine and International Health* 6 (10): 799–810.

Supramaniam, V., V. Belle, and J. Sung. 1984. "Fatal Motorcycle Accidents and Helmet Laws in Peninsular Malaysia." *Accident Analysis and Prevention* 16 (3): 157–62.

UNAIDS (Joint United Nations Programme on HIV/AIDS). 1997. *Blood Safety and AIDS: UNAIDS Point of View.* Geneva: UNAIDS.

UNDP (United Nations Development Programme). 2004. Thailand's Response to HIV/AIDS: Progress and Challenges. Bangkok UNDP. "Mauritius: 1999–2000 Budget Increased." U.S. Department of State, Washington, DC.

USAID (United States Agency for International Development). 2002. *What Happened in Uganda?* Washington, DC: USAID.

Walker, D., J. McDermott, J. Fox-Rushby, M. Tanjung, M. Nadjib, M. Widiatmoko, and E. Achadi. 2002. "An Economic Analysis of Midwifery Training Programmes in South Kalimantan, Indonesia." *Bulletin of the World Health Organization* 80 (1): 47–55.

WHO (World Health Organization). 1999. *Global Status Report on Alcohol.* WHO/HSC/SAB/99.11.Geneva: WHO, Sustance Abuse Department.

_____. 2000. *1997–1999 World Health Statistics Annual.* Geneva: WHO.

_____. 2002. *The World Health Report 2002: Reducing Risks, Promoting Healthy Life.* Geneva: WHO.

_____. 2003. "Antenatal Care in Developing Countries: Promises, Achievements, and Missed Opportunities: An Analysis of Trends, Levels, and Differentials, 1990–2001." Geneva: WHO.

WHO and UNICEF. 2001. *Model Chapter for Textbooks: Integrated Management of Childhood Illness.* WHO/CAH/00.40. Geneva: WHO.

World Bank. 1993. *World Development Report 1993: Investing in Health.* New York: Oxford University Press.

———. 2004. *World Development Indicators.* New York: Oxford University Press. Available annually.

Yuan, W. 2000. "The Effectiveness of the 'Ride Bright' Legislation for Motorcycles in Singapore." *Accident Analysis and Prevention* 32 (4): 559–63.

About the Editors

Dean T. Jamison is a Professor of Health Economics in the School of Medicine at the University of California, San Francisco (UCSF), and an affiliate of UCSF Global Health Sciences. He is also a Senior Fellow at the Ellison Institute. Dr. Jamison concurrently serves as an Adjunct Professor in both the Peking University Guanghua School of Management and in the University of Queensland School of Population Health.

Before joining UCSF, Dr. Jamison was on the faculty of the University of California, Los Angeles, and also spent a number of years at the World Bank, where he was a senior economist in the research department, division chief for education policy, and division chief for population, health, and nutrition. In 1992–93 he temporarily rejoined the World Bank to serve as Director of the World Development Report Office and as lead author for the Bank's 1993 *World Development Report: Investing in Health*. His publications are in the areas of economic theory, public health and education. Most recently, Dr. Jamison has served as the Senior Editor for the Disease Control Priorities Project, where he was involved with preparation of *Disease Control Priorities in Developing Countries*, 2nd edition, and *The Global Burden of Disease and Risk Factors*, both published by Oxford University Press in 2006. Dr. Jamison studied at Stanford (B.A., Philosophy; M.S., Engineering Sciences) and at Harvard (Ph.D., Economics, under K.J. Arrow). In 1994 he was elected to membership in the Institute of Medicine of the U.S. National Academy of Sciences.

Joel G. Breman, M.D., D.T.P.H., is Senior Scientific Advisor, Fogarty International Center (FIC), National Institutes of Health, and Co-Managing Editor of the Disease Control Priorities Project. He was educated at the University of Southern California, Los Angeles,

Keck School of Medicine, University of Southern California, and the London School of Hygiene and Tropical Medicine. Dr. Breman trained in medicine at the University of Southern California, Los Angeles County Medical Center; infectious diseases at the Boston City Hospital, Harvard Medical School; and in epidemiology at the Centers for Disease Control and Prevention. He worked on smallpox eradication in Guinea (1967–69); Burkina Faso, at the Organization for Coordination and Cooperation in the Control of the Major Endemic Diseases (1972–76); and at the World Health Organization, Geneva (1977–80) where he was responsible for orthopoxvirus research and the certification of eradication.

In 1976, in the Democratic Republic of the Congo (formerly Zaire), Dr. Breman investigated the first outbreak of Ebola Hemorrhagic Fever. Following the confirmation of smallpox eradication in 1980, Dr. Breman returned to the CDC where he began work on the epidemiology and control of malaria. Dr. Breman joined the FIC in 1995 and has been Director of the International Training and Research Program in Emerging Infectious Diseases and Senior Scientific Advisor. He has been a member of many advisory groups, including serving as the Chair of the WHO Technical Advisory Group on Human Monkeypox and as a member of the WHO International Commission for the Certification of *Dracunculiasis* (Guinea worm) Eradication. Dr. Breman has over 100 publications on infectious diseases and research capacity strengthening in developing countries. He was guest editor of two supplements to the *American Journal of Tropical Medicine and Hygiene: The Intolerable Burden of Malaria: A New Look at the Numbers* (2001) and *The Intolerable Burden of Malaria: What's New, What's Needed* (2004).

Anthony R. Measham is Co-Managing Editor of the Disease Control Priorities Project at the Fogarty International Center, U.S. National Institutes of Health; Deputy Director of the Communicating Health Priorities Project at the Population Reference Bureau, Washington, D.C.; and a member of the Working Group of the Global Alliance for Vaccines and Immunization (GAVI) on behalf of the World Bank.

Born in the United Kingdom, Dr. Measham practiced family medicine in Dartmouth, Nova Scotia, Canada, before devoting the remainder of his career to date in international health. He spent 15 years resident in developing countries on behalf of the Population Council (Colombia), the Ford Foundation (Bangladesh), and the World Bank (India). Early in his international health career, he was Deputy Director of the Center for Population and Family Health at Columbia University, New York, from 1975–77. He then served for 17 years on the staff of the World Bank, as Health Adviser from 1984–88 and Chief for Policy and Research of the Health, Nutrition and Population Division of the World Bank from 1988–93.

Dr. Measham has spent most of his career providing technical assistance, carrying out research and analysis, and helping to develop projects in more than 20 developing countries, primarily in the areas of maternal and child health and family planning, and nutrition. He was an editor of *Disease Control Priorities in Developing Countries,* 1st edition (1993), and has authored approximately 60 monographs, book chapters, and journal articles.

Dr. Measham graduated in Medicine from Dalhousie University, Halifax, Nova Scotia, Canada. He received a Master's of Science and a doctorate in Public Health from the University of North Carolina in Chapel Hill and is a diplomat of the American Board of Preventive Medicine and Public Health. His honors include election to Alpha Omega Alpha Honor Medical Society; appointment as Special Professor of International Health, University of Nottingham Medical School, Nottingham, U.K.; and being named Dalhousie University Medical Alumnus of the Year in 2000–01.

Sir George Alleyne, M.D., F.R.C.P., F.A.C.P. (Hon.), D.Sc. (Hon.), is Director Emeritus of the Pan American Health Organization (PAHO) where he served as Director from 1995 to 2003. Dr. Alleyne is a native of Barbados and graduated from the University of the West Indies (UWI) in Medicine in 1957. He completed his postgraduate training in internal medicine in the United Kingdom and did further postgraduate work in that country and in the United States. He entered academic medicine in UWI in 1962, and his career included research in the Tropical Metabolism Research Unit for his Doctorate in Medicine. He was appointed Professor of Medicine at UWI in 1972, and four years later he became Chairman of the Department of Medicine. He is an emeritus Professor of UWI. He entered PAHO in 1981; in 1983 he was appointed Director of the Area of Health Programs; in 1990, he was appointed Assistant Director.

Dr. Alleyne's scientific publications have dealt with his research in renal physiology and biochemistry and various aspects of clinical medicine. During his term as Director he has dealt with and published on issues such as equity in health, health and development, and the basis for international cooperation in health. He has also addressed several aspects of Caribbean health and the problems it faces. He is a member of the Institute of Medicine and Chancellor of the University of the West Indies.

Dr. Alleyne has received numerous awards in recognition of his work, including prestigious decorations and national honors from many countries of the Americas. In 1990, he was made Knight Bachelor by Her Majesty Queen Elizabeth II for his services to medicine. In 2001, he was awarded the Order of the Caribbean Community, the highest honor that can be conferred on a Caribbean national.

Mariam Claeson, M.D., M.P.H., is the Program Coordinator for AIDS in the South Asia Region of the World Bank since January 2005. She was the Lead Public Health Specialist in the Health, Nutrition and Population, Human Development Network of the World Bank (1998–2004), managing the HNP Millennium Development Goals work program to support accelerated progress in countries. She co-authored the call for action of the Bellagio study group on child survival, in 2003: *Knowledge into Action for Child Survival*, and the World Bank report on *The Millennium Development Goals for Health: Rising to the Challenges* (2005). She was a member of the What Works Working group hosted by the Center for Global Development that resulted in the report *Millions Saved: Proven Successes in Global Health* (2005).

Dr. Claeson coauthored the health chapter of the *Poverty Reduction Strategy* source book, promoting a life-cycle approach to maternal and child health and nutrition. As a coordinator of the Public Health thematic group (1998–2002), she led the development of the strategy note: *Public Health and World Bank Operations* and promoted multisector approaches to child health within the World Bank and in Bank supported country operations, analytical work, and lending.

Prior to joining the World Bank, Mariam Claeson worked with WHO from 1987–95, in later years as program manager for the WHO Global Program for the Control of Diarrheal Diseases (CDD). She has several years of field experience, working in developing countries, in clinical practice at the rural district level (in Tanzania, Bangladesh, Bhutan); in national program management on immunization and diarrheal disease control (Ethiopia 1984–86); and in health sector development projects in middle- and low-income countries.

David B. Evans, Ph.D., is an economist by training. Between 1980 and 1990 he was an academic, first in economics departments and then in a medical school, during which time he undertook consultancies for the World Bank, WHO and government. From 1990–98 he sponsored and conducted research into social and economic aspects of tropical diseases and their control in the UNICEF/UNDP/World Bank/WHO Special Programme on Research and Training in Tropical Diseases. He subsequently became Director for the Global Programme on Evidence for Health Policy and then the Department of Health Systems Financing in WHO where he is now responsible for a range of activities relating to the development of appropriate health financing strategies and policies. These include the WHO-CHOICE project which has assessed and reported the costs and effectiveness of over 700 health interventions, the costs of scaling up interventions, health expenditures and accounts, the extent of financial catastrophe and impoverishment due to out-of-pocket payments for health, and assessment of the impact of different types of ways of raising funds for health, pooling them, and using them to provide or purchase services and interventions. He has published widely in these areas.

Prabhat Jha is Canada Research Chair of Health and Development at the University of Toronto, Canada. He is the Founding Director of the Centre for Global Health Research, St. Michael's Hospital, Associate Professor in the Department of Public Health Sciences, University of Toronto and Research Scholar at the McLaughlin Centre for Molecular Medicine. Dr. Jha is also Professeur Extraordinaire at the Université de Lausanne, Switzerland.

Dr. Jha is lead author of *Curbing the Epidemic: Governments and the Economics of Tobacco Control* and co-editor of *Tobacco Control in Developing Countries.* Both are among the most influential books on tobacco control. Dr. Jha is the principal investigator of a prospective study of 1 million deaths in India, researching mortality from smoking, alcohol use, fertility patterns, indoor air pollution and other risk factors among 2.3 million homes and 15 million people. This is the world's largest prospective study of health (www.cghr.org/project.htm).

He also conducts studies of HIV transmission in various countries, specifically focusing on documenting the risk factors for spread of HIV, and interventions to prevent growth of the HIV epidemic. His studies have received over $5 million in peer-reviewed grants.

Dr. Jha has published widely on tobacco, HIV/AIDS, and health of the global poor. His awards include a Gold Medal from the Poland Health Promotion Foundation (2000), the Top 40 Canadians under age 40 Award (2004), and the Ontario Premier's Research Excellence Award (2004). Dr. Jha was a Research Scholar at the University of Toronto and McMaster University in Canada. He holds a M.D. from the University of Manitoba, Canada, and a D. Phil in Epidemiology and Public Health from Oxford University, England, where he studied as a Rhodes Scholar at Magdalen College.

Anne Mills, Ph.D., is Professor of Health Economics and Policy at the London School of Hygiene and Tropical Medicine. She has over 20 years of experience in health-economics related research in developing countries, and has published widely in the fields of health economics and health planning including books on the role of government in health in developing countries, health planning in the United Kingdom, decentralization, health economics research in developing countries, and the public private mix. Her most recent research interests have been in the organization and financing of health systems including evaluation of contractual relationships between public and private sectors, and in the application of economic evaluation techniques to improve the efficiency of disease control programs.

She has had extensive involvement in supporting the health economics research activities of the WHO Tropical Disease Research Programme. She founded, and is Head of, the Health Economics and Financing Programme, which has become one of the leading groups in the world developing and applying health economics' theories and techniques to increase knowledge on how best to improve the equity and efficiency of developing country health systems. She has acted as advisor to a number of multilateral and bilateral agencies, notably the United Kingdom Department for International Development and the World Health Organization. She guided the creation of the Alliance for Health Policy and Systems Research, and chairs its Board. Most recently, she has been a member of the Commission for Macro-economics and Health, and co-chair of its working group 'Improving the health outcomes of the poor'.

Philip Musgrove is Deputy Editor-Global Health for *Health Affairs,* which is published by Project HOPE in Bethesda, Maryland. He worked for the World Bank (1990–2002), including two years on secondment to the World Health Organization (1999–2001), retiring as a Principal Economist. He was previously Advisor in Health Economics, Pan American Health Organization (1982–1990), and a Research Associate at the Brookings Institution and at Resources for the Future (1964–81).

Dr. Musgrove is Adjunct Professor in the School of Advanced International Studies, Johns Hopkins University, and has taught at George Washington University, American University and the University of Florida. He holds degrees from Haverford College (B.A., 1962, summa cum laude), Princeton University (M.P.A., 1964) and Massachusetts Institute of Technology (Ph.D., 1974).

Dr. Musgrove has worked on health reform projects in Argentina, Brazil, Chile, and Colombia, as well as dealing with a variety of issues in health economics, financing, equity, and nutrition. His publications include more than 50 articles in economics and health journals and chapters in 20 books.

Advisory Committee to the Editors

J. R. Aluoch
Professor, Nairobi Women's Hospital, Nairobi,
    Kenya

Jacques Baudouy
Director, Health, Nutrition and Population
World Bank, Washington, D.C., United States

Fred Binka
Executive Director, INDEPTH Network, Accra,
    Ghana

Mayra Buvinić
Director, Gender and Development
World Bank, Washington, D.C., United States

David Challoner, Co-chair
Foreign Secretary, Institute of Medicine
U.S. National Academies, Gainesville, Florida,
    United States

Guy de Thé, Co-chair
Research Director and Professor Emeritus, Institut
    Pasteur, Paris, France

Timothy Evans
Assistant Director General, Evidence and
    Information for Policy
World Health Organization, Geneva, Switzerland

Richard Horton
Editor, *The Lancet,* London, United Kingdom

Sharon Hrynkow
Acting Director, Fogarty International Center,
    National Institutes of Health
Bethesda, Maryland, United States

Gerald Keusch
Provost and Dean for Global Health
Boston University School of Public Health, Boston,
    Massachusetts, United States

Kiyoshi Kurokawa
President, Science Council of Japan (SCJ),
    Kanawaga, Japan

Peter Lachmann
Past President, UK Academy of Medical Sciences,
    Cambridge, United Kingdom

Mary Ann Lansang
Executive Director, INCLEN Trust International,
    Inc, Manila, Philippines

Christopher Lovelace
Director, Kyrgyz Republic Country Office and
    Central Asia Human Development
World Bank, Bishkek, Kyrgyz Republic

Anthony Mbewu
Executive Director, Medical Research Council of
    South Africa, Tygerberg, South Africa

Rajiv Misra
Former Secretary of Health
Government of India, Haryana, India

Perla Santos Ocampo
President, National Academy of Science and
    Technology, San Juan, Philippines

G. B. A. Okelo
Secretary General and Ag. Executive Director,
    Africa Academy of Sciences, Nairobi, Kenya

Sevket Ruacan
General Director, MESA Hospital, Ankara,
    Turkey

Pramilla Senanayake
Chairman, Foundation Council of the Global
    Forum for Health Research, Colombo,
    Sri Lanka

Jaime Sepúlveda, Chair
Director, National Institutes of Health of Mexico,
    Mexico City, Mexico

Chitr Sitthi-amorn
Director, Institute of Health Research/Dean
Chulalongkorn University, The College of Public
    Health, Bangkok, Thailand

Sally Stansfield
Associate Director, Global Health Strategies
Bill & Melinda Gates Foundation, Seattle,
    Washington, United States

Misael Uribe
President, National Academy of Medicine of
    Mexico, Mexico City, Mexico

Zhengguo Wang
Professor, Chinese Academy of Engineering,
    Daping, China

Witold Zatonski
Professor, Health Promotion Foundation, Warsaw,
    Poland

Contributing Writers

William D. Savedoff and Anne-Marie Smith, Social Insight

Table of Contents, *Disease Control Priorities in Developing Countries,* 2nd edition

Table of Contents, *Global Burden of Disease and Risk Factors*

Index

Boxes, figures, and tables are indicated by b, f, and t.

blackfly control in Sub-Saharan Africa, 29
blindness
    cataract treatment, 141b
    river blindness, control of, 28–29
    trachoma control program, 34–36
blood pressure. *See* cardiovascular disease (CVD)
blood-related disorders. *See* hemoglobinopathies
blood safety measures, 53, 65, 137
Bolivia and Chagas disease initiative, 25b
Botswana and HIV/AIDS epidemic, 66
Brazil
    Chagas disease initiative in, 25b
    contraception, access to, 84
    diarrheal diseases in, 82
breastfeeding
    reduction of diarrheal diseases due to, 80, 82
    transmission of HIV and, 62
Burkina Faso, malaria in, 75
burn-related injuries. *See* unintentional injuries

Cambodia, primary health care services in, 172
cancer, 97–98, 104–106, 163
cardiovascular disease (CVD)
    as cause of death, 98–99
    diet contributing to, 99–100
    lifestyle changes in response to, 99–102, 101b
    medical interventions for, 102–104
    profile of, 97
    research and development priority, 163
Caribbean. *See* Latin America and Caribbean
Carter Center, 25b
cataract treatment, 141b
census data, 157
Center for Global Development's Global Health Policy
    Research Network, 23
Centers for Disease Control and Prevention (U.S.),
    25b, 158
Central Asia
    See also specific countries
    alcohol consumption in, 120, 121, 123
    CVD in, 98, 99
    vaccinations in, 78, 79
Chagas disease, 25b
childbirth conditions
    access to skilled attendance, 90, 91b, 92–94, 93b,
        169, 170
    cost-effective strategies for, 60
    inequity patterns in, 10
    maternal death. *See* maternal mortality
    neonatal death. *See* child mortality rates
    risk factors for, 31

childhood health
    integrated services. *See* integrated management
        of childhood illness (IMCI)
    nutrition. *See* nutrition
    school-based health. *See* school health programs
    successful programs for improving, 25b
child mortality rates
    diarrheal disease and, 79
    inequity patterns, 9–10
    infant and neonatal mortality, 7, 31, 83, 84, 88, 90–95,
        92b, 92t, 178–179
    lowering of, 3, 4, 135, 178–179
    malaria and, 74
Chile
    Chagas disease initiative in, 25b
    Hib disease prevention in, 33–34
    life expectancy in, 4
    public health improvements in, 7
China
    disparity of health status between regions of, 10
    food manufacture in, 102
    gender-related health issues in, 10
    incentive pay to doctors in, 171, 171b
    life expectancy in, 4
    malaria in, 75
    maternal deaths in, 88
    neonatal resuscitation program in, 93b
    salt iodination program in, 26b
    TB control program in, 26b
    tobacco use in, 114
    traffic fatalities in, 112
    transportation choices in, 100
chloroquine, 75, 76
cholera, 77, 162
chronic management, 45b, 46b
cigarette consumption. *See* tobacco use and control
clean drinking water, 81
client factors and gender differentials, 11
Colombia
    contraception, access to, 84
    stomach cancer in, 53
communicable diseases. *See* infectious diseases
communication needed for emergency medical services, 143
community level of care, 130–133
    decentralizing health functions to, 172
    onchocerciasis control program, 29
    Tanzania Essential Health Interventions Program
        approach to health planning for, 161, 161b
condoms. *See* family planning; HIV/AIDS
congenital and developmental disorders, 106–110
Congo, Democratic Republic of, and diabetes, 103

water service and quality, 81
weak health systems, progress in, 7, 27–28
What Works Working Group, 23
WHO. *See* World Health Organization
women
    childbirth conditions. *See* childbirth conditions
    death in childbirth. *See* maternal mortality
    HIV/AIDS and, 61, 62, 65, 66, 153
    inequity in health services and status, 9–11, 15
    life expectancy of, 3, 3f
    malaria and, 74
    prenatal care. *See* prenatal care programs
    reproductive health of, 84
        See also maternal conditions
    status improvements of, 7
    tobacco use by, 115
    water transport by, 81
World Development Report 1993: Investing in Health
    (World Bank), 161b
World Health Organization (WHO)
    Alma Ata Declaration on Primary Health Care
        (1978), 133
    Commission on Macroeconomics and Health, 133
    on contraceptive use, 85

    on eliminating antimicrobial supplements in animal
        feed, 149
    Expanded Program on Immunization
        (EPI), 77
    guidelines for national drug policies, 146
    guinea worm control program, 25b
    on HIV/AIDS treatment accessibility, 68
    IMCI program, 150
    Regional Office in Africa and integrated disease
        population surveillance, 159
    smallpox eradication efforts of, 28
    training of epidemiologists, 158
World Health Report (WHO 2002) on deaths due to CVD,
    diabetes, and related conditions, 99
worms, school health programs for deworming, 152

years of life lost, defined, 43b
yellow fever, 77
young adults, 153–154

Zimbabwe
    HIV/AIDS epidemic in, 66
    primary health care nurses in, 170
zinc supplementation, 80, 82

Photo Credits